THE
RICHARD PEABODY
READER

The
Richard Peabody
Reader

SELECTED POETRY & PROSE
BY RICHARD PEABODY

Edited by Lucinda Ebersole

Introduction by Michael Dirda

Alan Squire Publishing
Bethesda, Maryland

Alan Squire Publishing

The Richard Peabody Reader is published by Alan Squire Publishing, an imprint of the Santa Fe Writers Project.

© 2015, Richard Peabody.

Introduction, © 2015, Michael Dirda.

Library of Congress Cataloging-in-Publication Data

Peabody, Richard, 1951–
  [Works. Selections]
  The Richard Peabody reader : selected poetry & prose /
by Richard Peabody ; edited by Lucinda Ebersole.
     pages ; cm
  Includes bibliographical references and index.
  ISBN 978-0-9848329-8-9 (pbk. : alk. paper)
  I. Ebersole, Lucinda. II. Title.
  PS3566.E13A6 2015
  811'.54—dc23

                    2014027235

ISBN: 978-0-9848329-8-9

Jacket design by Randy Stanard, Dewitt Designs, www.dewittdesigns.com.

Photos: front cover—Richard Peabody, 1987 (photographer unknown); back cover—Peabody, 2008 (Dean Evangelista) and Peabody, 1983 (photographer unknown); spine—Peabody, 1997 (Andi Olsen); front inside jacket—left to right, Silvana Straw, Peabody, Jacquie Jones, Sharon Morgenthaler, Reuben Jackson, 1990 (Charles Steck); back inside jacket—Peabody, 1988 (Peggy Pfeiffer).

Copy editing and interior design by Nita Congress.

Printing consultant: Steve Waxman.

Printed by R.R. Donnelley.

Ordo Vagorum

be varied wordsounds, to merit Fats Waller's sometime elsewhere encomium: "Perfect, delicious, wonderful." —Michael Horovitz, Editor, *New Departures*

Richard Peabody has long been a mainstay of the D.C. literary scene, an inveterate supporter of writers. This collection is a perfect illustration of just what he can do himself. An incisive, often dryly witty observer of life, and most particularly of the relationships of men at that midlife tipping point. Men with their partners, parents, children, buddies, he takes a compassionate knife to them all in poems, short stories, and essays, and handles all the forms with glorious ease and sometimes startling images. *The Richard Peabody Reader* shows just how much of a master he's become. —Chris Nickson, author of *Gods of Gold* and the *Richard Nottingham* novels

This grand collection reveals the truth: Richard Peabody has a great big crush on humanity, zits and all. For decades he's been ready to use any form, brief lyric to long narrative, to explore our raptures, our terrors, our dangerous daring, our panic at everyday demands, and the everlasting battle between our vile bodies and our inconvenient, sweet ideals, as he's captured the impulses and consequences our twisting lives are made of. —Lynne Barrett, author of *Magpies*

The writer, it was once thought, was the bauxite of the book business, the laden ore that a publisher, an editor, a designer, a distributor turned into the aluminum can of pop. But Richard Peabody is a whole new element, is his own overhead, is a brand-new effervescence—miner, smelter, canner, deposit, and all. A sliver of his life's work, here encased, barely represented in this surface-scratching *Reader*, assays this alchemy, weighs out this collapse of categories—publisher, editor, agent—compressed into this diamond-studded diamond, this new precious metal, this new seamless seam of the writer's writer. From now on, writers, we must do everything, write everything, be everything. Richard Peabody has vertically integrated. Richard Peabody has infinitely widened every horizon, has deepened the deepest depth. Reader, he writes! He writes! He writes! He writes! —Michael Martone, author of *Four for a Quarter*

ALSO BY RICHARD PEABODY

FICTION

Paraffin Days
Open Joints on Bridge
Sugar Mountain
Blue Suburban Skies

POETRY

I'm in Love with the Morton Salt Girl
Echt & Ersatz
Sad Fashions
Buoyancy and Other Myths
Mood Vertigo
Last of the Red Hot Magnetos
Speed Enforced by Aircraft

EDITOR/CO-EDITOR

62 issues of the literary annual *Gargoyle*

D.C. women's fiction anthology series: *Grace and Gravity, Enhanced Gravity, Electric Grace, Gravity Dancers, Amazing Graces, Defying Gravity*

The Mondo anthology series: *Mondo Barbie, Mondo Elvis, Mondo Marilyn, Mondo James Dean*

DC Magazines: A Literary Retrospective

Mavericks: Nine Independent Publishers

Loose Change, stories and poems by Tina Fulker

Coming to Terms: A Literary Response to Abortion

A Different Beat: Writing by Women of the Beat Generation

In Praise of What Persists, stories by Joyce Renwick

Alice Redux: New Stores of Alice, Lewis, and Wonderland

Conversations with Gore Vidal

Sex & Chocolate: Tasty Morsels for Mind and Body

Kiss the Sky: Fiction and Poetry Starring Jimi Hendrix

Stress City: A Big Book of Fiction by 51 DC Guys

for absent friends:

Paul Bowles and
Edouard Roditi

Contents

3 WAR & PEACE   119

4 HOME & FAMILIES   177

Editor's Note

s a reader of anthologies, I find those long-winded essays by the editor to be a huge bore. The only people who read them are high school juniors who need info for their English term paper. Write your own damn term paper!

Here's what you need to know:

I first met Richard Peabody the way most writers met him; sitting in one of his classes. Mine was a private "home" class he often held sitting in his living room, surrounded by books. During the class he mentioned a story published by Joy Williams. I said, "If my husband were Rust Hills, I could get published." "How did you know she was married to Rust Hills?" he asked.

I just looked at him, because I was a writer and all writers knew that Rust Hills was the editor of *Esquire* and he often published his wife. I thought, maybe this is a waste of my time, or maybe, as they say in the movies, "I think this is the beginning of a beautiful friendship." In the end, I know it was.

Richard Peabody has published everybody who was anybody. Along the way he has published his own body of work. Poetry, prose, stories, criticism, and memoir are commingled in this reader.

So start reading. His work stands on its own.

Lucinda Ebersole
West Virginia, 2014

Introduction

Why read Richard Peabody? No one who has experienced the storytelling power, the wit, the striking turns of phrase, and the sheer sexiness of Peabody's fiction and poetry would ever ask this question. Those lucky readers will simply be grateful to possess, in one hefty and convenient volume, a mammoth selection from thirty years and more of his often breathtaking work. But what of others who have casually picked up *The Richard Peabody Reader* and are now idly glancing at this introduction before making a quick skim through the pages that follow?

In that case, I urge you to turn to the poem "The Other Man Is Always French." Don't protest that you don't like poetry. It'll only take twenty seconds to read. Here's the opening:

The Other Man Is Always French

The other woman can be
a blonde or a redhead
but the other man
is always French.

He dresses better
than I ever will.

He can picnic
and stroll
with a wineglass
in one upraised hand.

Munch pâté,
drink espresso,
and tempt with
ashy kisses.

He hangs out
at Dupont Circle
because the trees
remind him of Paris.

Did I mention sex?

Face it—
he's had centuries
of practice.

I'm an American.
What do I know?

He drives a fast car,
and can brood like
nobody's business,
while I sit home
watching ESPN.

He's tall and
chats about art—
I don't even want
to discuss that accent…

See? Don't you want to read the rest? Note the characteristic Peabody blend of just the right details, a dash of local color (Washington's "Dupont Circle"), and self-deprecation. The poem moves swiftly, without fanciness or obfuscation. The opening lines elicit a smile and that smile grows broader as the poem proceeds. Not least, like so much of Peabody's writing, "The Other Man Is Always French" hovers between genres: somewhat prosy for verse, comic but not just comic, a playful *jeu d'esprit* that nonetheless touches on the personal.

Though constantly suffused with an autobiographical air and profoundly grounded in Washington bohemia, Peabody's work—whatever its form—nearly always hooks us because it tells a story. Sometimes the structure of those stories may be complex, but many of them possess an almost O. Henry–like attention to plotting. The longer ones establish several narrative lines that gradually converge. They end with a bang, not a whimper.

Because Richard Peabody is a major figure in independent publishing, as well as the driving force behind *Gargoyle*, one of the country's best literary magazines, he might be expected to be wildly experimental or too demanding for ordinary readers. Nothing is further from the truth. A story like "Peppermint Schnapps" could have appeared in *Ellery Queen's Mystery Magazine*; it would have made a perfect episode for the old *Alfred Hitchcock Presents* television program. "A More Level Playing Field in Fallujah" opens with a grabber sentence—"I can't go out like this, Lieutenant Walker thinks. I didn't go to Yale to die like this in the fucking desert"—and from it sets up a *conte cruel* worthy of Ambrose Bierce. Another story—about an epidemic of fleas—mixes satire, domestic realism, and the faintly fantastic: It could stand next to "The Argentine Ant," Italo Calvino's account of a similarly unstoppable invasion.

Let me stress that by mentioning Bierce or Calvino, I don't intend to diminish Peabody's originality or the distinctiveness of his voice, but only to underscore just how clever, sharply worked out, and imaginative his stories can be. To call some of them almost genre fiction might seem a backhanded compliment, but it's not: Peabody's work is crafted, well made, as compelling as Maupassant or Maugham.

Of course, these aren't the only kind of stories Peabody writes. Not even James Salter describes hotter sex. Consider "Walking on Gilded Splinters," a spot-on, brilliantly detailed story of adultery. In it, Peabody conveys both the almost miraculous exhilaration of an illicit love affair and its attendant guilt and confusions. Given the sheer incandescence of lovemaking with Miranda Ballard, one can almost forgive the protagonist: Some experiences are worth damnation. But in the end, Peabody neatly brings home the damage caused by infidelity through the unlikely figure of a once-attractive bag lady who, he writes, "could still draw eyes, even if she could no longer hold them."

Isn't that neatly said? Such memorable diction recurs throughout Peabody's fiction and poetry. Sometimes a single adjective is absolutely right: Robert Mitchum's "bohunky face." Other times it's a detail. In "The Colonel," the manager of a legendary rock musician (an unnamed Elvis Presley) is so sybaritic that he hires flunkies to pull the handles of Vegas slot machines for him. Sometimes an image is unforgettable, as when cockroaches crawl into a condom and make it swell while they eat the semen inside. Peabody also comes up with perfect vignettes. In "Country Porch Lights," a writer at an artists' retreat in the South remembers his first meeting with a pretty "mountain girl":

> He'd sat and listened to her talk about her family's market and spent a lot of time studying her bare feet as she slipped off her sandals and stepped first one and then the other foot in and out of a mud puddle. She'd coat her toes with mud and then swirl them around in the water and wash them clean again. Over and over. And it seemed completely playful and unconscious. He couldn't recall saying a word.

In "Princess Daddy," a nonfiction piece packed with sharply observed details, Peabody recalls playing with his daughter:

> Twyla assures me that once we land on the Princess Planet we will find lots and lots of Barbies. So that's where they come from? Every time I walk that pink aisle at Toys R Us I have indeed left the cosmos. Watch a covey of three-year-old girls approach that aisle and learn what reverence is all about.

What's impressive is how Peabody in that first sentence makes us hear Twyla's serious little-girl voice—"lots and lots of Barbies"—before going on to comment on the endearing earnestness of childhood.

He achieves even more compact sentence magic in the selection called "Letters from the Editor." Here, Peabody sets down what are, apparently, comments by an editor or teacher on a series of short stories. Are they actual comments made to former students or simply fabricated ones that Peabody has transformed into mini–works of art? They do somewhat recall those "novels in three lines" culled by Félix Fénéon from a French newspaper's classified pages. Lacking any context, however, these punchy editorial remarks come across as comic and eerie, and also highly suggestive; they invite plots to be constructed around them. Here are just three, out of many: "I never would have guessed that you could get so much mileage out of apricot-colored clothing." Even better is "So much implied in this story, so much left inscrutable. The scene with the lunch pail is amazing." But my favorite remains, "Still, I did think you took the gunplay and the paranoia in the hat-drying scene too far."

As a writer, Peabody aims for what one might call a felt reality. In one of the essays included here, he summarizes his artistic credo, emphasizing that what is most important in writing is "some sense of everyday experience." Moreover, that experience should be grounded in a time and place—in his own case, Washington, D.C., since the 1960s. He goes on to say:

> I don't necessarily want to document anyone's life, but there are aspects of this city that aren't represented in popular novels and have little to do with the government. My D.C. is writers, artists, and musicians, struggling to be heard. Living in cheap apartments (for here), hitting the fern bar happy hours for the free food, hanging out at the 9:30 Club, d.c. space, or the WPA, attending art openings, free concerts, Redskins games, etc. One wishes more people were aware that there are Washingtonians here, be they Chinese, Salvadoran, or whatever, who are not living on Capitol Hill.

This other D.C.—the Washington that has nothing to do with the federal government, K Street lobbyists, or expense account lunches—becomes virtually a character in several stories. Place names imbue the action with a local habitation and some familiar names: Catonsville, Anne Arundel Community College, Lee Highway, the Severn River, Glebe Road, Silver Spring, the University of Maryland. But to categorize Peabody as just a D.C. writer would be as wrong-headed as calling Eudora Welty a Mississippi regionalist or Larry McMurtry the author of some cowboy stories. All literature is local, but Peabody's work is never provincial. He plays in the national league.

Still, Peabody is aware that "living in one town turns everything into a time portal of some kind." The short novel included here, *Sugar Mountain*, becomes a virtual catalogue aria of Washington landmarks—the Childe Harold restaurant, Second Story Books, the canal in Georgetown, Maggie's Farm head shop, Teaism, the House of Musical Traditions, the graffiti of Cool Disco Dan along the Metro's Red Line, even the vanished graffito over the Beltway bridge by the Mormon Temple that used to read "Surrender Dorothy," and many others. At one point, a young woman named Sealy asks her much older lover Hal about his obsession with Washington's past:

> "You know, Hal, you keep giving me a tour of the places that used to be here, but you never talk about what's here right now."

> "What?" Hal ponders her words. "I guess that's true."

> "It's like your D.C. is buried under a layer of India ink. Like you have to scrape at it to show me what you see when you walk around. It's bizarre. Like you're living in the past and the present at the same time."

> Hal has stopped walking. He's gazing across Key Bridge now. Watching vee formations of Canada geese fly south.

He can't even imagine M Street anymore. The different layers of time making its signs and buildings waver and change like an acid trip. Hours spent at Café de Paris, Au Pied de Cochon, Max's, or La Ruche, all running into one another along with the years. Sageworth House. Emergency. Commander Salamander. The Singer's Studio. The Biograph Theatre. Running in a loop like a Fritz Lang movie in color.

Sunt lacrimae rerum—there are tears in things. This thread of wistfulness in Peabody's work, of evanescence—"blink and you miss the years"—sometimes modulates into an actual recognition of failure or the harsh realization that one's life hasn't mattered at all. Older men mourn their lost youth or linger over bittersweet memories of the rose-lipt girls they once loved. After years of effort, once-young writers face the reality of having fallen far short of their dreams. It's no accident that Hal's long worked-on novel is titled "Gloom Patrol." At one point his daughter Taylor—Sealy's best friend—takes a surreptitious look at the manuscript, "Hoping against hope that it's not autobiographical. Highs & lows. Good & bad. Ultimately frustrating and disappointing. Not a masterpiece after all. Wanted it to be for his sake. Breaks my heart." Is it any wonder that Hal hates the movie *American Beauty* because he sees so much of himself in Kevin Spacey's character?

Obviously, too much of this could seem maudlin, mere self-pity. But Peabody's sensitivity to time's passage is usually muted into the autumnal and elegiac, despite the occasional *cri du cœur*. He himself seems to have always possessed a highly self-aware, slightly saturnine nature. Look at his rambling, free-associative letter to his friend George Myers Jr:

...if I want to make it?? (whatever that means?? say a family and house in Ireland and enough money to get by between books), then I have to push and finally make some coin. All of which sounds egotistical and awful but is a daydream shared by many [...] I mean you are not quite as near 30 as

I am and I feel that twinge...creeping...that fear that I'm going to be penniless, jobless, living with my mom like Jack Kerouac for the rest of my life and never doing anything... Seems like all I really know how to do is write and spend money on magazine and other publishing ventures and spend time with le femmes and they don't pay for that (and I wouldn't want them to)...but that's it...eat/drink and write [...] just that I'm bored with, no that's wrong, I'm impatient always have been and always will be...I want it now and by god I don't want to wait...

Few of us ever do. Still, age does bring with it some self-understanding and self-acceptance. Consider the poem "When She Walked in the Room." A teacher finds his eyes drawn to a provocative teenaged student, and though he wisely dismisses the girl's "sexual grandstanding," he cannot deny its power:

Not as smart as the rest.
Not beautiful yet at ease
in a way none of the other students
have achieved.

Arriving late.

A mean girl
comfortable with her body.

Sitting with legs open
panties on view to the world.

She flashed cleavage when she leaned over.
Had to be reminded about today's assignment.

Flashing flesh and a whiff of eroticism
as though she were in control of the entire class.

I'm a married man with two wonderful kids
and I no longer lust after teenagers

but her legs draw my eyes
over and over again. And she knows it.

They also draw the eyes of the woman
who'd invited me to lecture on poetry.

Afterwards we are both astonished
that no matter what we did we were drawn

again and again to glance between this
blonde woman's legs.

Ashamed of the control
she had over both of us.

Unable to comprehend how such a thing
is possible in one so young.

Angry at being so blatantly toyed with
when so many other women in the class

were so brilliant and creative.
And yet hours later it's the one who

stooped to sexual grandstanding that I recall.
The one who troubles my sleep.

The one I couldn't look in the eye.

While Peabody frequently shows us protagonists who are leading lives of quiet desperation—even those who are sleeping with beautiful younger women—he lets his anger really loose in his poems and stories about war. In "Military Fantasia" he writes:

Those who live by the sword
die by the sword.
And that's too good for them.

Those who don't live by the sword
also die by the sword,
too frequently for my liking.

In the story "Stop the War or Giant Amoebas Will Eat You," Peabody imagines a high school student who produces a series of anonymous antiwar pamphlets. They describe an invasion of Texas with the same rhetoric employed by the U.S. government to justify its own incursions into the Middle East. Here's a brief sample:

> "We will try to force the Bush regime to capitulate as quickly as possible with minimum damage to civilians," the Chinese military spokesman told reporters. "There is not a desire to destroy Texas. What we are going to do is liberate Texas from a dictator.

That sentence about liberating Texas from a dictator almost certainly dates this to the war against Saddam Hussein and thus grounds the story in a specific historical moment. Peabody is always doing this; he's constantly aware of time—time periods, the passage of time, the past, the present instant. When in a long essay, he describes short story trends, he's clearly writing in the 1980s when Raymond Carver was every young writer's model. When Taylor in *Sugar Mountain* is shown obsessed with raves, we know we are in the 1990s:

> This crazy woman in leopard skin skirt saying, "K would be da bomb about now." Skanky crack ho. Nearly biting through her pacifier. Looked like Lil' Kim on the worst ever bad hair/bad wig day.

Having now read through, with enormous admiration and pleasure, the stories, essays, and poems in *The Richard Peabody Reader*, three elements stand out: One, superb depictions of Washington life, especially the Washington of young artists, musicians, and writers; two, a seemingly effortless ease at capturing emotional experiences, whether the mad excitement of illicit love or the tenderness of a father for his children; and three, moving reflections on time and the passage of time and the failure of our youthful dreams to come true, occasionally even glimpses of "the ascendancy of despair over reason."

But there's certainly a fourth element, too, one that tempers despair and soothes reason: Peabody's humor. As should be clear by now, a pervasive wryness can be detected in most of Peabody's writing, and sometimes he can be almost surreal. In "King of the Zombies," a drunk emerges from a bar and imagines that the participants in a zombie walk are actual flesh-eating monsters. In "Chimichanga," Peabody—a fan of old horror movies like *Attack of the Crab Monsters*—fantasizes that his poem's portentous title word will summon Lovecraftian monsters from the primordial slime. In the even funnier "Valley of the Gods, 1994," he recalls a pink Cadillac convertible, with Texas tags, crashing into an arroyo and being buried two feet deep in the sand. Out of it emerge a pair of women with "big hair," quite possibly Thelma and Louise "if they'd been rich and Republican." Here's how the poem ends:

> The women wave. No big deal.
> One climbs out of the car in faux leopard skin
>
> and heels. Chugging a silver flask.
> Offering us a drink. "How y'all?"
>
> The other has whipped out a cell phone and
> is already yelling at somebody somewhere.
>
> And for all I know they're still there.
> Stuck up to their hubcaps
>
> in desert sand. Increasingly defiant.
> "Don't mess with Texas," you can
>
> hear one of them shouting.
> And Lord knows, no amount of sugar
>
> could ever sweeten that tea.

So, why read Richard Peabody? The answer is simple: He's a wonderfully entertaining writer. Open these pages and, as the old movie posters proclaimed, "you'll laugh, you'll cry."

If you're male, you are also likely to get all hot and bothered when he describes Miranda Ballard and Sealy. Should you be a parent, you'll immediately recognize how well he depicts the pleasures and horrors of caring for young children. And if you're a writer or would-be writer, you'll admire and envy his narrative drive, his eye for detail, his command of every kind of diction, slang, and lingo, and most of all, his air of easygoing nonchalance, the product, as we all know, of the most considered and thoughtful artistry.

Michael Dirda

Michael Dirda is a Pulitzer Prize–winning book columnist for the Washington Post. *He is the author of six books, most recently* Classics for Pleasure *and the 2012 Edgar Award–winning* On Conan Doyle.

SEX & LOVE 1

Trysting

(Dumbarton Oaks, Washington, D.C.)

skinny dipping
in the midst of power ties
and haute couture

I should come back in the daylight
view the relics

half-glimpsed
Byzantine moon

the word "Loggia" turns me on

Lest I forget:
damask skin
intimacy

luscious pool

Everything According to Plan

Tommy was infatuated with girls on the cusp of rebellion even though he always seemed to wind up being the whipping boy for their impulsive teenage acting out. Against mom, apple pie, the flag. So he was blamed for their preexisting tats, piercings, and infatuations with weed or wine or prescription meds. The last two times had been disgustingly messy. One girl's father, a Montgomery County cop, had threatened to shoot him. His life was fouled up enough without courting trouble like that.

And yet, Tommy had spent the entire summer painting himself into brilliant corners where Jessica Hall was concerned. Every time he considered the consequences of asking his old buddy Chip's little sis out he choked. Why? Her parents would freak of course. They'd lecture him and probably threaten to call the cops. His own folks would throw him out. Not that he hadn't been that route before, but he was broke right now. Had nowhere to go. No car. And was honestly peeved that he was always blamed for the havoc that so-called goody-two-shoes guys had wreaked before he even managed to get a girl's phone number.

It had been a bad winter and Geeks On Call had let a lot of new people go. Tommy survived the first round of cuts, but was finally axed in the spring, and with the thaw moved back in with his folks. The move was a step backward in his eyes, one he felt labeled him a failure. He'd been down and depressed, looking for a cushy job that would cover his student loan and mounting credit card debt and allow him to get out of his folks' hair ASAP—before they all killed each other. His parents, seeing his need to get away from the house, arranged for a family membership at the YMCA. Tommy complained bitterly about it at the time, but now silently thanked them. Because he'd just asked his old friend Chip Hall's little sister Jessica out to the movies.

Tommy had grudgingly gone to the old YMCA pool a couple times. All of the young hard bodies made him feel ancient. He had to admit that he'd been studying so hard in grad school that he hadn't exercised very much in the past three years. He knew he was flabby and soft. He contented himself with the occasional cannonball off the high dive during adult swim, swam a couple of lazy laps up and down the racing lanes, yet was mostly content to watch the little kids squeal and play. Everything changed when he spotted a teal bikini flying toward him and heard a high-pitched squeal, which Doppler-effected his name almost incomprehensibly past his ears, "TOMMMMMYYYYYYYYYY." He was met with a wet and wiggly girl—arms around his neck, legs around his waist. Damn.

"Tommy," the girl whipped her wet hair back and kissed him. "Hello, hello. When did you get back? Does Chip know? Of course he doesn't. He would have told me. Ohmygod, does he know?" She punched his shoulder. "You didn't come see me."

Tommy finally recognized Jessica's coltish smile. He started to say something and thought better of it. "Great tan," he managed and set her down on the wet concrete.

"Are you back for long?"

"All summer," he lied.

"Good, good, good."

Jessica's friends were gathering around. She introduced them. Tommy weighed the combination of smiles, curiosity, and ill will. Most were awaiting his departure. He stayed. They all swapped the usual small talk, shared histories like they were Chinese takeout.

"Chip's living in Catonsville with a Japanese girl he met in Wisconsin."

News to Tommy. Chip had always been unpredictable and they'd lost touch once Tommy hit grad school.

"And how 'bout you?"

"Nothing much."

"School?"

"Oh yeah, I'm going to Anne Arundel."

Jessica said it like she wanted to tell him something important, but Tommy felt the conversation slipping away and mumbled something about picking up a pizza sometime.

"Well, I could use a ride home if you're leaving soon."

"Sure, right now."

Jessica met him at the locker room door in a floppy orange cover-up, mirror shades, and sandals.

"It's the blue Tercel over there."

"Yuck."

"Yeah, well...It's my mom's car, you know."

Tommy wanted to say something memorable but his mind was blank. He felt stupid and creepy. Most of his women friends were married, divorced, and even remarried. In fact, most of the women his younger brother Alan's age were married now. He had been a college freshman when Jessica was still in elementary school. This would never work.

He held the door for her and then she was telling him, "You know, I've always had a crush on you. I used to love talking with you when you came over to visit Chip."

She leaned back. He studied the wrinkled fold of her leg where it joined the thigh and he wanted to stop the car. Jessica smiled, reached down, and moved the seat back as far as it would go.

"That was a million years ago. Your bro and I were still in high school."

Jessica arched her thick eyebrows. Tommy's mouth went dry. She'd been a cute kid who'd hung around outside Chip's room eavesdropping on their every word. So who was this sitting beside him?

She fiddled with his Smiths CD. Jumped back a few tracks to "The Boy with the Thorn in His Side," and surprised him by singing along.

Tommy couldn't believe she was really sitting there—vibrant, alive, a few inches away. The mirror shades made her inscrutable.

He parked in front of the old split level on the hill with the baby blue shutters.

"Well, thanks. Guess I'll see you at the pool."

Tommy started the car but sat there in park and watched her walk up the stairs. Jessica turned around and waved. She seemed glad that he'd watched her. She was flirting with him. Nah, you're being an idiot, she's just a kid, she's not that slick. On the drive home he glanced occasionally at the wet imprint her bikini had left on the seat.

Tommy stayed away from the pool for a few days. Too much stress. He called Chip and drove up to see him in Catonsville. Keiko turned out to be Korean, not Japanese, and was a taller, more imposing presence than he'd imagined. A practicing shrink it turned out.

They had a boozy dinner, shared common ground, and talked high school glory days, while she took them all in. It was mostly forgettable until Chip made some snarky comments about his little sis.

"Tommy here always had the hots for Jessica," he almost snarled. It sounded like he was on some sort of federal fact-finding mission. He also sounded jealous.

Keiko slipped Tommy her business card. "If you ever want to talk about it," she said. Tommy most definitely did not want to talk about it. Not now, or ever.

He asked Jessica out the very next day. Tommy watched for her trademark teal bikini amid the comings and goings poolside. Right when he was about to give up and go home, Jessica arrived like a cloudburst.

She waved, but he stayed put until she walked over to his lounger.

"How 'bout that movie?" he said.

Jessica smiled and her blonde friend shook car keys and giggled.

"Sure. What time?"

"Tonight?"

"Pick me up around eight, okay?"

"Think your parents will mind?"

"Don't worry, I'll handle it."

Tommy changed in the mildewed locker room. He was both psyched and pissed off. He took a longer shower than necessary. Watched a little boy throw a near-apocalyptic tantrum because he didn't want to go home. Covered up when a middle-aged father brought his toddler daughter into the stalls. He realized he was putting off leaving as long as possible because his brother had needed the car and had dropped him off at the pool. He had to walk six blocks home and he'd never felt comfortable in shorts with his skinny, too-pale legs.

Tommy was finally coming out the door facing the pool when he heard Jessica's voice. He hesitated. She was talking to the Ukrainian lifeguard.

"What are you doing tonight?" the lifeguard asked.

"Got a date."

"With who?"

"Alan Carpenter's older brother, Tommy."

The lifeguard laughed. "Old guy."

"No, he's not," Jessica said.

"How old?"

"Twenty-five maybe. He went to school with my brother."

The lifeguard reached around her waist and hoisted her effortlessly.

"Serious with him?"

"Are you kidding?"

"I come by later. Two a.m.?"

"All right."

Tommy waited what he thought was a diplomatic interval and emerged from the locker room with a tight smile glued to his face. The lifeguard released Jessica and turned away, but not before Tommy saw the smirk creeping over his face.

Jessica waved. "Don't forget, eight o'clock."

"I'll be there," Tommy said, though it came out hoarse. He hurried through the turnstile and thought he heard the lifeguard.

"Did he hear?"

And as Tommy pushed open the steel gate, Jessica's tenor answered as sweetly as ever, "No, of course not, silly."

Honeysuckle at Night

I fake sleep
while you strip

toss clothes
onto pine floor.

Do you always do that
when I'm not around?

Just clean up for me?
Your neatness fetish a big act.

Or is it my influence
this new sloppiness?

Full moon light
kissing your feet.

You walking
on ivory tiptoes

Virginia Creeper

She's so good looking.

A prolific climber
scaling the slippery walls of poetry.

Offering forked green tendrils upward
to those who don't need help.

Never looking back.

Never looking down.

Did she bruise your feelings?

Agitate your ego?

No worries. You'll see her again
on her way back down.

She thinks Daedalus.
Streaming wings of glory.

You think Salome.
A slippery Dance of Death.

She thinks bourbon and bon bons.
You think acrobatic geckos.

She doesn't yet realize—
the temple anointed
only view her as a shiny ornament.

Nothing more.

The Other Man Is Always French

The other woman can be
a blonde or a redhead
but the other man
is always French.

He dresses better
than I ever will.

He can picnic
and stroll
with a wineglass
in one upraised hand.

Munch pâté,
drink espresso,
and tempt with
ashy kisses.

He hangs out
at Dupont Circle
because the trees
remind him of Paris.

Did I mention sex?

Face it—
he's had centuries
of practice.

I'm an American.
What do I know?

He drives a fast car,
and can brood like
nobody's business,
while I sit home
watching ESPN.

He's tall and
chats about art—
I don't even want
to discuss that accent.

He's Mr. Attitude.

My fantasy is to call
the State Department
and have him deported.

Only he'll probably
convince you to marry him
for a green card.

No way I'm going to win—
the other man is
always more aggressive,
always more attentive.

The other man
is just too French
for words.

From now on
I'm going out
with statuesque German women

so next time we run
into each other
they can kick his butt
for me.

Walking on Gilded Splinters

You could tell at a glance that she'd been exquisitely beautiful in the not-so-distant past. Wilson did a double take the first time he spotted her moving dreamily through the intersection where he was stuck in traffic, late again delivering his son, Miles, to daycare. The sympathetic magic of her hair and her delicate features seemed to work like a momentary time machine, revealing the image of the young girl buried deep inside the woman. This illusion only lasted for an instant. She could still draw eyes, even if she could no longer hold them—people looked away embarrassed or filled with pity. Her spell too difficult to maintain for all of the rush hour traffic on Lee Highway. The idea that she might be homeless and pushing a shopping cart full of trash, that something must have happened to cause the long flowing locks to go ratty and gray, the angelic high cheek-boned face to go gaunt and ravaged, the mystique to turn inward, was tough for any observer to swallow. Most people don't easily accept such fallen grace. And then the light changed, and it was time to put the pedal to the metal until the stampede of cars stopped once more at the next light.

Wilson was late. He never seemed to get Miles strapped into his car seat before eight fifteen and even that was with plenty of resistance. Miles would begin by folding in on himself and then arching his back. Wilson would talk gently, admonish his son, and then escalate to sheer force. He'd push the thirty-pound boy back into the cushioned seat only to have Miles attempt to scoot down and slide over the lip of the car seat onto the floor. This daily struggle ended with Miles crying, snot covered and red faced, while Wilson ground his teeth and shook with frustration.

By eight thirty, or eight forty-five, Miles would be unstrapped, and Wilson would hand his boy over to Esperanza, the thirtyish Salvadoran caregiver, invariably with a modicum of screaming and kicking, until the door finally closed, leaving Wilson in the hallway alone. There would be a flash of guilt, of regret, and then Wilson would dutifully sign Miles onto the attendance roll at Sunrise Daycare and walk past the front desk where he would exchange perfunctory greetings with the staff before moving like a drowning man out into the oppressive sea of Washington area humidity.

Since Easter, things had been different. Wilson couldn't wait to unload his little guy. And once the door closed, once he was floating down the hall, a new energy kicked in. He was off to see Miranda Ballard. Sometimes they'd run into each other in the hallway—she with her Cinderella Princess daughter, Felicity, in tow. They never betrayed a hint of their infidelity at the daycare center, though within minutes his black Passat would pull up behind her dark green Lexus SUV and they'd race each other to her guest bedroom. They were becoming more brazen—the backyard deck and tennis court had been favorites before it became too hot, and now they frequently made it no further than the living room rug.

And the sex was good. They were both needy and the restrictions placed on them by time and possibility created a fast and furious coupling that threatened to ignite their very skin. Wilson wasn't getting any at home. Angie, his lawyer wife of five years, was pregnant again, and the baby was due in October. A fluke. He really couldn't remember having sex on more than one occasion since Miles was born and that almost three years ago. Miranda's husband was pressing her for another baby as well, though so far she'd managed to resist and distract him. They frequently compared notes in their lazy afterglow. Miranda talked of leaving Roger (who he'd always thought had about as much charm as a graveyard) when Felicity turned five, if not sooner, and moving back to her Southern California roots, while Wilson confessed that he felt like driving away from his family almost every single day.

"Where would you go?" Miranda asked.

"Anywhere." But the truth is he had no idea where he'd go, what he'd do, or if it was possible for him to abandon his wife and children. He wasn't that sort of monster. Was he? Time would tell.

☀

ON TUESDAY HE SPOTTED THE homeless woman again. It was hot for June. Already into the high nineties and the annual cicada invasion had begun. Miles would stop and point at every single husk on the driveway and it was all Wilson could manage to get Miles into the car. Late again. And there was the delicate homeless woman sleepwalking along Lee Highway. A beautiful lost soul. She wore a stripey pink dress today. One that looked so muted and new that Wilson again found himself wondering if she still lived at home. Or if there was really anything wrong with her. Maybe she was just a little eccentric? Like Lydia his nutso boss at Re/Max who was anal retentive about objects on her desk, arranging and rearranging them in some cosmic order that only she could ascertain.

"I saw her again today. She was wearing pink."

"Pajamas?"

Miranda was caressing his arm, his hip. Heavy blue eyes glinting. They had managed to make it to the bedroom today, but Wilson had stepped on a stray Lego and slipped, falling hard out of her arms. She'd stifled her laughter and comforted him momentarily before she straddled him on the red oaken floor and made him forget about his pain.

"A dress. A fashionable one."

"Hmm, the bag lady in Dolce & Gabbana?"

"J. Crew maybe, but she wears it well."

"I think you've got the hots for her."

Wilson coughed; he had begun dreaming about the woman. He'd walk into a cavernous ornate treasure room and she'd turn to face him and it was always something out of *Raiders of the Lost Ark*—the beautiful will-o-the-wisp turning with a flash into a vampiric harpy. And he'd wake. Lord knows he'd loved to have met her when she was twentyish.

"You know what?" Miranda said, grinning.

God he loved her wide mouth, her full lips.

"What?"

"Let's go away for the weekend."

"That's nuts."

"No, hear me out. Roger wants to take Felicity sailing."

"Where?"

"Annapolis. His folks have a house on the Severn River."

"So?"

"So?" Miranda laughed. "So?" She dipped her tongue down to his chest and started licking his nipples. "So, my studly one, I've got sooo much work to do at the art gallery I have just got to stay downtown and they can spend the July fourth weekend sailing on the bay, while I drain every ounce of sperm out of your body."

"Think you can?" Wilson asked laughing until Miranda lowered her blue eyes down to his, dead serious.

"Try me."

☀

WILSON WAS EXHAUSTED, FEELING OLD and burned out. Miles had been sick for a month. It had been sheer torture. Like living in a house of plague—nothing major, just low-level stuff—conjunctivitis, the Coxsackie virus, a sore throat, a head cold, conjunctivitis again, the Coxsackie virus again. He hadn't been able to get free to see Miranda. He and his wife had traded days at home watching Miles and he'd tried to fit his walk-throughs in on evenings and weekends. They literally handed Miles off and passed like ships in the night these days. And the July fourth weekend with Miranda had come and gone unrealized. He was sleepless and frustrated. But after a weekend brimming over with ghastly bodily fluids of all kinds, Miles appeared to be functioning a little bit better, and since the boy hadn't thrown up or had a fever in twenty-four hours, it seemed possible to take him to daycare. God knows they both needed a break from their son. Not that either could waste a second to relax or rest.

He led the young married couple through the five-bedroom McMansion, knowing they'd never be able to afford the bidding war that would invariably happen. He didn't waste his time very often these days, but moments like this one left him worried the real estate bubble was going to burst. Three-bedroom houses that had been going for $400,000 a pop had gone up to half a million, and then up to $600,000 and on to $700,000. Everything was out of control. Scrapped lots were being rebuilt from edge to edge along property lines and sold for double their initial cost. Even Lydia, a woman in his office whom he couldn't imagine selling water in the desert, was closing on house after house. The boom couldn't last forever in Arlington, yet so far there was no end in sight. Wilson was happy to be along for the ride.

On the drive back to the office, he saw the street woman again. Today she wore red Converse sneakers and a little black dress. She didn't look like a scarecrow despite having almost no meat on her bones; in fact, it was a complete mystery how she was functioning at all.

☼

ANGIE WAS IN THE LAST trimester and grinding him down. He was tired all the time and sleepless and his mind was exploring avenues he hadn't known existed until after Miles was born. Ever since Miranda asked the question, he'd been imagining possible exit scenarios. More and more he found himself wondering if such a thing were possible. Not that he could, or would, or was even contemplating it. Yet the mental game of possibility was in full swing. What would he do? Where would he live? Can he walk out on his wife and kids? He'd failed at everything he ever tried to do. His son was the only area in his life where he didn't feel some sort of self-pity. Would he risk ruining that, too? Absolutely all he was really good at was attracting a certain kind of woman, he thought. After all, Miranda wasn't his first affair. Affairs by their nature never last. Never. So why risk playing the asshole by leaving his family? Maybe he'd be good at that? he considered. It's something?

His cell sprang to life with Queen's "We are the Champions." It was Miranda.

"Now."

"The coast is clear?"

"Where are you?"

"Over by the college—Marymount."

"Be here in ten minutes."

She hung up before he could respond. He was going to say BUT. Angie was going in late today after dropping Miles off. He was supposed to try to wrap up his showings and clear the decks for sex with her. His wife had made a rare gesture in that direction. Most of the kid's ghastly bodily fluids had wound up coating her over the weekend. He was sure she needed some TLC now herself. And sometimes he found he still loved her, the petite blonde 'five foot two eyes of blue' woman he'd met in a jury pool, before she became a mother and became so preoccupied with her role she seemingly forgot about him.

Miranda greeted him at the door in a barely buttoned iceberg crisp white shirt and skimpy black lace panties. Her long inky hair framed her face in luxurious curls that swept off the shirt's shoulders. She looked expensive, Pre-Raphaelite, and eager.

"God—" he said before she locked her thick mouth on his and hauled him inside by his belt buckle. They were the same height and her daily tennis regimen made her his physical equal.

"We only have half an hour but I've got to get laid, got to got to."

And then Wilson's cell erupted with Queen's anthem once more.

"Let it ring." Miranda was pulling him down onto the floor, one hand inside his shirt, one cupping his erection through his pants.

"I have to, I have to…"

"Ohhhhhh," Miranda beat her fists on the floor in frustration and then lowered herself onto her back and crossed her arms over her face.

Wilson was on his knees awkwardly hovering over her. It was Sunrise Daycare. This couldn't be happening. Miles had been fine when he'd dropped him off. How does a kid develop a fever in half an hour? And while he studied the oval indentations Miranda's stiff nipples were making in the cotton shirt, he listened to Esperanza. Miles had a fever of a hundred and two. Could Wilson come get him?

"No. It's been a month." Miranda glared.

"Miranda, honey, I have to pick him up."

"I know I know but when can I see you?"

"Honey, I—"

She grabbed his cock through his pants and squeezed tight. "I have to see you."

☀

WILSON LOVED THE OLD MANSION on Dittmar Road. Wished he could buy it. Old-style wraparound porch. Victorian gingerbread. About an acre right in the heart of the posh Country Club Hills community next to the country club golf course. Most houses in Arlington sold before the Open signs were even up in the front yard. But this one hadn't sold in a week. They were asking a million. Wilson could see a developer buying it and scrapping the house. Putting in two McMansions and selling each for $750,000. Or more. They'd make their money. Hell, they might even get the zoning and put in three houses.

Nobody wanted a lawn anymore. Wilson could relate. His Lyon Park neighbors seemed to compete to see how many times they could mow their lawns during a week. He was lucky to manage it once every two weeks. He couldn't wait until Miles was old enough to push the mower for allowance money.

☼

WITH THE BABY DUE IN two months, Angie was deep into the name game. They had foresworn the amnio this time around. She was set on Robin or Antonio for a boy. Wilson argued against Robin. A name guaranteed to make life tougher. Every kid was going to pound on a Robin. And he disliked Angie's unhealthy obsession with Banderas. This time around he was drawn to basic names like Alan or Kurt. Angie wanted Charity or Juliet for a girl. And Wilson knew better than to argue with her about either. Though he floated Charlotte, a name he'd always loved, past her. Only to be crushed when Angie said, "I'd never name a child after a place." She hadn't talked to him for twenty-four hours after he said, "But a bird's okay?"

Mornings were getting a little easier. Miles seemed to go to daycare more willingly; at least the constant car seat struggle was easing. In fact now Miles seemed to cling to Wilson's legs, wanting him to stay, too. Esperanza always peeled Miles away but Wilson would tarry, kneel and kiss his boy's cheek.

"I love you pop-pop," Miles said.

His son's small voice brought tears to Wilson's eyes. Oh my God, he thought. Oh my God. What am I doing thinking about leaving this kid? His insides were melting. Not that things were any easier on the Angie front. Nor were they running smoothly with Miranda, a much stronger woman than he'd imagined.

Still, some things remained constant. The homeless woman was patrolling her post at the corner of Glebe and Lee Highway. Nobody had found a buyer for the Dittmar Road house. And he still dropped Miles off and then drove to Miranda's. True, his ardor may have cooled, but they were still a very comfortable fit—a habit that was getting harder and harder to break.

☀

"YOU KNOW WHAT I FOUND out?"

Miranda was eating sliced peaches. She'd dribbled them with cinnamon and after covering his genitals with the sticky concoction had gone down on him. He was flat on his back relishing the aftershock as she sat crosslegged by his side eating the rest with her fingers, occasionally guiding a slice between his lips. They were fresh peaches, sweet and soft and at their peak of ripeness, quickly browning in the broiling air. Miranda's a.c. had broken and so she'd opened all the windows and strategically aimed a couple of box fans at their naked, sweating bodies.

"Hmm?"

"She was a junkie."

"Hmm?" Wilson was drifting off to sleep. Bad idea. He had to show the Dittmar house at ten thirty. "Who was?"

"Your bag lady."

"What?" He eased up on both elbows.

"Yeah, and you know what else?"

Wilson was alert now; his skin tingled with sweat and the sticky peach juice. He sat up, wanting a shower in the worst way.

"She's your age."

"My age?" He thought of the haunted eyes. "Impossible."

"No, she's forty-two, the drugs just turned her inside out, I guess. She used to be rich, married to some contractor guy who built most of the houses over by the country club." She pushed the last slice into his mouth, surprising him; he opened his lips involuntarily and choked for air.

"Sorry." She rubbed peach juice from his face, and then kissed him wetly. "Anyway, she was in a car accident. Got hooked on morphine for her back pain, something like that."

"And the husband?"

"Left her for a trophy wife," Miranda smiled, using the back of her hand to move her curls away from her eyes.

"Why didn't he try to get her some help?"

Miranda sucked cinnamon and juice off her sticky fingers one by one and studied him with amusement. Wilson thought that he'd probably even pay to watch her eat with her fingers, as seeing each finger slide in and out over her thick lower lip, now shiny and wet with peach juice, might be the single most erotic act he'd ever witnessed. And then those lips parted into a toothy smile as she put the white bowl, its blue fish design visible for a second, down with a clunk, and turned to face him. "Umm," she said licking her lips. "Delicious." And then reaching up slowly, seductively, she pulled her black curls back out of her face into a ponytail, exposing her breasts, which were still perky, unlike his wife's, which had gone saggy and lacerated from nursing. Miranda had weaned in the first few weeks and that several years ago, and the differing results of nursing styles were pronounced. "Now," she said, smiling again, noting with approval his tentative arousal, "why do guys leave their wives? Hmm?" She finished fiddling with her hair, whipped the ponytail back and forth, and then paused. "I mean what exactly is going on down here, mister? Hmm?" And with that she leaned forward on her hands and cat crawled over him, slithering her breasts lightly across his skin, before taking his cock in her mouth again. She held him in her teeth momentarily, lifted him out, kissed his glans, and then teased him with a rapidly flicking tongue before turning her head back his way. "Do you want to help me, silly man?" she said, with a throaty laugh. And then she settled her full weight onto him, her knees bent, both shapely athletic legs in the air, hovering for only an instant before scissor kicking languidly back and forth and then lowering gently down into position on either side of his face, her curvy white bottom rising up off his chest, scooching closer and closer, her thighs lifting, her tan legs spreading wider, wider, revealing her black tuft, her meaning very clear.

❀

IN THE SHOWER AFTERWARDS, WILSON wondered about affairs and why people have them. For men it was easy, he considered. All you had to do was listen to a frustrated wife complain about her husband and then make it your goal to be everything he was not. If the husband was strong and forceful, you had to be passive and let her lead. If he was passive, you had to take her. If he never talked, you expressed yourself. If he talked too much, you went silent. Women may have seen through the charade, but they welcomed the change, the variety, and embraced all the things they'd been missing. Still, watching the water wash over Miranda's taut body, her tiny waist and tight ass a total contrast to his wife's thickening middle, it wasn't difficult to see why men cheated. Was it always about sex and age and looks? Was he really that shallow?

❀

ON THE DRIVE TO THE house on Dittmar Road for his appointment, Wilson pondered the passage of time and women's looks, and simultaneously noted that the homeless woman was no longer at her post. At first it didn't register that something was different. When it did, he realized that he sort of depended on her. She'd been a constant fixture—there from the very first day he'd followed Miranda home. She'd always been there. Coming or going. A direction he'd never before driven that early in the day—south down Lee Highway against the flow. And he found himself feeling a tremendous sense of loss—missing the homeless woman, the constancy of it, his junkie angel, as though she were watching over him somehow. Didn't it even sort of figure that he'd have a junkie angel? He laughed out loud, punched on the CD player, and got Raffi singing "Baby Beluga." Miles loved Raffi.

☼

THE COUPLE WAS ALREADY WAITING at the house, and surprisingly, so was Lydia. In too much makeup and a beige dress that made her look like a puffball. What the hell? This was his walk-through.

"Angie called the office. Something wrong with your cell phone?"

"Huh?" Wilson checked his phone. The power light was off. His phone had gone dead. Damn, when did he charge it last?

Lydia handed him her Nokia. "Call her on her cell. I'll handle these two."

Angie answered on the second ring. "Where are you?"

"I just got here. I grabbed a bagel at the Lee-Harrison shopping center. My phone's dead. I'm using Lydia's. What's going on?" He paced to the end of the porch where red and white roses were climbing a stanchion halfway up the side of the house. They were breathtakingly aromatic and beautiful.

"Meet me at Dr. Bennett's. Miles fell down the courtyard steps at the playground. They think he may have broken his nose on the bricks."

"What? Where are you?" He turned and watched the young couple follow Lydia through the front door.

"En route. I'll be there in five minutes."

☼

THE FALLS CHURCH PEDIATRICIANS' PARKING lot was nearly full, much as it had been during their son's solid month of plague. Daycare was a great way to pass colds from kid to kid, from family to family, and, he'd learned, from family member to family member and back around again. So far he'd been lucky.

The waiting room was full of children—newborn to twelve years old—in various stages of wailing, whimpering, and whining, some with snot dripping green eddies down their faces, others hacking up a lung.

Angie was nowhere to be seen. He walked to the info desk. He'd been in so frequently of late that even Cindy the candy striper knew him by name.

"Miles has already gone back. Dr. Bennett is examining him now."

Wilson thanked her and she smiled, revealing her braces. Cindy was just a kid herself, a teenager taking care of kids. He hurried around the corner past the scales, the posters on height and weight, the eating charts, past a mother whose tiny infant was playing with the drinking fountain, past another who had a death grip on the arm of a screaming toddler who was stretched out across the floor as though mommy had been dragging him down the carpeted hallway, and into Dr. Bennett's office, where he collided with her bulging stomach. It was neck and neck as to who would deliver first—his wife or Dr. Bennett.

Wilson apologized and ruffled Miles's hair, but his son pushed his hands away and said, "No, Daddy. No," before saying "Mommy" and tucking his head sideways into her chest. The little guy looked miserable.

Angie had an ice pack in one hand and bloody Kleenex in the other. Most of the blood had been wiped away, and Wilson was relieved to discover that there wasn't much visible damage after all.

"I'd keep some ice on it, if Miles will let you. Do you think you can do that, Miles?" Dr. Bennett asked. She was young and fresh out of Georgetown, but she'd won Angie over when she sat on the floor during Miles's very first visit. She engendered trust in the kids she saw by dealing with them on their level. Miles nodded slightly. "Yes, there's no concussion. The nose doesn't appear to be broken. Kids are made out of rubber at this age. He's resilient; he'll be fine in a couple days."

"Will there be a scar do you think?" Angie asked.

His wife would be worried about that, he thought, before accepting that of course he was concerned, too.

"I doubt it. Obviously there are contusions to the face. Next time you come in, we'll have a look see. You might want to ensure that Miles's nose gets a generous coating of sunscreen when he goes outside. And make him wear a hat. The skin will be a little more sensitive for a while, and the lost skin will cause it to burn more readily. He'll also need Tylenol for a day or two."

"I gave him some right after it happened," Angie said. "But we're all out. Can you drive to CVS and pick some up, honey?"

Both pregnant women turned to face him, Miles sheltered between them like a pillow.

☼

WILSON SETTLED UP THE BILL while Angie took Miles home. The waiting room was just as full as it had been when he'd arrived. Maybe fuller. He coughed. Oh no. He coughed again. He even felt a little dizzy. No, no, no, he thought. He hadn't touched anything, had he? The doorknob. He'd touched the doorknob. Looking out on the bedlam of snot and coughing, he thought of Dustin Hoffman in *Outbreak*, a movie he'd watched one night while Miles coughed fitfully and finally fell asleep on his shoulder. The germs must be airborne by now.

Cindy the candy striper handled his bill and he was out of there, down the stairs, and back into the humidity. Angie was still in the parking lot, laughing, talking to somebody. Miranda. Shit. Miles was ready to go home, his head tucked just under the curve of Angie's belly. Wilson wanted to go home, too. Miranda held her daughter's hand. Felicity had a fever. After what he'd been through over the past month, Wilson could spot a fever anywhere.

"Look who's here," Angie said.

"Hi Will," Miranda said, her eyes sparkling. She was wearing a white V-neck tennis top and red tennis skirt with black piping, complete with visor, in sharp contrast to his wife's maternity dress—today's was the color of lemonade. And Angie definitely looked like five more minutes outside away from air conditioning might do her in.

Wilson began breathing again. "Hey Miranda," he said. And then he coughed a loud chest cough.

"Oh honey," Angie said, with arched eyebrows.

And then Felicity, her pigtails shaking from side to side with the force of it, coughed the exact same chesty cough.

☀

"THANK GOD," ANGIE SAID, CLIMBING onto the half-circle of brown couch that dominated their living room. "He's finally asleep."

Wilson was watching baseball highlights. It was eleven fifteen. Miles was supposed to be asleep by eight thirty. He noted his wife's saggy yellow maternity jammies, and then coughed. She laughed.

"It's not funny."

"Oh I suppose not," she said, kissing him on the cheek. "Better you than me."

"I'm sure you'll get it, too."

"I'm sure I will." And then she reached over to hug him closer. "Hello stranger."

"What's going on?"

"Oh, I'm just exhausted and we're preparing some new case and it's making me crazy."

"Why? What is it?" Wilson normally blanked on Angie's cases. She'd cut her hours down so much of late and lost so much time to Miles's being sick that he was almost surprised to find that she was working on anything at the moment.

"Do you know the big old mansion on Dittmar Road?"

"Well, yeah, I do, I was trying to sell it today when you called."

"Oh dear, we really haven't been communicating very much, have we?"

"What about the Dittmar house?"

"Well, I'm representing the wife. She's trying to get the house back from the estate. Mind you, I'm not at all sure she has a prayer. She's a pretty sad case. Her husband was Clark, the local contractor."

Wilson whistled. Lydia had been handling everything through an intermediary. Or maybe she'd known all along and simply not informed him. "Clark? I see those signs on almost every construction site, every big hole in the ground in Arlington."

"That would be the one."

"So what's the story?"

"She'd gone missing for several months—went off her medication or some rigmarole."

"I heard a story something like that recently. I used to see this homeless woman every day at the corner of Glebe and Lee Highway, but she's gone missing. Does your client have waist-length gray hair?"

Angie straightened herself and studied him. "Well, she used to be a bag lady, I guess. She doesn't have long gray hair. Have you actually talked to her?"

"No," he shook his head.

"My client's staying with her sister right now. And it was her sister who approached me about the case. Clark died a few months back. A heart attack I believe." And then his wife laughed. "The old guy had a trophy wife. Apparently died like Rockefeller, in the act. Anyway, we're contesting the will."

"There goes my commission."

"Hey," she punched his arm. "Just what are you doing at the corner of Glebe and Lee Highway every day?"

"Dittmar Road's in Country Club Hills off Glebe past the country club."

"Every day?"

"I like the Starbucks at Lee-Harrison, too."

Angie studied him.

"Do you still love me?"

Wilson gasped. "What?"

She punched him again. "Do you love me?"

"Of course. Of course I do."

"You aren't cheating on me, are you? You aren't sleeping with Miranda?"

"Miranda?"

"Yeah, Miranda Ballard. You know, the unnaturally thin witchy chick in the doctor's parking lot this afternoon. The one with the scanty tennis duds your eyes burned holes through."

Wilson freaked. He'd hoped she hadn't noticed his hesitation at joining them in the parking lot. Hoped he hadn't stared. Trying to keep his face immobile, he kissed Angie's forehead. "No, I'm not sleeping with Miranda."

Angie brushed her bangs and his kiss away and studied him hard. "You bastard, if I find out you are, I'll—" and then she was crying and crumbled into his lap.

"I'm having a baby."

"I know, I know."

"Soon."

"Yes."

"I'm scared."

And despite the tears, Angie took one of his hands and placed it on her bump. Wilson could feel the powerful kicking immediately.

☼

THAT NIGHT THE HOMELESS WOMAN came to Wilson in his dreams. She was riding some kind of elaborate barge, like a prop out of *Cleopatra* with lots and lots of oars. She had her arms outstretched as though she was trying to capture the sun. And then she seemed to be holding a burning hoop over her head. And this time she didn't transform into a monster as she approached, she seemed to get younger and younger. Her long flowing hair grew blonder now. And the motion of the rowing, of the barge, whipped her beautiful hair about her head like an aura. And then he realized that Dr. Bennett was seated to her left and his wife was seated to her right, and the homeless woman's hair wrapped itself behind their heads like a banner. And he thought of an Aubrey Beardsley print Miranda had in her study. And when the ship came to a stop directly in front of him, the homeless woman took the burning hoop and lowered it around him where it stayed miraculously in place at chest level like an antigravity Hula Hoop. The flames did not burn or harm him as he feared. They simply fluttered against his arms like paper fire. And when he looked up again, the homeless woman had transformed into Cindy the candy striper. And then the barge glided on, as the women waved, and Wilson felt as though they were carrying all of his pain, and restlessness, and frustration away with them. Once they were out of sight, the spell was broken and the burning hoop dropped to the ground, shattering into a universe of paper flames.

Wilson was too sick to go to the office. Too sick to get out of bed. He was groggy and out of it for several days, so his wife stayed home and babied him until she decided he was a bigger baby than Miles and went back to work. He was just getting back on his feet, watching *The Matrix* on his DVD player, when Miranda called.

"Just checking in."

"Going to bring me some chicken soup?" Wilson paused Keanu in mid leap.

"Something like that."

"Angie's onto us." He hadn't meant to blurt it out.

Silence.

"Shit."

More silence. Wilson glanced out the window at the neighbor's dog. That little dachshund really hated the mailman. He'd barked on cue every single day Wilson had been home.

"Does she know or suspect?"

"Suspect."

"Are we over?"

"You think?"

Miranda sighed. "I've really enjoyed your body, you know."

"I'm sorry."

"I'm a big girl. I can handle it. It's been fun."

"Yes. I'll miss you. Take care." Wilson hung up. Then he hit play again and Keanu completed his leap.

☼

THE NEXT MORNING WILSON WOKE up relieved, his life less complicated, and felt well enough to get back to work. Miles even shared his banana with him at breakfast.

"Pop-pop better?" Miles said.

His son was beaming at him from his booster seat. The face scrapes had healed quickly, though the nose still had some serious scabs. Wilson went on and on about the magic banana his son had given him and how it must have cured his cold. Anything to get Miles to eat more fruit. Angie was happy to relinquish drop-off.

"What do you think of Irene or Coral?"

"So-so. How about Nicole?"

"I was tormented by a girl named Nicole in Girl Scouts."

"Crystal?"

Angie laughed. "Crystal?" She shook her head and went out the door with a bagel in her mouth, her purse in one hand, and a bulging briefcase that contained her laptop and legal documents in the other.

Miles didn't run into Miranda in the hallway as he feared—he wasn't sure he could resist if she refused to end things. Nothing but blue skies so far. And for a late August day, the temp wasn't set anywhere near the usual liquefy-all-life forms stage as yet.

Wilson had been in the habit of driving to Miranda's for so long now that he did indeed subconsciously continue his drive toward the intersection of Lee and Glebe. The gray-haired woman was still nowhere in evidence. He picked up a mocha grande at Starbucks. Felt a sexual sort of tug when he drove back near Miranda's Crescent Hills neighborhood, sighed, and drove to Re/Max, where he learned that the Dittmar Road house had indeed been pulled off the market. The intermediary he'd been dealing with had told Lydia that there was now a sizable lien on the estate. Something legal had come up.

So Wilson spent the rest of the morning rescheduling some walk-throughs for later in the week, while outlining plans for an opening on a new house that was completing construction. He felt good enough later to contemplate a swim at the YMCA, and on a whim drove into the parking lot of his wife's Lyon Park law firm. Maybe she'd want to get some tacos for lunch?

His phone rang as he slammed the car door. It was Miranda.

"Look, Wilson—"

"Miranda, honey, I can't—"

"No, listen to me."

"But—"

"Will, just listen. I can't go cold turkey like this. I just can't do it. There must be a way for us to get together once a month or something."

Wilson watched the traffic on Old Dominion. He turned toward Lee Highway. He watched the vapor trails in the sky, the way the shadows fell on the concrete in the parking lot. What was he going to do?

Miranda's voice had a little meanness in it. "C'mon, you know you want it, too. Hmm? You know you do."

Wilson had to be the boss, had to say something decisive. "I'll call you around three p.m. Is that good?"

"Are you coming over?"

"What? No, no."

"Unhh."

"I'll call you."

"You better... We need to talk."

"We will," and Wilson punched End, closed his eyes for a moment, and then walked quickly across the parking lot.

☼

"WELL, LOOK WHO'S HERE," ANGIE said, eyes lighting up a little. She kissed his cheek and then turned to the two women seated by her desk.

"Honey, I'd like you to meet the Blake sisters, Whitney and Amanda."

They were like a younger version of the silent film actresses—the Gish sisters. Wilson couldn't take his eyes off either one. The dream transformation seemed to have truly happened with Whitney. Where he had seen a homeless woman with graying hair and a haunted, time-ravaged face before, it was as though the missing inner lifestyle, the years of privilege, had been poured back into her and restored. Her demeanor, her carriage, all modified and amplified. The split ends were gone, and the gray hair had been cut, dyed white-blonde, and shaped to accent her eyes. Where they had looked washed out before, they now seemed magnified by a pair of horn rims revealing a beatific intelligence. Her thin legs were hidden in Katharine Hepburn slacks, and she looked like she'd be perfectly at home in boardroom, casino, or limousine. She watched him intently like somebody who remembered a story told long ago.

"I used to see you every day," Wilson said, and instantly regretted it. His wife gripped his arm tightly.

"My husband was one of the Re/Max Realtors trying to sell your house," Angie said.

"I was thinking that I knew you from somewhere," she said. "Life on the streets has run a little roughshod with my memories, I'm afraid." Her voice was at once raspy and sophisticated.

"I'm afraid Whitney has had quite a distressing adventure. She's back on her medication now," Amanda said, patting her sister's arm, but Whitney brushed her off.

"I'm not finished," Whitney said, staring her sister down, and returning her focus to Wilson. "Life on the streets was hard," she said. "Of course. It wasn't something I'd do by choice or again. I never gave up hope that things would change for the better. And as you can see, they have." Content with her little speech, she shook her head almost imperceptibly.

Meds? Wilson was confused. Hadn't that been her problem in the first place? "I was sorry to hear about your troubles after the car accident," he said. "Do they have you on some new kind of painkiller?"

All of the women stared at him, and it took a few seconds before he realized he might have put his foot in it.

"What car accident?" Amanda inquired, shocked.

"Honey, what are you talking about?" Angie asked him, using her Earth-to-Will voice.

"I meant I just heard that…well, there were rumors about the Dittmar Road house and…"

"The truth is the only accident I participated in was marrying Frank Clark." Whitney laughed. "After that accident I was desperate enough to need some antidepressants. I stopped taking them for a while and well, hit a rough patch. Everything's better now." She smiled at him, that joke still perched on the edge of her lips.

Whitney was indeed a clotheshorse and Amanda had taken her shopping. She wore leather slip-ons and an expensive belt of what looked like interlocking strands of golden chain. The pair looked like sisters straight out of the Bloomsbury era his wife so idolized. Their portrait would fit comfortably alongside Virginia, Vita, and Vanessa.

Angie was keen on the lunch idea, and so Wilson killed time with a *Newsweek* in the office while the women finished their business. He'd made a pit stop to the bathroom, spent too long staring at himself in the mirror, worried that his affair with Miranda was actually somehow visible, and had stopped by the giant window at the end of the hallway to watch the traffic, when he felt a hand on his elbow.

It was Whitney. A secret still looking like it was trying to escape from her mouth. "Will, was it?"

"Yes, Whitney, that's right. What's on your mind?"

"I used to sleep in a tree house."

Wilson laughed, thought maybe she really did have a screw loose after all, and said, "Uh huh."

"An abandoned tree house not too far away." Whitney seemed to choose her next words very carefully.

"Yes, go on."

"In some woods in Crescent Hills behind a big house with a tennis court."

And Wilson's heart sank. There was a thick woody area behind Miranda's house. There might be a tree house. In the winter he would have seen it. In the spring and summer the trees would have hidden it.

"I've watched you."

Wilson didn't know what to do or say. Where was Angie? Why hadn't she come looking for him?

"When's the baby due?"

"October."

"Don't do to your wife what my husband did to me."

"I—"

"Do you understand?" She took off her glasses and looked at him again as though she couldn't see him clearly enough.

"Yes."

"Well, then," she said, tapping the folded glasses against his chest dismissively before turning her back to walk into the ladies bathroom, leaving Wilson stunned and mute in front of the oversize hallway window, the afternoon sun blazing like a fireball behind him.

Rendezvous in New England

A blue wheelbarrow.

Out of place
on a gentle slope.

What paint remains
fading.

A pint-sized pumpkin
shriveled

on the rusted bed.

Bag of Bones

I love
Bag of Bones.

She's not a Supermodel
only eats like one—

water and air
the gaze of strangers.

Bag of Bones
tugs my tie
whispers,

"Roll me."

Who can resist?
animal-vegetable-mineral.

Bag of Bones
loves Tim Burton.

Always looks perfect
at Halloween.

"You don't really love me,"
she says.

"While you sleep
I sing lullabies to your bones

and they love me."
Oh Bag of Bones

take me home,

take me home.

Astro City

rom the bouncy spring rocket ship ride on the playground where he sits, Sean watches the orange-suited convicts rake litter and brush from the shoulders of the asphalt that wraps around the crescent-shaped beach. He remembers that Key West's motto is "One Human Family." Sean doesn't know why he remembers this but it comes to him seated here now, watching his children run loudly from the swings to the colorful slides, which despite being made from some sort of space-age polymer designed to remain cool to the touch in direct sunlight are, he knows, already too hot for their tiny hands. Too hot before noon even this time of year on a disastrous Christmas vacation. Disastrous because Sean is hung over, because he feels so genuinely guilty about drinking again last night after two years on the wagon that he's caved to his wife Carmen's demands, and taken the kids to Astro City Park, the only playground they could find, and guilty because he knows that the convicts aren't included in Key West's tourist brochures, though he is just now beginning to believe that the convicts in their orange suits have more freedom than he does.

Sean tries to resist this train wreck of thought, when it is flicked from his consciousness like an errant mosquito as Chai, the younger of the children, trips, falling head first into the steps of the playground slides. With a quickness that amazes him, Sean has moved across the hot sand and is scooping up his toddler before she realizes she's hurt, actually bleeding. She's got a bloody nose and Sean knows it's got to be painful as he brushes sand away, and rocks her gently in his arms. Bobby, the oldest, appears simultaneously in the opening of the tunnel slide at Sean's feet. His son's glee quickly turning to concern, fear. Sean can see his boy

39

pointing. He looks down. Chai has bled all over Sean's brand-new Hawaiian shirt.

As Chai's two-year-old wails increase in volume, Sean thinks he'll go completely deaf only to be somewhat saved by the even louder zooming engines just overhead—another in an endless procession of prop planes shuttling tourists back and forth from the southernmost tip of the U.S.A. The airplane momentarily distracts Chai. Sean knows there's a box of Kleenex somewhere in the rental van and begins power walking toward the playground gate and the parking lot.

"Bobby, here's the key, open the door. Hurry now."

His son catches the key ring, scrambles ahead, and is now painstakingly depressing the latch to pull the door open. The inside of the dark blue van is already set on broil, too hot to put the kids into, but Sean has no choice. He sets Chai down on the driver's seat and he can see that the hot vinyl is making things worse, the singed air almost impossible to breathe.

"Find the Kleenex, son. There's a box in here someplace." Sean puts the key in the ignition, opens the windows, and cranks the a.c. all the way.

Miraculously, Bobby finds the Kleenex and hands the box over. Sean pulls out a wad, wets them with the now-warm water from the water bottle in the diaper bag. He cleans Chai's face and is astonished that the damage isn't more severe. No need for the emergency room after all. A lot of blood; still the damage is relatively minor. She's bitten through her bottom gum a little. He holds the wet wad to her mouth, her scraped-up nose. Leans her head back to help things clot. The cool air blowing on her calming her down.

"You want some ice cream? Would that help, honey?" Chai's still crying and burbling. Sean finds the bottle of Infant Tylenol in the diaper bag and gives her a dose. Then he lifts her tiny crumpled bird's body and straps her into the car seat. Straps Bobby in the other car seat. And off they go to Sean's friend Leo's house where they're camped out for the week. There's a small market on the corner, so Sean leaves the van in park, idling, something he'd never do back home in Chicago, and gets a box of ice cream sandwiches from the punky young Indian behind the counter. The place reeks of chicken curry, today's carry-out special.

Back in the van, Sean pulls an illegal U-turn, drives one way the wrong way up the driveway and back into the compound parking lot. He's supposed to park in the space labeled Bednarek, though the sign is missing or conveniently deep-sixed, and there are cars parked all over the place that don't seem to belong to any of the people who actually live in the small houses that years ago housed cigar factory workers. Sean lucks out and finds another signless spot.

Bobby, released from his car seat, races through the brush, scaring a multitude of cats, over the paving stones, up the wooden back steps, across the concrete deck which is covered with yesterday's chalk scribbles, and into the screen porch. "Mama Mama," he yells. The techno-dance crap the gay couple next door plays incessantly is already omnipresent above the cries of the roosters and chickens, the cats, and the rustling of the coconut trees in what passes for a breeze. Old Man Rayburn, who owns the cabana-sized blue house beside the abandoned unfenced concrete pool, watches with red-rimmed eyes as Sean carries Chai up the steps. And just as Sean slips inside the porch door, he notices a motion to his left. A woman standing on her stoop wearing only a bra and panties smoking a cigarette. She waves the smoke in a circle. At him? His buddy Leo had told him the place was a rental, that he had no idea who was living there from month to month—it turned over all the time, he'd said.

"What's going on? What's happened?" Carmen bursts out of the house, oozing efficiency. She strokes Chai's black curls and doesn't really take her from Sean as much as she vacuums her daughter into her own maternal orbit. Carmen and Chai are one. Sean is never aware of letting go.

One second Chai is cradled on his chest and the next she's wafting across the room in his wife's arms.

Bobby is standing underfoot, so much so that Sean almost trips over him, and then he remembers the ice cream sandwiches, and he opens the box, pulls one out, hands it to the boy, and roughs his hair. When he looks back at the stoop, bra-and-panties woman is gone. Sean follows his family into the bedroom where Carmen is nursing Chai on one of the twin beds they've pushed together to create enough space for parental sleeping. Their daughter is almost weaned, so this is a surprise—Sean waves an ice cream sandwich and breaks her concentration. Chai wants the ice cream and snatches out for it, her mouth still tugging on the nipple, eyes and hands focused elsewhere. The ice cream wins, and Chai lets go of Mama to reach it, but not before stretching the nipple like a piece of elastic. Sean waves another.

"I don't want one," Carmen says, adjusting her bra, her tangerine-colored blouse. "It's almost lunchtime, honey."

"Think of it as medication."

Bobby has joined them and all four climb on to the beds.

"What happened?"

"She fell. Right into the steps," Sean says, unwrapping a sandwich for himself.

"She's been falling down a lot lately. Maybe her shoes are too small?"

"What does that have to do with anything?"

"Just a thought."

Chai points at her lacerated nose and says, "Boo-boo nose."

"You got a boo-boo honey, a big boo-boo," Carmen says and kisses her daughter's hair. "Do you think she needs stitches?"

"Nah—she's not really hurt that bad. The blood made it look a lot worse than it is. There are tons of veins just under the skin on the face."

Now Chai has ice cream mashed all over her lips, mouth, and cheeks. She's smiling and happy again.

Carmen wraps her fingers around Sean's ice cream, and he allows her to pull it from his mouth. She licks all the way down one long edge, coating her tongue with vanilla. This is typical. She hands it back. Wipes her fingers on his shirt. Laughs.

"Take your shirt off and let me soak it. Maybe we can get the blood out." Then his wife moves out of the bed, turns the window unit up to high, takes the box with the remaining semi-melted ice cream sandwiches with her, and disappears into the kitchen. "I'm making tuna fish sandwiches for lunch," her voice trails back.

"With pickles? With pickles, Mama?" Bobby shouts, and is out of the bed and in pursuit.

"With pickles."

Sean finishes his ice cream, unbuttons his shirt, and wads it up to clean Chai's messy face. She protests a little, but he knows she's okay now, because as soon as he's done, she bounces out of bed and races after her mother and brother. Sean feels almost competent. Relishing his role as a father for a change. A role that is increasingly hard to define. At lunch, though, he will take pleasure in watching a rejuvenated Chai eat her way through an entire tray of frozen French fries.

When the rest of the family crashes for nap time immediately after eating, Sean moves onto the screen porch. He's got an ice tea. He's relaxing. Knows he's got two hours before his brood is up and energized. Time to ponder what he's gotten himself into. Old Man Rayburn is sitting in a lawn chair playing with a big orange cat. He has a catnip mouse on a piece of braided nylon fishing line and he's flipping it just out of reach. Bra-and-panties woman is nowhere to be seen. The techno softer now. The gay couple doesn't seem to leave for work until around two p.m. Sean reaches into his glass and pulls out a piece of ice to plop into his mouth and suck on. His head is still throbbing. He's trying to figure out if he should keep an appointment. He'd met Irina last night on his solo reconnoiter. Last night in the doldrums, he'd wandered the streets in search of something to do, something to distract him from Carmen's big news.

☀

SEAN COULDN'T EXPLAIN WHAT HAD happened. He couldn't tell you what he was doing in Key West, either. Carmen had wanted to go somewhere warm. She was sick of the Chicago winters. So was he. A stiff breeze coming off Lake Michigan could turn your blood to ice on a summer day. In the height of winter, it acted more like a chilly reciprocating saw. Carmen had tossed some names about and he found himself infatuated with just one—Key West. And so here they were, only to discover that it wasn't a place to bring preschoolers. Carmen was furious enough about that. Sean had been kind of dimly aware that something was up, though what he couldn't guess. So after pizza last night, he'd been putting puzzles together on the floor with the kids when Carmen disappeared. He'd given both children a bath. Not a job he relished, though he could manage in a pinch. Carmen must have gone for another walk. She'd been leaving him with the kids more and more lately. The White Rabbit, the children's bookshop she owned, wasn't sunk yet but it had begun listing seriously to one side and it was only a matter of time. One of the chains had opened a new location two blocks away, and the competition was killing her. In one of the more bonehead moves of their early courtship, Sean had taken her to see Tom Hanks and Meg Ryan in *You've Got Mail*. He hadn't read any plot summaries, he'd just figured it was a chick flick and she'd forgive him for that particular week's transgressions, yet as the plot relentlessly drove the two stars together, she got angrier and angrier. "That would never happen in real life!" Carmen had shouted in the lobby. "She would have killed him before she'd have slept with him." Even the sentimental part of him had to admit that romance seemed impossible given the situation—Hanks being the owner of a chain superstore while Ryan was a small bookshop owner. Carmen wouldn't let it go—her ranting lasted for hours. Sean had apologized, and they'd married, and Bobby was en route almost immediately after their Irish honeymoon. A short honeymoon. Because Carmen never left her shop in the hands of her assistants for very long. A bookstore is a 24/7 proposition, and Carmen was almost always working.

Sean swayed slightly. His balance shaky after lifting the kids in and out of the tub and drying them off. They were calling to him now from the bedroom, asking him to read to them, to put them to bed.

"We're pregnant," Carmen announced, as she stepped inside from the screen porch. Carmen was smiling. Her white teeth with the gap in the top middle. She was electric with excitement. Sean felt like he was watching a Hollywood version of what a happy woman was supposed to be.

"Did you hear me?"

That plea in her voice. Doubting him.

"I heard you," Sean said. His words bitten off. Why? He was excited. Surprised. Why should his words have teeth? Rip into her?

Tears starting to form in her root beer–colored eyes.

"Honey?"

Sean's arms automatically encircling his wife's hips, hips that seemed to widen a little every time his arms went around them. But she wouldn't stop crying. The kids were shouting from the bedroom, and Sean couldn't see a way out.

"I'm going for a walk," he said. And he removed himself from her and the clamor of the children, vanishing out the back door, across the concrete porch, under the coconut trees, past the raggedy cats in the sand by Rayburn's house, past the empty concrete pool with the cracks running across the bottom, down the driveway to the street, turning left at the graveyard, and from there toward the tourist congestion on Duval Street.

☼

SEAN HAD BEEN WATCHING THE cruise ships, watching the tourists, pondering his life's new complications, when he spotted a mime of sorts. While other people at Mallory Square were performing dazzling illusions or trying to separate tourists from their cash with some kind of music, jokes, or pet tricks, she was standing on a white pillar in white makeup, white robes, holding a white bell and clapper. She barely moved. She was minimal when everybody else was in a frenzy of motion. Calm in the midst of chaos. You had to slow down to really notice what she was doing. So Sean leaned on a bulkhead and watched.

The elongated woman in white was slim and trim and had the catlike grace of a trained athlete. She was more tantalizing moving one foot from side to side than most women are naked. At times her act reminded him of ballet exercises. That unconsciously graceful, that routine. Even the prune-faced Key West natives seemed to drink up every sensual sway, bend, and flex. When tourists put money in the white bowl at her feet, she struck the white bell with the clapper. The peal cut right through Sean's bad ear. When tourists put a wad of money in the white bowl the woman in white clasped hands around the bell and clapper and made like she was praying. She was good. Very winning. Very subtle. Little kids were captivated. The woman in white caught them with double takes, and after a kid jumped, she'd smile. They adored her.

Sean had been wearing his Blackhawks jersey; it was ludicrous for daytime, but the evening chill justified bringing it along. He couldn't take his eyes off the woman in white. She was supposed to be an angel or goddess or something. How on earth did she haul that pillar with her every day? So he waited for her to step down off her pedestal. At sunset, when the tourists began to thin, return to their cruise ships and hotels, or head for dinner and drinks, the woman in white slid down onto the wharf. That's when Sean walked up and put a ten in her white bowl.

"Great act," he'd said. Would she continue playing the part or not?

"Thank you," she'd said. She had an Eastern European accent.

"Russian?"

"Ukraine."

"How do you manage to schlep all of this stuff for your act?"

"The hotel. They let me store."

"Can I give you a hand? Buy you a drink?" Sean was surprised that he was so excited. He wondered for a moment if she cleaned off the white makeup or did she go home just like that.

"Tomorrow. You choose place."

"You live here."

"You choose."

"Hemingway House?"

"Is good. Noon?"

Sean knew his kids almost always napped between twelve and two p.m. "No, make it one p.m." He'd started to walk away and then realized he hadn't asked her name. "I'm Sean."

"Irina."

☀

AFTER THAT, SEAN HAD WANDERED around and found a used bookshop that was some sort of front for porno. Part of the store was legit, but as you walked deeper inside, the building seemed to swallow you up, the shelving arrangements became more and more labyrinthine, while the shelves grew higher and higher, eventually towering above even his basketball big–man physique, with titles he couldn't hope to reach without a ladder. Miles of Books was the name of the place. It should have been Miles of Porn. Though Sean hadn't had a drink in two years, not since he swore to Carmen that he would quit drinking and become more dependable before Chai was born, he was drawn like an iron filing across the street where people were gathered in a parking lot and wound up at a derelict bar with some of the lowest life forms he had ever seen. What do you call Trailer Trash that has inbred for a century? Whiteout?

And there Sean had sat knocking back a shot and a beer, and then another. He'd promised Carmen he'd never drink again. Something Leo and his other sports buddies thought was nuts. He had managed until now. How could she be pregnant? Sean didn't think they'd had sex more than three times in the past six months. Chai was still nursing and pretty much glued to mama whenever Carmen was home. They had two bedrooms, but the place was still pretty small so opportunities were limited. Hell, between their work schedules there weren't any opportunities to speak of, were there? Mrs. Morales had babysat for them a couple of times so they could celebrate their anniversary, their birthdays. And here I am, Sean had thought, turning thirty-five and I need a date. What's happening to me? Why aren't things going my way?

☼

SEAN WATCHES A LIZARD SUN itself on the cinderblock wall of the porch, plops the empty ice-tea glass on the soggy napkin atop the wicker table, and then scribbles "Gone for a walk. Love you." The Hemingway House is a fairly straight shot down Olivia Street from where they're staying. Sean's walked past it a few times and likes the walls and the giant trees. He's acquainted with the basic outlines of the Hemingway legend, without actually having read any of the books. He vaguely remembers a George C. Scott movie but that's the sum total of it. And when it came to Key West and a place to meet Irina, this was the only landmark he could muster. Everybody knows the house. He mentally thanks Leo for lending them his dead mother's old place. Maybe this vacation is what he really needed after all? He's been so restless lately. Apartment building supers never get away anymore than bookstore owners, but Carmen had pushed. He'd left Esteban in charge. The brownstone on North Lake Shore Drive faced Lake Michigan. Sean could walk the kids out the door to the lakefront beach. He liked their two-bedroom super's apartment. In the winter he watched an endless white vista from his kitchen table. Carmen was content. Or had been. Where would a new baby sleep? They'd have to buy a van. Book Mrs. Morales for more daycare. His dream had been that the kids would go to nearby Northwestern. How on earth would they pay for everything now?

Hemingway House proves a major rip-off and disappointment. Sean is pretty depressed. He watches the tourists, watches Hemingway's six-toed cats that have now mutated into seven-toed cats. And when a pasty-looking woman with bangs eventually finds him sitting on the steps to Hemingway's office studying the pool, she is unrecognizable as Irina. Where he'd imagined blonde she is brunette. Where he'd remembered curves there is muscle. Where he'd remembered soft eyes there are chiseled coal splinters. Her English is more fractured. Sean yearns for the white makeup, the wings, the pillar, the bell, and the clapper. What was he doing? he wonders. Irina doesn't betray a hint of emotion as she guides him across the street to a coffee shop.

"What are you thinking?" she asks once they are situated.

The hip-hop on the radio is really loud. Sean's left ear aches. He'd ruptured it when Bobby was two. His son had pushed the door open as Sean had been digging a Q-tip in his ear and he'd poked it straight through the eardrum. His hearing has never been the same. "My kids," Sean says, surprising himself. Not like he'd hidden his wedding ring or anything.

"Children?"

"Yeah."

"How many?" The barista brings them their espressos.

"Two. With one on the way."

"You feel sorry?" She hitches one leg over the other and offers him a cigarette.

He shakes his head. "No. No. Not at all. They're great kids. I guess I'm just not ready to give up my free time again so soon."

She nods. "I have child." And then raises her head toward the ceiling and exhales a great flurry of smoke straight up in the air.

"You do?"

"Alina. Two year old."

"Was she born in Key West?"

"No. Only here one year."

"Why here?"

"What's not to like?" she laughs, spreading her arms wide. "I come to America to get married. End up here. Is okay."

"And your act pays enough to raise your daughter?"

"Enough."

"But you're looking around."

"You married?"

"Yeah."

"Happy?"

"Yeah."

"You live where?"

"Chicago."

"Cold?"

"Very."

"Tak, I think so."

"Where is Alina? I mean, it's none of my business but who takes care of her?"

"Babysitter. Sleeping now."

"Me, too. I mean mine, too."

"Good, everybody sleeping." Irina leans forward conspiratorially, puts a hand on his arm, and says, "Sean, you sleep with me?"

The music is really too loud now. Sean's ears are quaking. He's imagined this moment, though realizes he has to leave. As much as he enjoyed the fantasy, he's not going to go through with this. He's too scared. "Irina, you're beautiful but no. I'm gonna go."

Irina pulls her hand away as he stands up. Studies him for a second. "Okay, go," she says and exhales some smoke, then stubs the cigarette out in her saucer.

Sean doesn't know what to do. He realizes Irina isn't beautiful; it's all about her innate sensuality. It's how she moves that's so attractive. When was the last time Carmen moved with anything approaching that smoldering sensuality? What's he doing? Falling for Irina's act? Tempting fate? Sean hesitates but eye contact has ceased, and so he leaves.

☀

AN AMBULANCE IS NESTLED IN the parking lot behind the house. Carmen and the kids are standing among a group of men, everybody concentrating. A pair of medics are on their knees around Old Man Rayburn.

"What happened?" Sean asks, one arm circling Carmen's waist.

"He fainted and cracked his head on the concrete."

"Daddy, Daddy," Chai says, pulling on his shirt, pointing. "Boo-boo."

"Where were you?" Carmen asks.

"You don't want to know," Sean says, surprised when one of the gay men from next door lifts Chai up and holds her. Chai never lets anybody pick her up. Not even Carmen's folks in San Antonio. Right this second though, his daughter looks supremely confident and happy.

Carmen is pushing the double jogger they rented. Sean's carrying the diaper bag and lagging far enough behind her that he can almost imagine he's watching somebody else's family.

Bobby is pretending to fly down the cemetery's asphalt runways, while Chai herds chickens from one whitewashed section to another. The sky is a vivid blue, spotted with a few white clouds, like markings on a giant blue cow. And the air is filled with fragrance from exotic flowers. Sean knows nothing about flowers, but Carmen has been pointing out hibiscus, oleander, bougainvillea, and frangipani blooms.

Chai is no worse for wear, though she looks like she's been abused. Sean is afraid somebody will call child services and have them arrested, but most people just stare at her wounds and then give him the raised eyebrow.

Two gravediggers are plying their trade. They are bitching, moaning, and complaining. Help the same everywhere. Sean unable to really relax and vacation, he can't forget that elderly Mrs. Mason needs a garbage disposal, that the Ingrahams need the a.c. checked out. At least he doesn't own the building. God, that would really put the kibosh on things.

The cemetery is an endless chessboard of activity with joggers and women with strollers, dog walkers, and families replacing flowers on crypts or weeding around tombstones. There are service roads looping back and forth between the palm trees through sections that seem to be separately roped-off subdivisions for families, or war memorials, or city districts. Though Sean at first believes it's some kind of elaborate heavenly hierarchy or another—the people with fortresslike mausoleums obviously most favored and blessed. So much for "One Human Family." The motto didn't apply. Sean remembers that the Spanish called the place *Cayo Hueso*, or "island of bones." "One Human Cemetery" suddenly seems much more fitting.

☼

KEY WEST AQUARIUM IS THEIR next stop. Bobby is rambunctious, and Carmen takes him by the hand while Sean holds Chai up high so she can see all of the sharks and manta rays.

There are signs everywhere that warn against standing on the raised platform area near the tanks. Sean pays no attention, and after the guide has led the rest of the tourists out the back to the outdoor enclosures where the swordfish and other cool exotics are, he steps up and dangles his daughter over the water. "Look at the big fish, honey, look." Chai's eyes are focusing on the water, until Sean steps back off the dais as a surge of water wets his feet and one of the sharks rises high in the tank. Close. Close call. Almost. Chai is giggling about the water on Daddy's shoes. Sean's not laughing. That was too damn close. He's been a fool. He's stupid and he doesn't deserve to live. Risking his daughter's life that way.

☀

SEAN WANTS TO WATCH THE Bears game. They're playing the Washington Redskins at four thirty today. So he finds a sports bar and sets Bobby up with a basket of shrimp while Carmen takes Chai out to buy new shoes. The game is close, closer than it should be until Brian Urlacher and the Bears defense wrest control. With one quarter to go, Bobby's head is resting on the table and Sean pays the bill and gathers his son up to carry him home. Sean loves this aspect of having a son. He can't wait until Bobby's a little older so that he can take him to see the Bears, Blackhawks, Bulls, and Cubbies. He would never admit it, but one of his greatest fears in life is that Bobby's adolescent rebellion will be to root for the White Sox. Sports Sundays will rule. Carmen pretty much dominates Sundays now because she sees so little of the children during the week. Once they're a little older, Sean hopes he can amend things.

☀

AFTER THE KIDS ARE DOWN for the night, Carmen comes out on the screen porch where Sean's reading the newspaper by the light of the Tiki torches, Cuban music turned low on the radio.

"Hold me," she says, curling into his lap and looping her arms around his neck.

Sean embraces his wife.

"I'm so worried," she says.

"Me, too."

"I smelled the booze on you last night."

"Don't start."

"Why?"

"Dunno."

"I'm not going to put up with it again, Sean. We had an agreement."

"I know. I know."

"What does that mean? That's how you react to a new baby?"

Sean is silent. Mulling it all over.

"What are we doing here, Sean? I mean you dragged me down here—"

"Dragged you?"

"—to this place that isn't child-proofed—"

"What? Key West was on your list."

"—and there's nothing we can do with little kids."

"Yeah, yeah, I know."

"I should have flown to Texas, spent Christmas with my family."

Sean's family is dead. All Irish, all Catholic, all alcoholic, all gone. His wife's family is prolific and, save for Carmen, hasn't roamed far from home.

"It's not right for the kids to miss Christmas."

"You're right."

Leo was going to retire in Florida and had told him all about Key West. Moderate temps, great food, kayaking, sailboats, scuba, coral reefs, whale watching, fishing, all of which sounded great to Sean. Of course you can't do most of these things with real small kids. Sean had thought he might get to do at least one of them alone. And then there was the very visible gay and lesbian community. Not so easily explained to kids. Maybe they could come back again after Chai was at least ten?

"Don't you want another child?"

"Yes. No. It's a total surprise is all."

"Come to bed," she whispers in his ear.

"No, I'm going to find a meeting."

"What?" Carmen pushes away from him. Locks her eyes on his. "Are you serious?"

"Yes."

☼

SEAN CAN'T BELIEVE HE'S TURNED down sex with his wife to go to a meeting, but he really doesn't want to end up like the rest of his family. He knows this. He still can't figure out why last night got to him so much. Finding a meeting is not easy, though even a party town like Key West has one or two and eventually Sean stumbles into the basement of a Presbyterian church where six desperate souls are sitting on metal folding chairs sipping really sludgy black coffee out of tiny vending machine cups. The Sunday school Christmas tinsel and decorations add to Sean's sense of grimness. He listens to their stories, the comfort of the familiar, and opens his story with a bang.

"I always drink Cutty Sark," Sean says.

"Why's that?"

"Because the Kennedy family owned it."

Sean is laughing at his own Irish joke, when a young woman sweeps into the room and joins them. He knows her. It's bra-and-panties woman, the renter next door. Clothed for once in a brown Turtle Kraals T-shirt. She's probably a waitress at the restaurant.

"Oh, it's you," she says. "You parked in my space. I had your van towed."

☼

CHRISTMAS IN KEY WEST. SEAN thinks of Venus flytraps, that velvety sort of hellishness. Apart from the occasional manatee dressed like Santa, the ubiquitous strings of colored lights and tinsel, it's hard to imagine the Christmas spirit anywhere in the entire state. Key West seems to be where people run to avoid the holidays. As though Key West is always on holiday. Unless you're a local. Sean tries to imagine denizens of the Conch Republic flying to the UP, the Upper Peninsula of Michigan, for the holidays in a geographical reversal of desires. But that's ridiculous. Do sun bunnies ever dream of being snow bunnies? Do Florida kids want to ride sleds and ice fish?

So after the endless hassle of getting the rental van back, Sean takes the family to the beach at Fort Zachary Taylor in the morning on Christmas Eve. The beach really is beautiful. Sean watches as Chai collects tiny pieces of coral and shells. He's not sure how he's going to get them away from her. This is a national park and you're not really allowed to remove things. And Bobby is playing with a balsa wood glider. Throwing it up in the breeze and trying to keep it out of the palm trees, off other people's blankets. Carmen is reading *Girl With a Pearl Earring*. Sean wistfully watches the fishing boats make their way down the channel and out to sea. It's mostly new mothers on the beach this early, though there are a couple of dynamite Cuban chicks on a blanket to his right. He glances from time to time, keeping tabs on them. They don't look like the type who get wet but they surprise him by running across the rocky beach into the surf. Their bikinis have that high cutaway style and they are both all leg. Sean watches for a while and when the kids return and nag Carmen for snacks, he lays back and shuts his eyes. And he dreams that the woman in white comes to him. Only something's wrong. It's not Irina but bra-and-panties woman in the white makeup, the white robes. And just when he's all hot and bothered, she takes out the bell, raises the clapper, and strikes.

"Sean."

"Hmm?"

"One of the guys next door told me that Mr. Rayburn is in critical condition."

"Yeah. With what?"

"His heart. Shouldn't you tell Leo?"

"You think?"

"I'm sure he'd like to know."

"Okay."

"I've got something for you."

"Hmm? What?"

Carmen puts something in his hand. What is it? He opens his eyes and looks. A pregnancy test strip.

"I thought I better make sure, so I did it again this morning."

"It's blue."

"It's blue all right."

Sean starts counting on his fingers.

"September."

"September." Sean sighs—there goes next football season.

☀

EVENTUALLY THE SUN GOES IN and it gets so overcast and cold that they can't sun. This gives Carmen the opportunity she needs to go buy some gifts for the kids. Since bringing wrapped packages through airport security after 9/11 was going to be impossible, Carmen decided they'd do most of Christmas when they got back to Chicago. Still, they didn't want the kids to go completely cold turkey with no tree and nothing to open, so they'd been caving to their whims all during the trip. There looked to be an entire new duffle bag full of beach gear and toys that was going to make the flight back north. Sean would handle lunch while Carmen ran out to buy a couple of larger items that could be wrapped and opened on Christmas Day.

Today's lunch is your basic McDonald's. Bobby wants a chicken nugget Happy Meal, wants to play in the ball room. Chai is too little to get on the apparatus, never eats Happy Meals. French fries will keep her occupied, and some milk. Sean's hungry, so he orders a pair of Big Macs. He loads up the drinks, the straws, the napkins, the ketchup for Chai's fries, and heads for the ball room. Bobby is right under his feet—he's hungry and trying to snag some fries off the tray. Sean is carrying Chai in his left arm, balancing the large drinks and the tray with his right. When they get to the door, he pushes it slowly with his right elbow and Bobby jumps up and bumps his arm from underneath. The drinks start to tip, and he overcompensates just enough to right them but the wrist movement sends them cascading over the other direction and the Sprite and the pink lemonade— their lids flying—land right on his son's head, and everybody's soaking wet. Sean manages to hold onto the tray, soda splashed all over the fries, the rest of the food on the ground in a wet pile. Sean's jeans are wet all the way down his crotch.

"What the fuck do you think you're doing?" he explodes at his son. He drops the tray on top of everything else and his right arm flies out and slaps his son into the glass door of the ball room, just as a mother comes rushing to help out and pulls the door inward, so that Bobby sprawls into a heap at her feet.

"Oh my God, I'm so sorry, I just wondered if you needed any help—" and then the woman stops as she registers what she's just heard, witnessed. She studies Sean's face and backs up a step.

Chai is crying and slides down out of Sean's grip. A manager is running over. Sean realizes that every eye in the place is on him. Bobby is crying. The woman holding the door can't let go. If she does the door will bang into his son. Her tiny twin daughters now hugging her legs. They look scared, too.

Sean's right arm is shaking. He says, "Lady, I..." and then stops. Lunch is ruined. It's not like lunches haven't been ruined before. "I'm sorry. It's just an accident. No big deal. C'mon Bobby, get up."

But the boy lies in a heap on the floor crying. Chai, sitting by Sean's feet, crying as well. Sean realizes he'll have to buy more food. He'll have to start over. He reaches in his pocket. He's only got five dollars. Damn. He can't buy lunch for them all. He'll have to find an ATM. This is unbelievable.

The woman is still standing there. "Do you need—?" she stops.

"We're okay. We're okay."

Now the manager is beside him. There's a cleanup crew bustling to mop and a bucket is on the floor beside Chai. Sean reaches down and picks Bobby up, and the boy doesn't resist. He's holding his red swollen cheek. And Sean nestles him in his right arm and then he reaches down with his left and gets Chai around the waist. The manager opens the outer door, and Sean says, "I'm sorry, thank you," and head down, embarrassed, carries his children out to the van.

☀

LEO HAD TOLD HIM THERE was a sign for the second parking place. While Carmen does damage control on the kids at the house, Sean explores the heaped-up shells and rubble that make up the barrier between the parking lot and Old Man Rayburn's yard. He finds half a sign, which reads—Bedna. Well, that's something at least. He puts the termite-chewed wooden sign in front of the van at the second parking spot. A rooster crows. A couple of chickens have flown halfway up a tree. Sean didn't know chickens could fly. Bra-and-panties woman is back on the stoop. He's going to ream her out and starts walking toward the house as one of the gay men from next door pops out of the gate.

"I'm just back from the hospital."

Sean stops. "Really? How's Old Man Rayburn doing?"

"He's dead."

"I'm sorry."

"Time just caught up with Bayard. He was eighty-five, you know."

"I didn't. And the cats?"

"Oh Ward and I, we'll feed them. He loved his cats so."

Sean watches as the man climbs on a bright yellow motor scooter, starts it up, and then with a wave speeds off down the driveway. When he looks back to the stoop, bra-and-panties woman is gone again.

Carmen is waiting for him on the porch.

"What the hell's going on, Sean?"

"I don't need this right now."

"Look, you haven't lifted a finger to make a single meal on this so-called vacation. You didn't help me child-proof. You haven't helped in the kitchen. You haven't called Leo to tell him about Mr. Rayburn."

"He's dead."

"What? How do you know?"

"One of the guys next door just told me."

"There was the van fiasco."

"Not my fault."

"And now you abuse the children."

"I'm stressed. You know I'm stressed out."

"Then there's the drinking."

"I went to a meeting. It was only one night."

"We had a bargain. You'd quit drinking and being such a bastard when your teams lost and I'd be the breadwinner and we'd have another kid."

"Right, one more kid. Not two more."

"I don't have to tell you that the new baby was an accident. You know it is."

"How do I? Huh? Tell me that. How?"

"And how do I know after the little stunt you just pulled that Chai fell down the steps at the playground? Why should I believe you?"

"Ask her. Ask Bobby."

"Listen, I'm going to let the kids nap a little and then we're going to the playground and try to tire them out, and then we'll go out for dinner before coming back and putting out the presents. I'm not going to jeopardize their

Christmas, what little holiday spirit there is left, by arguing with you."

"Fine, suits me."

☀

SO TO MAKE AMENDS, SEAN drives his brood to the playground. He feels like shit. He loves his family, he really does. The fact that there are no shade trees shouldn't matter now that things are so overcast, but of course by the time he pulls into the packed parking lot the sun is breaking out of the clouds and starting to heat everything up again. Well, at least the kids will tire themselves out before dinner. Maybe they'll forget about McDonald's?

Sean halfway expects to see the orange-suited convicts again and is almost disappointed when they're not picking the area outside Astro City. As he watches, Carmen helps Chai swing from one bar to another on the parallel bars. She's too tiny to reach them for another couple years at least so Carmen helps their little girl maintain a fantasy. And his daughter's face is splitting, her grin is so huge. There're a lot more children at the playground today. Somebody has organized a birthday party and a troop of vans has taken most of the parking spaces and deposited a group of moms who are busily setting up the typical "hot dogs, hamburgers, and cake" party under the only shade trees at the rear of the fenced-in playground. When was the last time they'd thrown a big birthday bash for one of the kids?

"You know, Sean, I'm wrong. I don't think I can handle this right now. I need some time to think. I'm going to leave."

Carmen is holding Chai, who has both hands wrapped around a sippy cup, lips sucking furiously.

In his blurry uneven state, Sean thinks Carmen means she's leaving him at Astro City.

"You don't care about the children."

"Don't be ridiculous."

"Sean, if you really loved them you wouldn't spend so much time trying to keep away from them. I love you, but I'm not going through the motions for this or any holiday."

"Well, merry fucking Christmas," Sean says. He doesn't know why he says this. It just seems like the right thing. Seems somehow to sum up all of the fear, disappointment, and self-loathing he's got locked inside him. And he prays for a miracle. Anything. And is startled when the noise from the party seems to audibly crank up a few notches. "So now what? What are you going to do?"

"Have the baby. Manage on my own. Maybe sell the shop and move to Texas with my folks."

Sean's eyes dart past Carmen to the laughing children, the moms playing chaperone. There's singing and cake and in the middle of it all his eyes focus on a familiar face. And as Sean watches, Irina walks toward him. What a sensual blur she is as she moves across the sand like a jeans commercial or a daydream. Carmen is still talking but Sean moves away now, toward Irina.

"Look, about yesterday. I'm sorry. I need to apologize. You see, I really just wanted to ask you what the deal was with all the white stuff. I wanted—" His head swivels as Irina walks past him. Whiplash. No hint of recognition. And as he turns, Irina stops and bends down to heft a small child, a little girl with butterscotch-colored skin, not a day older than Chai. Irina turns, her shades a shiny white mirror, and walks back toward the party.

Carmen watches a moment and then hoists Chai a little higher in her arms, grasps Bobby's hand, and begins walking toward the parking lot, to the rental van, as the Conch Tourist Train slithers past, while the Astro City Park plastic bakes in the relentless Florida sun.

As Bees in Honey Drown

There's still honey in your voice
when you answer her unpredictable
late night phone calls.

A sympathetic counterpoint
to her breathy whispers.

She has always been able
to make you quiver.

And don't think
your new lover
hasn't noticed.

If a voice could give life
perhaps this is the wavelength
it might
choose.

Burnished sweet as clover honey
—that split-second hesitation
before sliding over the lip
of the jar—folding back onto
itself in golden ribbons.

Reasons to Live

A meadow behind the red and white house
opens up to sunlight and a teenager—
maybe sixteen in a purple T-shirt
with a heart as big and noisy
and unforgettable as Kaaterskill Falls—
swings in a hammock to the rhythm
of their own quivering Walkman.

It is good to stand just so
and contemplate the beauty
just out of reach and unobtainable
like a son, or daughter, or an unrequited love.

Their purple shirt matches the
meadow flowers, and you,
lazy in the humid embrace of late
August, have forgotten what
you were on about. Happy
to be alive and simply standing
in such a special place.

Perhaps you have always stood
poised at this exact moment,
sunlight turning to shadow.
Perhaps now, you, too,
will find a reason to get up tomorrow,
relax, and continue your journey.

POP & CULTURE ^{2}

I'm in Love with the Morton Salt Girl

I'm in love with the Morton Salt girl.
I want to pour salt in her hair and watch
her dance. I want to walk with her through the
salt rain and pretend that it is water. I want to
get lost in the Washington Cathedral and follow her
salt trail to freedom.

I want to discover her salt lick in the forests of Virginia.
I want to stand in line for hours to see her walk on in
the middle of a movie only to have the film break and watch
    salt
pour out and flood the aisles. I want to sit in an empty theater
up to my eyeballs in salt and dream of her.

When I go home she will be waiting for me in her white dress
and I will drink salt water and lose my bad dreams.
I will seek the blindness of salt, salt down my wounds,
hang like a side of ham over the shower rod in the bathroom
and let her pour salt directly on my body.

When she is done I will lick her salty lips with my tongue
and walk her down the stairs into the rain, wishing that I
could grow gills and bathe in her vast salt seas.

E Is for Elephant

Nothing scared the Colonel more than tight spaces, so it took a hell of a lot of sweet talk to get him into the tunnel of the MRI. One young intern had been pretty convincing, and so the Colonel sighed and rolled his bulk off the gurney to please the blue eyes, big lashes, and black hair, took a deep breath, and climbed onto the platform.

"Are you Italian?" He liked Mediterranean types.

"No Sir. Greek."

"Greek, you say." The Colonel swished the word behind his teeth like a new mouthwash.

"What's your name, son?"

"Nick."

Then Nick warned him that the noise would be so loud he'd have to wear the proffered thick gray headphones. The Colonel had balked at that, too. The machine was formidable enough.

"But Nick, what if I can't take it in there? What if I need to have you pull me out? How will you hear me, son?"

"We won't leave you alone, sir. Someone will be standing right here by your side. There's really nothing to fear."

☀

THEY ALWAYS SAY THAT. THERE'S never anything to fear, the Colonel thought. A year ago he'd fallen and he'd had only the vaguest notion of something slamming into him. His right arm and shoulders were numb and he was aware that something was very, very wrong. An electric door had been opening into him, where he had fallen. And his bulk had somehow confused the electronic mechanism. The door opened and closed, over and over again. Banging into him with the regularity of a porch swing. And yet he couldn't move. And he'd been afraid. Afraid like he'd been in the hole of the freighter, a stowaway en route to America, beginning all over again in America. One of RCA's well-dressed young men had finally lifted him out of harm's way. He'd been mortified. How on earth did such a thing come to pass.

☀

THE GREEK ORDERLY CONVINCED HIM to get inside. The noise was impressive—an infernal clanging like one of those no-talent British rock groups. The metal crunching seemed to crawl right under his skin, wending its way down his body like a dog's teeth on a bone, all the while maintaining a racket that seemed more internal than external. A psycho gong from hell or perhaps something from the movie *Metropolis*. The Colonel licked his lips. A bead of sweat traced a line down his forehead.

☀

THE COLONEL FOUND HIMSELF THINKING about his youth. He'd slept with a hooker named Marte in Amsterdam, before the carny days, the midget weddings, the elephants. Before the kid. The kid was nothing more than a big elephant. The big E. He laughed. The Colonel had crawled into Marte's boyish arms and tried, really tried. But he couldn't shake the sight of the cockroaches. He'd faked sleep and positioned himself so the streetlights made a pool on the floor. And there in the light where it had been flung after the grunting, after the slapping of skin on skin, lay a condom, a little trail of cum on the linoleum floor around it. And something moving. Cockroaches. Fucking cockroaches. Crawling all over each other to squeeze inside that tiny opening. The entire membrane coming to life with them. Fucking cockroaches eating somebody else's cum. He'd jumped out of bed, put on one boot, and stepped squarely in the middle of the seething mass. Watched the roaches pop out both ends of the latex, leaving a sticky glaze of cum and carapaces adhered to the sole of his boot and to the tile.

☀

THE COLONEL COULDN'T TELL YOU why he'd worn a Hawaiian shirt and baseball cap to the kid's funeral. It's true that he used his poor health as an excuse to avoid being a pallbearer. But really, the idea of supporting the person whose career had supported him for twenty years just didn't sit well. And while most of the mourners were preoccupied with the spectacle, he was thinking. There had to be a way to make more money out of the kid's empire even with the kid cold and in the ground.

Still, he could be excused. Surely the media would forgive him. The boy meant everything to him. Everything. The kid's father had inherited the estate. But the Colonel had badgered him. Vernon was in line. No problems there. When the white Cadillac hearse deposited the kid at the cemetery, he thought it was all going to work out. Hell, there was money to be made off of all of this. Lots of it. Once the eulogy started, he drifted away. Sat on a cop's motorcycle.

☀

OF COURSE HE'D KNOWN BETTER. Knew he didn't have to push it to the limit like that. The same way he knew the films were awful. But who cared? The idea was to make money and they'd done that. Hell, he'd made tons of money. He couldn't believe he wasn't gambling in Vegas even now.

☀

"BUT I WANT TO DO something serious. I want to star in the James Dean story. No more songs. No more girls."

"But your public wants to see you sing. They love you."

"I mean it, Colonel."

"Look. Why do you want to be James Dean? James who? He died young. Nobody will even remember him in a couple of years. You're better looking. Isn't he, Bitsy? Isn't he better looking?"

☀

IT WAS AMAZING HOW WELL he'd fooled everybody. The Dutchman. They never guessed that he wasn't really a Louisiana colonel and not one of their own. He thought about nights in Amsterdam. That city never slept. He'd never gone back of course. No passport. Wouldn't have been able to get back into the U.S. Would've risked everything. Of course now it was out. That bitch Priscilla had seen to that.

☀

THE THOUGHT OF THE GERMAN hookers draped all over the kid in Berlin was too much, though. God. The shower scene in the army movie. Pure beefcake. And the kid's lips. A shiver started at the base of his neck and traveled quickly to his waist. He was getting an erection. The robe was parting beneath the burgundy tie and even with his girth the erection was touching the top of the machinery. Right here in the damn MRI.

☀

MOST OF THE BOY'S AUDIENCE never realized the Colonel was a fraud. He'd fought hard to fool them. Of course the kid knew. Of course he did. But it was part of their act. Their sweet act.

☀

HE FOUND HIMSELF WISHING HE could undo everything. He missed the kid. That was no way for anybody to go. Dying on the toilet! Like his face had stretch marks.

☀

"HOW LONG YOU PEOPLE GONNA keep me in heah? Hello. C'mon now, stop joking around. Somebody get me out of heah."

There was no answer. The claustrophobia was getting worse. He couldn't move. And his erection was brushing the metal. He was going to cum unless he could move. And of course, the flogging scene slipped into his mind. The kid getting whipped in the jailhouse. It would come to him now. Trapped in this machine. He couldn't move, couldn't lift a hand, and his jowls were sweating under the metal, under the awkward gray headphones. His nose itched and he tried not to think about it.

☼

MARIE HAD NEVER UNDERSTOOD. HE'D provided for his wife, but it was all for show. Your typical celebrity wedding. The kid, on the other hand, had to get married. The media would have destroyed the kid for playing around. No way the Colonel would let that happen. Too much riding on it. Too many people depending on him.

☼

ONLY IN THE CASINO WAS he completely alive. The croupiers smiled, called him Colonel. He liked that. Free drinks. Free room. He sent some of the boys ahead and then he'd pick a machine for each one. They carried baskets of change. It made all the blue-haired women from Peoria and Oshkosh stare. He'd stroll behind with his good cigar and he'd bark orders. The young men would crank those handles for him. That was the life. He didn't have to crank handles on slots anymore by god, he paid people to do the work for him.

☼

THE KID WAS JUST ANOTHER lost puppy. The Colonel had witnessed his share of pet funerals at the Tampa Humane Society.

Running the kid's life was like running his father's horses around in circles. Or the elephants. Who didn't want to control, really control, a big dumb animal? That was everything.

☼

THE COLONEL COULDN'T DROWN OUT the clanging but when it stopped, his mind wandered to the Ferris wheel stopping at its pinnacle and the wedding march bombarding the assembled crowd from makeshift speakers.

"Why don't you come back to my wagon later," the Colonel's pseudo-bride teased. "You look like you could do with a little honeymoon."

The Sears catalogue wrapped in black crepe looked like a Bible to the crowd, and they'd never guess that the justice of the peace in the car below them was just one of the roughneck crew, that the bride was a coochie dancer. The Dutchman knew that his stunt had worked. He was pulling crowds. P. T. Barnum was right about suckers. Every tarheel sucker in the vicinity of Charlotte, North Carolina, was assembled around the base of the wheel watching this weird wedding. And then they would stay for the rides and see the shows and spend all of their money.

☼

"WE CALLED HIM, COLONEL."

"And what did he say?"

"He said you can rot for all he cares."

The Colonel snorted. The kid was really mad at him this time. He'd signed him into another couple months of touring. Took the cash right up front. And now the kid was tired and cranky.

"Now here's what I want you boys to do. You call the doctor to see me here in the hotel. I'm sick, I tell you. It's my heart. You tell him that. Tell him he's killing me with this nonsense."

☼

"WHY ARE YOU DOING THIS, Colonel?"

"Doing what, boy? I'm sick, or haven't you heard."

"Sure Colonel, you're sick. All right."

"Haven't I made you rich? Haven't I made you famous?"

"That's true but—"

"No buts about it, son. Just trust me on this."

"Why can't we tour Europe?"

"It's too cold over there. How about we set up a concert in Hawaii instead? You'd like that, wouldn't you? All those hula dollies."

☼

BUT PRISCILLA AND THE LAWYERS had really fixed him. Just like some straggly-assed stray cat. They'd cut him out of the estate, cut him out of the easy ride, the casinos on the Vegas strip. Here he was now in Palm Springs with no reason to live. Stuck in a machine that had stopped working forever ago. Had they forgotten him after all?

"C'mon now. Stop joking. Get me out of heah. I want to get out. Somebody. Please get me out. Help." His voice was muffled because of the headphones. He didn't know if he was shouting at the top of his lungs, or if anybody could possibly hear him over the sound of the machinery. His pants were getting cold from his ejaculation. He didn't know how long this test was supposed to take, but he was cracking up. He felt like he'd been in the machine for hours.

"Please somebody. Please."

And for the first time in a long time...the Colonel actually cried.

She Discovers Jazz

stumbles over it
        more likely

purloined letters

as though love
is spelled

Wynton

and jazz
something
that never existed

your records
invisible
all those years

a moon
whose gravity
she refused to obey

until his ears

more interesting
than yours

heard

what she
was trying
to say

Fiji Water

Kyra's addicted to Fiji Water.
Something about the taste
It's sweeter, mellower.
More profound.

At first I think she's joking,
And then wonder if she's been
to Fiji and smuggled some
contraband home.

She hands me a square bluish bottle.
Fiji Water it says on the label.
Is this the new Frusen Glädjé
or Häagen-Dazs? An exotic fake name
invented by some nefarious
company's marketing department?

God only knows what's in this water.
Byproducts of nuclear spillways or
chemical plants? Something scary
and straight out of James Bond?
Or maybe just water from the dog's dish?

I close my eyes and sip the Kool-Aid.
I'm surprised. It doesn't taste
like other bottled water at all.

How can that be?
Is it flavored?
If so, it's awfully subtle.

In a flash I'm tripping
about the island of Fiji.
The all-knowing tropical water
teaches me how to surf,
how to speak the language,
weave grass mats, huts,
go naked without getting sunburned,
even enjoy coconut milk and lychee nuts.

I beachcomb and actually find complete
shells. Driftwood in the shape of animals,
ships, even bottles, lay around my feet.

Wait, the Fiji Water bottles drift
in on the actual tide where
the natives harvest them.

I'm riding the crest
of a wave along with 10,000
blue bottles of Fiji Water.

"Eureka," I say.
"This is the best
agua I've ever tasted."

"Good, ehh?" Kyra laughs.
"You know I peed in that water."

Before I can react,
Kyra says, "I'm joking."

Bad Day at IKEA

A few hours before April Stevens's philandering husband finally left her, she strollered the kids over to the IKEA store and promptly lost Bear.

Bear was a raggedy gray stuffed ragamuffin, passed down from April's older sister Janet to April, and then to April's daughters Emily and finally Easter, known as Pie for short. Emily had never been very attached to Bear. He'd lost an eye along the way, been left out in the rain, squashed by traffic in the street, and run through the sprinkler and washing machine so many times he'd become a miracle worthy of the best survivor narratives. No heroine cult or splendiferous sewing circle was going to be able to adhere one more patch to his disintegrating hide. April would be hard pressed to find a single remaining thread of the bear she'd come to know and love, which is precisely why Emily had passed the rough-hewn object on to her little sister, knowing for a fact that she would be getting Felicity, an American Girl Doll, at Christmas. So Bear may have been expendable and seen better days, but Pie loved Bear because he was a legendary misfit and an outcast. That's how she felt already at three, though she didn't have the precise grasp of words to make herself understood.

April had gone to IKEA to finalize preparations for her husband's fortieth birthday party. Preston had long opined that he didn't understand why only kids were allowed to frolic in the colorful ball rooms at IKEA. He wanted to take off his shoes and roll around too. Despite the fact that the more April researched play rooms like the ones at IKEA and McDonald's, the more the rumors about people finding all kinds of horrible things submerged beneath the red and blue and yellow balls—from syringes to hardened feces—seemed to be true. But Preston was an artist and a dreamer, and considerations like health and litigation were deemed unnecessary roadblocks to his freedom of expression.

The IKEA staff had been leery of an adult party, and their wrinkled brows only relented after April agreed to pay more than a thousand dollars for a full hour and signed numerous waivers. Further, April had arranged for sushi to be delivered, along with a bartender. The entire thing was to be a surprise.

While the girls chased each other around the ball room and the mat room, April made sure the IKEA staff understood that thirty adults would be transforming the fishbowl of the store into an adult party area at precisely 7 p.m. The girls were upset that they weren't going to be attending, but they were to be part of the pre-party party, at home, where they'd give Preston a mural they'd spent a week working on in secret, which included rainbows and tulips and puppy dogs and dolphins. As well as outlines of the girl's bodies, even Bear's, filled in with rubber stamps and stickers. April was very proud of the effort and imagination that had gone into the mural and hoped Preston would appreciate it. He'd been pretty distant lately, and April suspected he was going to push her soon to try for a boy, a third child. He grew up with a brother, and it was clear to her that he felt uncomfortable around his own daughters. Did she really want to be fat and constipated again for nine months? She was ambivalent. They'd traveled quite a distance since she'd been his T.A.

☼

BACK IN COLLEGE PARK, PRESTON, Artist-in-Residence and star attraction for the new Fine Arts Department, was engaged in scheduled late afternoon meetings with senior students, and his encounter with surreal sculptor Piri Lindquist had been like something out of a dream. Her efforts during the semester had been fairly rudimentary in terms of color and space, and he'd been thoroughly disappointed by her attempts to capture the surrealist gestalt. So to have her standing there in his gleaming new office was a bit of a downer. That is, at least until she opened her mouth and said the long-imagined— "Professor Stevens, I'd do anything for an A in this class."

Preston had spent a summer in Vicuna in the Upper Elqui valley of Chile. He'd been entranced by the Torre Bauer, a medieval German-style tower that a German-born mayor had imported stone by stone in 1905. And he'd become addicted to pisco, the strong national spirit of Chile. When Piri made her proposal, Preston opened one of the two remaining bottles of Ruta Norte he'd brought back, and scavenged vainly to find two glasses.

"I have glasses in my studio. Let me show you my new installation," she said.

Preston gleefully followed her into the bowels of the Fine Arts building, a Circle of Art Hell he tended to avoid during the semester. His nose was thoroughly burned out from decades spent with oil paint and paint thinner, so that he normally didn't notice strange scents even in this context, yet here among the stunted art projects of doomed Painting 101 students, he had a new appreciation for benzene and brimstone. One of Piri's classmates was trying to recreate the burning city of Centralia, Pennsylvania—a nightmare of twisted shapes, sinkholes, smoke, burning coal, and ash. Even Preston had to admire the devious nature of the work, though spending ten seconds with the piece was more time than he felt the artist deserved. He'd never think of the piece again, though his curiosity about the actual town was renewed.

"Here we are," Piri said, stopping in front of a colossal coil of corrugated silver and red sheet metal folded like a labyrinthine paperweight and large enough to practically fill a ten-by twenty-foot space.

"Why, it's an actual room," he said, awed. "A space within a structure."

Piri smiled, handed him a glass, and said, "Follow me."

He watched her stoop slightly, revealing entwined roses tattooed on the bare strip of skin above her waist, and enter the cleft in the twists and turns of silver and red metal, disappearing altogether into invisible inner workings.

That's not a room, you dolt, it's a vagina, Preston realized, as he followed close behind. Piri, god bless her, had just given his waning libido a jolt of more than five hundred volts. Now this was his idea of a fortieth birthday present.

Deep inside the intricate folds of the sheet metal vagina in the basement Circle of Art Hell in the Fine Arts building, Preston entered a mysterious cocoon of a room. Piri was already disrobing. The curved space was suffused by light exuding from a fold in the metal, revealing a futuristic-looking bed with a low-slung aluminum frame, plus an iPod stuck into a docking unit with speaker system vibrating to techno music by a group, he would later learn, that was known as Aphex Twin.

Preston filled the glass with the frothy yellow grape brandy and handed it to Piri, who turned around to reveal an athletic hairy body, reminiscent of some of the gals he'd fantasized about while cruising the hippiegoddess.com website in a fit of midnight despair. He fixated on the jagged black lightning bolt tattoos on either side of her unshaved pussy, lightning bolts acting as directionals, leading the way to her landing strip.

She took a sip.

"What do you call this installation?" he asked.

"I call it 'Preston's giving me an A.'"

Her eyes became glittering prizes he longed to possess.

☼

NOW, PISCO IS A STRONG drink that comes on pretty fast and is not for the faint-hearted. Even somebody with Piri's long history of collegiate alcohol abuse might be surprised, and it was pretty clear she'd gotten a little more than she'd bargained for at first blush.

So while Preston was determined to push and push until he reached China, or the womb, whichever came first, Piri tried to lock her eyes on anything substantial that would stop her spinning head. She tried the ballet gambit, fixing on a spot, but there was faint hope of that in the metallic curvature above her head. She'd neglected lunch in her eagerness to lock down her grade, and they'd polished off the bottle of pisco. The semester was coming to a close and she'd been very worried. Her art had made no impact on the faculty or her peers, save for the lunatic who'd dubbed himself DJ Ripple. He was the one behind the fiery homage to the Centralia mine fire. Piri was getting so queasy. Puking at a time like this was definitely going to cost her a grade point. So as Preston continued to push, Piri tried gamely, like all sailors do on a stormy sea, to keep the roiling pisco inside her.

☼

DJ RIPPLE HAD LONG AGO given up any and all hope of getting a single B in his art classes. He was looking at solid Cs and worse. So with a week to go in the semester, his Goth girlfriend off to Ocean City with her BFFs, he tried to cram for his art history final. Nothing doing. Resigned to his fate, he went off to IKEA. He'd surprise Goth girl with something new. A whisk? A spider plant? A cracked mirror? He knew he'd get an idea once he walked around the place.

☼

APRIL HAD A DIFFICULT TIME keeping the guest list to thirty. She'd invited a mix of faculty wives, some of Preston's more civilized artist buddies, and Silver Spring neighbors. Preston hadn't mentioned any students, but she had lined one up to look after the girls during the party.

April took a shower with her daughters, let them play with her makeup while she got dressed, and checked her watch. Where was the babysitter? Where was Preston? And where on earth had her cell phone got to?

That's when the screaming started. That's when Pie noticed that Bear was missing. Pie was hysterical. April tried to soothe her. Emily even tried to soothe her. But Pie wasn't having any of it. She wanted Bear and she wanted Bear right now. So April located the cordless house phone and called IKEA and asked if any of the ballroom staff had noticed a stuffed bear. It was nearly impossible to hear them over Pie's constant screaming. She had somebody look in the parking lot. No. She had somebody look through the ballroom. Nada. No babysitter. No Bear. April felt like stuffing her head in the oven.

Then she had a brainstorm. She'd get Preston to buy a new doll. He'd have to get two—one for Emily as well. She knew that Preston was capable of buying two stuffed hippos or aardvarks. But she'd make him see it her way. The new doll had to be something powerful enough to distract and conquer the still screaming Pie Pie.

She called Preston at the office. No answer. The phone just rang and rang. She called his cell. Nothing. She called Piri, the student she'd lined up to babysit.

☼

PRESTON HAD FINALLY REACHED A point with Piri that he'd never managed with any other woman. He'd somehow lost the condom inside her. Exhausted, his cock raw and painful to the touch from the friction of her hairy steel wool briar patch, he gave up. This was new. He'd pushed and pushed and pulled and pounded and he still couldn't get off. He collapsed beside her and his eyes shut.

☼

PIRI'S CELL PHONE WAS RINGING. She managed to wake up and extract herself out from under the beached whale of her art professor. What a disappointment.

"Hello?" she whispered.

"Piri? Where are you? The surprise party starts in half an hour."

"Shit," she said as the lost condom slipped partway out of her.

"What?"

"I forgot all about it, Mrs. Stevens. I'm so sorry. I'll be right there."

"Too late for that. Can you meet us at IKEA? I'll transfer the kids there. Okay?"

"Absolutely. I'm on my way."

"And have you seen Preston? Do you have any idea where he is? He was supposed to be home an hour ago."

☼

DJ RIPPLE LIKES THE BLUE and yellow IKEA building. He walks past what looks like a party in the ball room wishing he'd had that idea. You can rent the ballroom? Wow, amazing. He walks around the store and finds nothing that makes his kind of statement. Hell, he has to pee. He wanders off to find the bathrooms and despairs when he sees the tiny yellow double-sided sign on the floor. Somebody's cleaning the men's room. The other bathrooms are clear across the building, and he really needs to go right now. He knocks on the women's room. No response. He looks around. Nobody's watching. He disappears inside and locks the door. He takes a long pee and then washes his hands. In the mirror he notices something on the toilet tank inside one of the stalls. A beat-up stuffed bear. The thing has more stitches than Frankenstein's monster. This is perfect. Goth girl will adore it.

☼

PRESTON WON'T WAKE UP. PIRI shakes him, shakes him again. God, is he still breathing? She puts an ear to his chest. Whew, yes. But he's out like no man she's ever witnessed before. She's got to go. Fuck it. She'll figure a way out of this predicament later. She'll tell him it was the best sex she's ever had. No wait, he'll know that's a lie. Better to go the other direction. Tell him she's disappointed they can't do it again. That should ensure the grade. She climbs back into her jeans and fringed T-shirt and finds her way back out into the studio.

The minute she emerges and hits the foul odor of DJ Ripple's Centralia project, she loses control of the gorge inside her and crawls from the sheet metal wreckage to an accompanying spray of vomit. Oh god, she wants to die.

DJ Ripple applauds. "Damn, that was fantastic. You should do that every time you come out of there. People would pay to see that."

"Fuck you. Hand me a towel."

All of the towels he finds are filthy.

"There aren't any."

"Ahhhhh," she screams.

DJ Ripple turns on a faucet and wets a paper towel. He squeezes it out and walks it over to where Piri has rolled away from her spew and onto her back like so much road kill.

"What the fuck happened to you?"

"You wouldn't believe me," she says. Piri cleans up as well as she can. "Brilliant," she says.

She lifts her arms and DJ Ripple helps her stand and then stagger to the sink, which she turns on full blast and buries her face in, before taking a long drink.

"Hey, help me out. I'm late and I'm supposed to be baby-sitting Professor Stevens's kids."

"So? You need a ride?"

"No, but he does," and she points at the sheet metal vagina.

☀

DJ RIPPLE SCRATCHES HIS HEAD. What did she say? He hangs Bear by the neck with some gray duct tape midcenter over his assemblage. Classic. He'll bring Goth girl over when she gets back. Tell her he has a surprise for her. This will be great.

DJ Ripple is a large man, and the idea of crawling into Piri's metal cunt, because he's way too tall to make it standing up, to find god knows what, just doesn't sit too well. Now he hears somebody groaning. Great. He turns another fold in the sheet metal and his skull belt with all of the metal studs and key rings dings off the wall and hooks onto something. He tries to go forward. Nope. He inches back, and that's another nope.

☼

GUESTS HAVE BEGUN NIBBLING ON sushi and mingling. Shoes have come off, and a couple of the more adventurous partygoers have climbed into the slides and maze structures in the ball room. Alcohol is flowing. Sloe gin fizz, whiskey sours, and Glenmorangie, while others content themselves with more traditional sake, or even Ichiban beer.

Emily and Pie beg their mother to play in the ball room and she relents, looking at her watch, trying a guest's cell phone. Still no Preston. Pie screamed the entire way to IKEA but once she had the opportunity to play in the ball room, she became her old ebullient self. The girls are sliding into the balls, avoiding the adults, and having a splendid time.

☼

PIRI HAD HEARD A LITTLE about the surprise party, but since she was to be home with the girls, she had no idea about the lavish spread Mrs. Stevens had arranged. She apologized to her and explained that another friend of hers, also a student, would be bringing Preston shortly. At least she hoped DJ Ripple showed soon.

"Have some sushi," Mrs. Stevens directed. "There's some Sprite and bottled water as well. Let the kids play another ten minutes or so, and here," she handed Piri a hundred dollars. "Find a toy store and buy them each a new doll. We lost Bear, Pie's pride and joy, today. Offer her a new stuffed bear, but if she has her heart set on something else within reason that's fine. Okay?"

"Got it." Piri said, and then it was clear that she was dismissed. Fine. The sushi looked lovely, but she knew she couldn't handle anything but kappa rolls in her condition. She tried one, drank some bottled water. Palatable. Such a pity. All of this free sushi and she couldn't have any.

☀

PRESTON WOKE UP WITH A crick in his neck, one arm asleep, and excruciating pain in his cock. Why did he want a woman with a natural pussy? He needed his head examined.

Piri was gone. What time was it? He located his cell phone. The charge had run down and it wouldn't light up when he opened it. He sat up and put one bare foot on the lost condom. He sighed. Preston tried gingerly to get his underwear on, but the pain was too excruciating. He tried to remember everything. Piri had been fantastic. Hadn't she? Well, she certainly looked great.

"A little help?"

What? Somebody was yelling. Who the hell was that? Preston left his underwear on the bed, slipped his pants on, and buttoned his shirt. Then he stooped and tried to find his way out of the labyrinth.

"Who is it?" he shouted back.

"Who are you?" the voice came back.

And then Preston saw the problem. It was the thuggish kid who went by the stupid pseudonym. DJ something or other. And his fat ass was stuck, blocking the exit.

"Uhhh. Hi, Professor—"

"Can you move?"

"No."

"Should I give you a push?"

"No."

Preston took his one hundred and seventy-five pounds and tried to shoulder DJ Ripple's easily two hundred and fifty pounds. Nothing budged. He tried to pull him forward. Nothing doing.

"What are you doing here, anyway?" he asked the student.

"I suppose I could ask you the same question."

"Don't."

"Piri said I was to drive you to IKEA."

Preston was baffled. "IKEA? What for?"

"No idea."

"So you're supposed to give me a ride?"

"That's what she said."

"I have a better idea." If the student stretched out and made himself as flat as possible, there might be barely enough room for Preston to climb over top of him.

This worked to perfection except that every time his cock rubbed against his Dockers, he was in agony. Once Preston was on the other side, he unhooked one of the key rings on the student's belt, which had somehow become stuck on a rivet, and the two men made their way out to the car.

☀

PRESTON WALKED RIGHT PAST BEAR without even looking up.

☀

THE DJ KID DROVE A beat-up Tercel. When he opened the front door, a mountain of trash cascaded onto the pavement. Then he spent five minutes apologizing for the mess and another five shoveling it all into the backseat. Preston felt scrunched in the car. He had no idea how the larger student managed.

"I want you to drive me home so I can pack and then I'd like a lift to BWI."

"The airport?"

"Yeah, I've got a flight to catch."

"You do?"

"Yeah I'm going to Chile." He hoped his passport was in order. Was it even possible to just show up at the airport and leave in these days of Homeland Security? Why not? He'd fly down to Vicuna for a few weeks. Tell April he'd had a midlife crisis and had to reassess things. Then she'd fly the family down to join him and they'd spend the summer months there. He liked the plan. He'd email his final grades to the department.

The DJ kid raced down Route 1 toward IKEA and the Beltway, and pulled over near Berwyn Heights into a motel parking lot.

"What's going on?"

"I want an A."

Preston looked at the kid. "That's blackmail."

"Yes, I believe it is."

"Okay, fine, you've got an A."

DJ smiled and sped off.

What a dunce, Preston thought. He doesn't have it in writing. It's his word against mine. Amazing. He's got a D if I don't flunk him.

☼

PIRI HAS A DIFFICULT TIME getting the girls away from IKEA. She can tell that Mrs. Stevens is particularly stressed. And Piri's pissed at DJ Ripple for not bringing Preston. Where the hell are they? Her cell says it's 8 p.m. now. It takes Piri twenty minutes to install the car seats. She's never messed with them before and it's a disaster. She doesn't know how to use a locking clip and she's about to scream when a mother of three sees her travails and comes to her aid. Finally under way, she tries Preston's phone. It's ringing. She hears him pick up.

"Where the hell are you?" Piri yells.

☼

APRIL NOTICES AN IKEA CLERK walking a cell phone over to her. Preston. Something's happened. The clerk hands her the phone.

"Hi, Mrs. Stevens. Has your husband shown up yet?"

It's Piri. "No, where is he?"

"One of my friends was picking him up right after I left College Park. Look, I'll take the girls by and see if maybe their car broke down."

April closed the phone. A silver Cingular just like mine, she thought. She walked it back to the clerk who shook his head no.

"Oh no ma'am. You left that phone here at this morning's meeting. We forgot all about it until it rang."

"But this isn't my phone. My phone has black Sharpie on it from when Emily was three..." April stopped. She scrolled down through the phonebook. There she was. This is Preston's phone. But Piri called...? "That rank bastard," she said, stomping a red ball flat, and then she reached up and yanked her daughters' wonderful mural off the wall.

☼

IT TAKES A WHILE, BUT Piri convinces the girls that she has a chic modern playhouse they must see at the college where their daddy teaches. That's met with a truly lukewarm reception until she also promises McDonald's immediately afterward. Both girls cheer, and now they're excited and willing to go anywhere. Piri knows that the right thing to do is to make this as exciting and mysterious as she can without scaring the girls. So she tells them to close their eyes, and she takes each by the hand and leads them across the studio until they get to the sheet metal structure. However, she's forgotten the stench of DJ Ripple's Centralia project, which makes both girls flinch, open their eyes, and then scream.

Piri looks at the girls. Pie is pointing to something. DJ Ripple has hung something nasty and gray over the center of his demented project.

"Bear," Pie screams, "Bear." And she charges into the messy assemblage.

Emily grabs her arm. "No, don't."

"Oh god, no, child. Don't run in there. It's not safe. The artist has booby-trapped this thing with holes you can fall through."

Piri gets the folding yellow ladder from the wall and opens it up. Pie is hysterical. Screaming. She's so red it looks like she's going to pop blood vessels in her face. Emily is crying now, too. The stench. What was she thinking? Kids can't handle something like this. And what the hell is DJ Ripple doing with Bear?

She climbs the ladder. She can't lean out far enough to reach Bear.

"Emily, listen to me. I need your help."

Emily nods.

"See the broom?" Piri points.

Emily nods again.

"Can you fetch it for me? That's a big girl. Take your sister with you."

So Emily bravely makes a beeline for the rear wall, grabs the broom, and returns with Pie in tow. She hands the broom up to Piri.

Now Piri is able to swing the broom out and draw Bear over close enough to stretch and grab hold. She drops the broom into DJ Ripple's tar pit hellhole. Oh well, tough. And then she gets a firm hold of Bear's leg and yanks as hard as she possibly can.

☼

GOTH GIRL IS BESIDE HERSELF. DJ Ripple leads her into the studio with a flashlight, promising a surprise so splendid, she'll take it with her everywhere she goes, forever. The room is completely dark and spooky. Something smells. Ugh. Did he buy her a ring? Her girlfriends put him down quite a bit at Ocean City, but she was loyal. He's a little misguided, she thinks, yet he has a lot of potential. Their sex life could be better, though she does cut him some slack. He has been stressed out trying to complete his assemblage. She went to Centralia with him and took photos so he could try to capture what it felt like. She knows this was a brilliant idea but realizes DJ's down on himself because he just doesn't have the money or the materials to really render his vision. That's okay. After they're married they'll move back to Glen Burnie and it'll all work out.

"Here ya go, hon," he says, "Now stand still. Don't move. I'm going to go back and switch the light on. Open your eyes when I say so, and look up, okay?"

"Okay."

She's so excited she's got goose bumps up and down her arms under her leather jacket. "Hurry up." She's actually quivering.

"Here ya go, ta-dah."

The light comes on and Goth girl looks up to find? What? She starts to cry. What a shithead. Her girlfriends were right.

DJ Ripple runs the final couple of feet to her side. "See," he says, putting one arm around her waist, raising the other arm in the air, "didn't I tell you—"

Goth girl steps back and slaps him as hard as she can. And then she punches him in the stomach and double-times it for the door.

DJ Ripple (aka Elihu Lawrence McPeters) blinks his eyes. This can't be. Above his ambitious assemblage hangs a pair of black jockey shorts stuffed with cotton batting from which a long distended condom hangs like an elephant's dangling trunk.

Introducing Snakes to Ireland

When the sack opens
the first snake walks out.

No need to crawl.

Others follow.
The air is clean.
The people friendly.

They will all
drink Guinness.

For Zelda
(Forty Years Gone)

We all still miss you Zelda.
What were you thinking
as flames consumed the building:

How to make a palette of fire?
How to dance toe-to-toe with death?

He'd been courting you
for some time by then.

I liked you better
as the sunny Confederate belle
before you turned into Ophelia.

So come on back,
tender heart.

Come back
and shake up
our safe little lives.

Edge your way
behind the wheel.

Take us drinking all night,
dancing (though we can
barely walk) and wading
through fountains.

When the sun comes up
we'll share mimosas
on the roof of a hotel
and laugh at stupid jokes.

Zelda, honey,
we all miss you.

Memories just
aren't good enough.

Audrey in the Rain

She's not as splashy
as the women I'm
usually obsessed with.
The girl next door
with class. Black gloves.
Eyes in sync with
the orchestration.
A name that implies fashion.

When the sad rains come
she stands breathlessly
perfect, despite
the runny mascara
and tears.
I could freeze-frame
this second
and capture her forever
with a sloppy kiss.

But when I offer
my sorry coat
the patented laughter begins
and those small bones,
those delightful bones,
rattle my heart
until I know
I'm blessed.

Another Stupid Haircut

You wish just this once
the mirror would lie.
What was the barber
thinking about?
You felt ridiculous enough
carrying a Peter Gabriel
album into the shop—
visual aids never help.
You clip away with
nail scissors
and soon it looks even worse.
Conservative, square,
totally hopeless,
as though the ones
who cut hair were
really Martians with
only a rudimentary
idea of what humans
are supposed to look like.
Hair like topographic maps,
tv antenna, inverted
umbrellas, poodle dogs...
or else the great hair
disaster of Krakatoa—
poking out in
so many directions
that only the
end of the world
will make you feel
at all fashionable.

Louise Brooks

Her famous
black helmet
triggers autonomy.

A glandular avalanche.

You can relax.
Comb her eyes
for hidden metals.

The war is over.

Telephones ring in all
the holy cities of America.

Torn curtains
hung out to dry
on a windy day.

Waiting for the Popeye Effect

No amount of spinach
does the trick

Cartoons lie to me
on a daily basis

Essence of Mitchum

I'm having one of those typical days when I can't summon the energy it takes to open some frozen waffles and instead stand in the kitchen contemplating the way the rain is cascading down the Andersen windows. I discover a cabinet ajar in the bathroom, and think maybe I'll at least shave, make some tiny impression on this day, and discover Cynthia's deodorant where my shaving cream usually sits. What's this? Mitchum? I heft the pastel green canister. Is Cynthia cheating on me? Did some guy leave his...? Oh, now I see the daintier pink and white letters wrapping around the boldface Mitchum. This is *Lady Mitchum*. What nutcase thought of naming a woman's scent after Robert Mitchum? Those ad execs at Revlon must be high on crack.

☼

CYNTHIA CALLS ME FROM WORK. She's in a foul mood.

"I got a ticket."

Typical Cynthia. Always talking about consequences and never her responsibility in setting any particular ducks in a row.

"So what'd you do? Run a stop sign?" I say.

She's got this new habit of rolling through stop signs that really scares the pants off me.

"That's not funny, Chip."

I can sense her lip quivering. My clue to stop being a wise-ass.

"Sorry, babe. Tell me what happened."

She's been driving with her Walkman on. No big whoop. Her Honda is such a piece of shit that the stereo system has been D.O.A. since I've known her. But this driving around with the Walkman on is new. Of course, she didn't know it was against the law. And I can't say I've ever heard of anyone being busted for doing it.

"What's the fine?"

"Ouch," I say, though I'm thinking, there go the weekend pizzas. Damn.

☼

SOMEHOW HER PREDICAMENT PUMPS ME full of energy. I get creative. Open the fridge. Bang some pans together. I make some soup from scratch. Drop veggies in the pot. Let it simmer all day. I can see Cynthia's pissed off when she comes in the door, but she's a sucker for cumin and pleased that I've made dinner.

"I'm sorry your day was so shitty," I say. I hold her. Kiss her cheek. Bury my nose in her walnut-colored hair and breathe deep.

"I'm gonna take a shower," she says into my armpit. And I let her unpeel from my arms.

I slice tomatoes, sprinkle them with oil and basil. I cut open our last two baguettes. And then I ladle the soup into the only nice bowls we own. Off-white with cerulean blue stripes.

Cyn surprises me by coming from the shower to join me still wrapped in plum-colored towels.

The soup is good and I relax and watch her eat. Reenergized, she becomes more talkative. But I've tuned out her meaning. I'm locked into the musical quality of her voice and I can't make out the individual words. Plus, I'm not used to eating dinner with a woman displaying this much flesh and I'm having a hard time pretending I'm not staring. Because I am, every chance I get. Staring at the little folds on the inside of her knee where one leg cocks over the other, at the place where the towel pulls away from her thighs, still steamy pink from the shower, at the way she's tucked the towel into her cleavage.

"Chip. You aren't even listening."

She looks hurt. So I gather my wits.

"Sorry, babe. I was just thinking about you and that cop this morning." She shakes her head. "Thanks for making the soup. Next time add a little more garlic. Okay?" She pushes away from the table. I snatch at the purple cloth around her waist as she walks past. She swats my hand but giggles and soon we're on the beige carpet in the living room and our two disgusted cats jump down from the futon and walk away, ashamed of their owners.

☼

THAT NIGHT I DREAM ABOUT Robert Mitchum. I'm in the middle of the street. Old Tucson or something. And he's walking toward me obscured by this swirling sand. He's also singing. I can make out the words to "Thunder Road." I can see the black cowboy boots but I can't quite make out his bohunky face. He's maybe twenty yards away before the wind begins to die down. And then I see him. It's Mitchum all right, and he's still singing. I can't move. My feet won't obey my brain. I want to run. Because Mitchum is wearing a dress. One of those *Gunsmoke* Miss Kitty numbers. Ostrich plumes and fishnets. Ultima II Lip Sexxxy red on his thick lips. He stops in front of me. A Spaghetti Western moment. And then he says, "Pucker up."

I wake in a cold sweat, stagger out of bed, and wander into the bathroom where Lady Mitchum awaits. I open the "Powder Fresh" canister. Sniff it through the trio of medieval vents. Not very memorable. Must be that aluminum zirconium tetrachlorohydrex gly. Whatever the hell that is. I automatically try it out. I don't feel any different. Tomorrow, I promise myself, I'll get a haircut and maybe look for work. There is definitely too much free time on my hands. Then I stumble back to bed.

King of the Zombies

The first Thursday in June had started well. Dean dealt with the endless line of painting contractors that began lining up in front of the door of the Sherwin-Williams at six thirty a.m., mixed and matched colors, sold tarps, brushes, and ladder pads, scrappers, and colored caulk. At lunch he'd skipped out from behind the counter to get a pink aluminum baseball bat for his daughter Tracy's birthday. He expected his boss to cut him some slack when he came back a half hour late, and was surprised to be fired. Hell, he was too old to be working retail at his age. That's what the bartender at Martin's Tavern told him. And he agreed, knowing he'd be replaced by a college kid for the duration of the summer. Life had become a spiraling series of disappointments. Five hours later, after drinking everything from gin rickeys to shots of Stoli with Red Bull, he felt an urgent need to head on home.

Dean pushed open the door into the bright lights of Georgetown. He stretched both arms behind him with the pink baseball bat and tried to make sense of what he was seeing. No traffic. A mass of people swaying and growling in a slow march past the bar to M Street. Hundreds of them. And blood. Lots of blood. He needed to focus. There was a woman with an ax in her back. A high school kid with his head split open. A tall man with a blood-stained white shirt. More of the same everywhere he looked.

Somehow while he was drinking, the zombie apocalypse had begun. He'd seen enough movies to know what to do. He hefted the pink bat and began swinging it into the crowd. Zombies wailed. He loved the metallic ring of the bat as it thudded solidly against skulls, against ribs. Right and left. He poked, he prodded, finally clearing a circle in the middle of Wisconsin Avenue to make his stand. Zombies groaned and bled at his feet. Dean perfected his golf swing, scattering blood splatter and teeth across the blacktop. Some zombies fled, others tried to tackle him. He kept swinging the bloody pink bat until he was overwhelmed, and dragged to the ground.

A gun cocked. "Police. Drop the bat. Drop it now."

Dean let go. His hands were cuffed. Somebody lifted him to his feet. Zombies were pointing at him. The evil undead were crying, screaming, yelling obscenities. There were bodies crumpled all over the street.

"It's a zombie walk, you fucktard."

"C'mon," the Mustache cop sat him down on the curb.

Other cops were taking info from the crowd. An ambulance siren was coming closer.

"Drunk guy here thought they were real."

"Nutcase. No such thing as zombies."

"My daughter's bat?" Dean whispered.

"That pink bat?" Mustache cop looked at Ray-Ban cop. "Evidence."

"It's not Halloween," Dean said.

"Every day is Halloween, buddy," Ray-Ban cop said. "Every single day."

Spaghetti Western Sestina

I worry about the bags of dollars
left by "Blondie," the Man with No Name
after all of the bad guys have taken a bullet,
worry about the bags after it's clear Tuco won't die
in the graveyard where the big gundown has transformed the West
with gold coins and spilled blood and highly operatic desert.

I want to live in that place, that's really Spain—Europe's only desert.
And somehow I want Tuco to collect all of those dollars
from the bags he split open with a shovel in the imaginary West.
Because without a horse I can't imagine how he's going to carry
    them, name
or no name. And I wonder how Lee Van Cleef can just die.
And oh my God are those flies crawling on his face. One bullet

and he drops. I expected him to be more diabolical than that. One
    bullet.
and "Angel Eyes" drops like a solitary crow circling the endless desert.
And I wonder what it's like to be Eli Wallach, a nice Jewish guy who
    doesn't die
in this movie, but who also starred in The Magnificent Seven for
    many more dollars.
An actor's an actor no matter what, no matter how big their name.
But c'mon would you ever guess he'd play in two of the best Westerns

ever made? No way. The only West Eli knew was West
Brooklyn. Am I right? I'll bet he wouldn't let flies crawl on his face
    or take just one bullet.
I've seen every Spaghetti Western by now. The ones with name
stars and the ones with actors like Edd Byrnes or Alex Cord, shot in
    the same desert
towns in Almeria, Spain. I love the Sergio Leone Dollars
trilogy, and his classic *Once Upon a Time in the West*. The way Henry
    Fonda dies

is fabulous. I'm sure he was tickled that he got to gnaw scenery and die
on screen. Not something he did often. And is it just me or does the
    old West
make more sense with Leone at the helm. Bandits shooting up the
    place for dollars.
Blood flying everywhere. Family, kids, bystanders taking a bullet.
I heard they had to film new footage for TV versions of these desert
shoot 'em ups. Harry Dean Stanton's intro about the Man with No
    Name

assures the American audience that he's not really a bounty killer
    sans name
but a U.S. government trained agent. Censors should just do the
    right thing and die.
Thank God, the Italians shot all of these movies in the '60s, in the
    desert.
Django, My Name Is Trinity, Sabata, Death Rides a Horse. The old West
just isn't the same without Ennio Morricone's soundtrack complete
    with bullets,
harmonicas, and soaring choruses. But back to the bags of dollars.

Sure Clint left all those dollars, the Man with No Name was fair in
    his way.
The Good? An ominous question mark. Better than a bullet or
    dying under the big sky.
The Ugly gets off easy—wandering mythic Western deserts with a
    fistful of dollars.

The Stillness of Apples, or Jean Genet Meets the Sphinx

You saw the painting in a gallery window every day on your walk to work and wanted it, so you smashed the store front with an elbow and grabbed the frame. The painting was the real genuine article—a Magritte oil of two green apples. One wore a mask, the other was au naturel.

A mask on a piece of fruit? What could be more ridiculous.

You lost yourself for hours contemplating masks. Became obsessed with Carnival, Mardi Gras, those masquerade balls in period art films. Of course people wear masks, but why an apple?

What does an apple have to conceal?

You scoured the library in search of a key to the mystery of Magritte's apples. Every image search revealed pairs of masked green apples.

Why only one apple with trappings?

You were no closer to solving the riddle. You thought about apples. Stolen apples of youth. The Garden of Eden. Apple picking in Washington state one timeless summer.

Could the second apple wear a mask as well? Was its back turned to disguise the fact?

Two weeks and the mask mocks you. You throw a drink at the painting and smash the glass. Lose control and break the frame across the back of a chair. Magritte's folly a messy pile at your feet. In the debris you see the cursed mask. That catalyst. You gather the scattered pieces and throw them in the fireplace. You set fire to the priceless canvas and watch it burn. For an instant the masked apple seems to mirror you. And as you watch, the apple curls in the center and turns to ash, concealing nothing.

On the Road to Georgia O'Keeffe

Georgia's
Irish hands
with a cup
and a crust
of soda bread

imagine
translucent
lavender hands

hands
that have more
grace and agility
at ninety
than some hands
ever do

those hands
floating
above
a dark table top

a cane
propped
like a shadow
against
a white chair

piñon
crackling
in a fireplace

long hands
with pronounced veins

that see
with eyes
in both palms

the last
three fingers
on each hand
moving as one

flying
like birds
around
the black kimono

the silver halo
of her hair

Georgia's
industrious fingers

coiling
rolls of clay
or kneading
dough

killing
a rattler
with a shovel

or tracing
the ridges
in a cliff face

Georgia's
exquisite fingers
captured in a photo

ghost hands
dancing forever
like wings

Chimichanga

Something stirs
beneath the ooze...

You lie awake nights
searching for
the precise incantation.

Find it in a taco joint.

Chimichanga.

A name that summons monsters.

H. P. Lovecraft stuffing
his face with jalapenos.

Chimichanga.

Rising from primordial slime.

Tortillas and hot sauce
conspire against us.

Chimichanga.

Last monster in the desert.

With one word
we will empty villages.

Peace Cross

We smoked a pile of weed
and went down to the Cross Roads
in Bladensburg, Maryland.

Eric Clapton had discovered
a hotshot redneck guitar hero
in this seedy crab house joint.

Talk about a time warp.
The waitress didn't want to
serve a table of hair trees.

Crewcuts were all the rage inside
those four walls. Pulchritudinous
gals with big hair, clamdiggers,

cigs, and short tight dresses,
ruled a dance floor smack dab
in the middle of the place.

We ordered serious blues and were
served "Spinning Wheel" and other
crapola from Top Forty AM radio.

The guitar hero had zero stage
presence, taking a backseat to
a rowdy piano player who was

too old school to have ever heard
Jimi Hendrix, Jimmy Page, Jeff Beck,
or any of our other rock idols.

These guys were SQUARE. Like
something out of *American Graffiti.*
When a Snidely Whiplash guy

grabbed a girl in white Go-Go boots,
twirled his mustache (for real) and said,
"What a nice ass, you have my dear,"

we were out the door. The place was a
total dump. We were so much hipper than
that band of old losers. As we opened

the car doors, the first sinewy strains
of "The Messiah Will Come Again"
infiltrated the parking lot.

We waited, stoned out of our minds,
and shivered in the January chill,
until the final notes circumnavigated

a busy traffic circle behind us,
the memorial Peace Cross shimmering
like a shiny tuning fork for the soul.

The Masque of the Red Death

I went out trick or treating one year
dressed as the Red Death.

I loved Vincent Price movies.
Loved watching him gnaw the scenery.

I smudged red crayons on my hands and face
and my mother made me a cheap

burgundy hooded cloak. Like most kids
I was disappointed in the overall effect.

My costume was okay, but didn't
make nearly the impact I'd hoped.

We'd ring doorbells and families
would kind of stare at me and guess

Little Red Riding Hood? Agghhhh.
I suffered the death of a thousand

paper cuts that Halloween night.
Nobody ever came close to figuring it out.

No amount of candy was a big enough
reward for my failure to strike fear

into even the tiniest elementary school
ghost or skeleton. I sulked for weeks.

Maybe I'm still sulking? My literary bent
too much at thirteen for my neighborhood.

Poe's allegory on the inevitability of death
lost in a tsunami of Disney costumes and sugar.

Thelonious

I want a jazz solo to ride

like a spike through a photograph

of six grungy kids on a toboggan,

like the small rosy flowers

of trailing arbutus, like

a bicycle wheel hanging

over the edge of next week.

And when it happens

with a burst of coriander,

I want to have to smack

my ears with both hands

to drain the notes

and smell something slick

like chlorine

afterwards.

Valley of the Gods, 1994

Seventeen miles of dirt road
once we turn off the highway.

"What's a dog doing way out here?"
my companion, a city girl.

"That's a coyote," I say.
And when I raise the binocs

for a closer look, he turns tail
and blends into the sandstone.

We're stopped
in the middle of the road.

No tourists.

And then in the distance
a plume of dust

like something in a B-movie.

"They're moving really fast
whoever they are," she says.

This dirt road—
one slightly overweight lane.

We're parked beside a wet arroyo.
There are rocks in the bottom

that could rip the transmission
out of any American car.

A strange apparition materializing
among the desert flowers.

A pink Cadillac convertible.

And the driver hits the arroyo
doing fifty miles per hour,

soaring into the air,
crashing with a muffled thud.

Two women with big hair.
Texas tags.

And they've buried the Caddy
two feet into the sandy banks.

They aren't going anywhere.

And it's not like we've seen
a tow truck since the highway.

Plus the water appears to be rising.

I'm getting the feeling that we're
witnessing the further adventures

of Thelma and Louise.
If they'd been rich and Republican.

The women wave. No big deal.
One climbs out of the car in faux leopard skin

and heels. Chugging a silver flask.
Offering us a drink. "How y'all?"

The other has whipped out a cell phone and
is already yelling at somebody somewhere.

And for all I know they're still there.
Stuck up to their hubcaps

in desert sand. Increasingly defiant.
"Don't mess with Texas," you can

hear one of them shouting.
And Lord knows, no amount of sugar

could ever sweeten that tea.

The Ten Most Misleading B Horror Movie Titles: A Found Poem

10. *Beast with a Million Eyes*
    (It has two)

9. *Frankenstein's Daughter*
   (It's a man)

8. *She Gods of Shark Reef*
   (No Gods, no sharks)

7. *Robot Monster*
   (No robots)

6. *Blood of Dracula*
   (No Dracula)

5. *Teenagers from Outer Space*
   (No one in cast under 30 years old)

4. *The Indestructible Man*
   (He's destroyed)

3. *It Conquered the World*
   (It doesn't)

2. *Teenage Zombies*
   (No teenage zombies)

1. *Frankenstein Meets the Space Monster*
   (Has absolutely nothing to do with Frankenstein)

Hillbilly Music

A skinny man is reading poems.
Rush hour radio serenading the alley.
A little Hank Williams in the night.

My father appears in the doorway.
His angry heart no longer able
to cry, cheat, or eat gumbo.

I don't believe in ghosts.
So maybe he's really stopping by
having developed a taste for poetry

in the afterlife.
Not that I can hear many words
seated in the back of the gallery.

The skinny poet reads slower than
most children do when learning how.
So what to make of my charismatic father

as he mouths silent words at me.
The fractured English of the poet
at the podium, Hank Williams' yodel,

fusing together on the first warm spring night,
thirteen years after my father's fatal heart attack.
Here I am now in Arlington just a few blocks

from the first apartment he lived in
with my mother and their brand-new baby boy
born fifty years and a couple weeks ago.

What to make of silence and coincidence.
As Hank honkytonks into the night sky
and the spaces between the skinny poet's words

get more and more lonesome and blue.

WAR & PEACE 3

Civil War Pietà

Dear Walt:

Did you ever embrace feet? The absence of feet?
Hold poor wounded feet captive in your hands. Caress them.
Ankles, instep, foot-ball, toes, toe-joints, the heel.
Attempt to mold the damaged clay of muscle and bone
until it once again resembled the perfect feet of newborns.
My dancer girlfriend had the most desirable legs imaginable.
Yet I cried when she stripped off her shoes and I learned
that she only possessed three remaining toenails.
She couldn't paint them like my daughters do now.
Couldn't wear open-toed shoes. Once she painted
my nails bloody red. Not like the brownish real blood
you saw daily at Armory Square Hospital
on your rounds from cot to cot. Tears in your beard.
Tears falling onto mangled sinew, the pale flesh of those
brave-hearted boys. Good brave boys, many of them
doomed amputees. My relationships with dancers
were always doomed for less dynamic reasons.
Bloody scabs woven into pink silk ballet slippers. Stripping off
her shoes thread by thread after she danced to reveal
her torn pitiful feet. I'm not a foot fetishist but a woman's feet
are extremely appealing, glorious, mystical.
A curve, an arch, a flexing of toes, a rocking of legs.
Bathing a soldier's feet, did you think analogous thoughts?
Give me to bathe the memories of all dead soldiers.
Did you wish you could heal them with a laying on of hands?
Long for some of the expensive perfume that sinner woman
        used
on the savior's feet? *Perfume therefore my chant, O love!*
immortal Love! Did you dream that by soothing these
men, by handling their wounded, ravaged flesh, their

121

stumps, their broken, savaged, gangrenous toes,
you could somehow make them whole once more? Free them?
Feet of war, feet of warriors, feet that nobody would ever kiss
or even touch again. Did you think why then I shall kiss them.
And parted the shirt from my bosom-bone, and plunged
your tongue to my bare-stript heart.
I shall touch them—these wounds, these wounded. Blue or gray
no longer an issue in a landscape fraught with cannon fire,
     pestilence,
and death. Nothing mattering but pain, and new worlds of pain,
combined with a hunger to paint a new reality via your
brain and heart, your tears. Did you stoop then, heft the boy
up into your arms in search of breath? Curl your body
     around his sad form?
Hospital linens draping you both, freezing you momentarily.
Sweet are the blooming cheeks of the living!
Before you rocked gently like a tired ship on an ocean of tears.

Peppermint Schnapps

inter sucks. Almost lunchtime and nobody absolutely nobody has been in to talk with Brent about any of the sleek new Mercedes M-class SUVs baking in the soap-streaked showroom window sunshine of a January day. No way can he accept this as he glares in Gabriel's direction. That tight-ass low-class antifreeze-sucking metrosexual excuse for a human is chatting up one of the best-looking absolutely divine black women Brent has ever seen off screen. Fuck me, he thinks. Why today of all days?

At breakfast, his Maria Conchita Alonso wannabe Puerto Rican wife read him the riot act about their sex life. Brent feels like shit. He's smoking too much again (he can't resist those Montecristo No. 2 Habanos), his dot.com stocks are tanking, he's having trouble making payments on his condo, and he's gotta gotta gotta make a sale today. Old man Focke Wulf and Messerschmitt, the Nazi CEOs of EuroTrash Motors called him on the carpet last week. Shit. Fuck. Piss.

When Gabriel opens the door for the woman (Who does she look like? Vanessa Williams? No, younger, darker.), Brent is beside himself. Gabriel's last-minute wink kills something deep inside him and covers it with dirt. He's boiling in his own juices and so pissed he doesn't even notice another customer walk in the opposite side of the showroom and up to his desk.

"You working?"

Brent, distracted, turns to the metallic-sounding voice. Looks like an ex-cop. That tell-tale barrelhouse chest. Only cops have that. Denim jacket. Blue jeans. Blue eyes. Converse shoes. Small black gym bag.

"Yes, sir. Put you in a coupe today?"

"Doubtful. Very doubtful. But talk to me about this SUV. Mercedes has an SUV? Why?"

Brent knows this guy isn't going to spring for the price tag. He kind of pops the replay button on his mental tape machine and runs down the features on the ML320. He could do this in his sleep. Fuel injection, 215 horses or you can move up to 268 with the ML430 and opt for the Sports Package, the Bose speakers, and 3rd Row seats, or move up again to 342 horses with the ML55 and all of the amenities. The guy does the predictable shtick, kicks the tires, slams the doors, the whole bit. Why do I get these retired guys when Gabriel Angel Face Salesman of the Month gets the babes? Brent catches a glint of a reflection in the windshield. Of course if any more of my hair goes down the drain, it'll be time for Rogaine. (Who does she look like? Tyra Banks? Right age but wrong eyes, smaller tits.)

"Mind taking a spin in one of these?"

Oh shit, the rube wants to go for a ride. "Sure, why not." I've got nothing better to do, Brent thinks, than sit here and work on an ulcer, and so he gets the keys to the road machine in the lot off a ring by his desk, swoops his black leather duster off the back of his chair (his *Matrix* look), and away they go.

Thirty minutes later, Brent finds himself halfway to Leesburg on some side road in the middle of nowhere. He looks out at the bare trees, snow on the ground. I fucking hate winter, he thinks, and pushes his Ray-Bans up his nose.

"Do you scuba?"

Brent lurches back. "What?" He'd given up on his sales spiel after Tyson's Corner. It's been quiet for a while now.

"Ever go scuba diving?"

"No."

"Young man like you should take it up."

"Why's that?"

"You get to travel some amazing places, see incredible things."

"I'll think about it." Amazing, incredible. Maybe it is genuinely possible, Brent thinks, to be bored to death.

"You remind me of some of the guys I knew in the islands who would scuba during the day and then hang out at a bar the next day. Nothing else to do really. They'd tie chunks of meat to steel line. The shark would take the hook and swim away as fast as it could until it hit the end of the line. Full stop. Then they'd just reel the shark in."

"I remind you of them?"

"Yeah, they'd just sit there every other day and drink in the hot sun and fish for sharks."

Just what I need. Time to wrap this up. "So..." and Brent draws a blank. What was this guy's name? Had they even talked names? "I'm sorry, I'm kind of having a brain-dead day. What was your name again?"

"Smitty."

Figures. "So, Smitty, what do you think of this baby? Can you see yourself hitting the links in one of these? Maybe driving up to Vermont for some fine powder?"

"Out of my price range."

No shit Sherlock. Brent eyes his Rolex. "Well, got to get back to the showroom soon or I'll miss lunch."

"Wouldn't want that. I just wanted to try one out. It's a swell drive."

Swell. Brent has never had such a swell time.

"Hey I gotta take a leak, any objection to my pulling over there in the trees."

"Sure, whatever."

While the guy crunches snow into the woods, Brent contemplates leaving him. Sighs—it would never wash. Focke Wulf would start World War III and fire him the minute he heard about it. Messerschmitt would have him publicly flogged. Brent thinks of his wife. She was almost as hot as that black woman when they first met. Nah. He's lying. She was never that hot. (Who does she look like? Naomi Campbell? Right shade, but younger with larger tits.) The wife had been hammering him all morning about having a kid. A kid? She was crazy. The last thing he needed to worry about was having a kid right now. And then he gets an idea. A doozy. Why not a puppy? That's kind of like a kid, right? Hell, yeah. He'll go home at lunchtime and surprise her with a little winter afternoon delight. Stop at the pound on the way and pick out one of those floppy-eared mutts, the kind no woman can resist. That might be just what she needs. Might buy him some breathing room.

Smitty is standing by the passenger door, so Brent rolls down the window. Now what? He has a flask in his gloved hand.

"Care for some peppermint schnapps?"

Peppermint schnapps. That brings back some memories. College days. The frat parties. Damn.

"Why not?" Brent says.

Smitty passes him the flask. Expensive. Classy. The guy's got more taste than he thought. Gotta get a flask like this. And Brent takes a hit. Then a longer one. He is pleased the old man let him drink first. He doesn't like sharing spit with strangers.

"Thanks. That's a blast from the past."

"Really?"

"College stuff."

"Coeds?"

Coeds? How old is this guy? "Them too." And he thought of Kim. How he'd never ever met anyone else with such perfect breasts. Not real ones anyway. He seemed to be daydreaming.

"Took me a while to track you down, but I've always been a patient man."

"What's that?" Brent must be hearing things.

"You've never amounted to much, Mr. Sullivan, have you? And you always lived off one woman or another, so your name was never listed in the phone book."

Mr. Sullivan? Brent tries to itch above his eye but his hands are heavy and he's moving slow, slower than slow. What's the old guy talking about?

"But these days with Yahoo People Finder you can find anybody and with your fancy new job, hell you're legit. You even have a wife. Though she is screwing that French guy you work with."

What the fuck? Gabriel? She's fucking Gabriel! Brent tries to speak "How the—" but his lips are sluggish and rubbery. Almost feels like his mouth has been sewn shut. He can't move. He really can't move and Brent panics.

"Oh, you can't talk. Amazing stuff, puffer fish venom. Works fast. You'll be pretty much paralyzed for about twenty minutes and this shouldn't take that long." Smitty reaches into the black gym bag at his feet and pulls out some rubber tubing. He bends down to the exhaust pipe and fiddles and then brings it around to the back window and pokes the tubing through.

"I knew you must have given her some sort of Mickey Finn 'cuz I never could believe she'd sleep with a guy like you."

Her? What is he talking about?

"Have you ever seen what someone looks like after they've been dead for twelve hours? The face is swollen. The skin so blue. So cold. Like packed snow."

Brent tries to get his tongue to move, tries to focus on the man.

"No, I don't suppose you have. It's kind of ironic, isn't it? Your one chance to see that, and you won't be able to."

Brent's body shifts a little and he slumps over against the window. He can no longer make eye contact. But the man's words keep coming.

"A couple of your frat brothers told me how you guys did it. Met them for a drink in Brooklyn. Once a Phi Delt always a Phi Delt right?" He holds the flask up again. "Peppermint schnapps. Mixed into the hot chocolate after skiing. Absolutely brilliant, Mr. Sullivan. Brilliant." And Smitty tipped an imaginary hat. "I'd figured you for grain alcohol."

Peppermint schnapps. Brent should have guessed. He was just a little out of it. There was still time. He'd give Smitty the SUV. Let him take it. Leave me by the side of the road. He'd say he was jacked and then he'd get even with Gabriel. He'd fix that low-life metrosexual motherfucker.

Smitty duct taped the glass opening around the tubing and rear window. "A pity to be wasting this stuff on you," he said, and then poured some of the schnapps on Brent's thinning hair. Next, he threw the flask into the front seat. "Your fingerprints are on the flask of course." While Brent watched, he couldn't even turn his head to follow, Smitty slid behind the wheel, leaving the door open and cranked the motor before pressing a button closing all the windows.

"You're having a bad day, Brent old buddy. A pisser of a bad day. Gabriel's got your wife, your stocks are in the toilet, you're losing your condo, trouble on the job, and there was just no easy way out."

Smitty steps down and stands there for a second, his calm blue eyes screwing up tighter and tighter. "My daughter, Kimberly, she dropped out of freshman year, came home pregnant, and though my wife and I would have done anything to help her, she couldn't face all the pressure. Couldn't decide whether to have the baby or get an abortion. So she offed herself. Pills. All your fault, buddy boy."

Kim? Pregnant? Kimberly had gotten pregnant? A baby. His baby? What? Brent tried to motion his head to the keys, tried to tell the man he was sorry. He was crying. God she'd been a virgin. She'd been so afraid. He tried to imagine her eyes, the same blue eyes. Of course. Of course.

"Almost forgot." The man reached in a jacket pocket and pulled out a folded envelope. He propped it on the dash. "Your suicide note. Typed."

No no no. This isn't happening. This isn't happening. Not today. Not now. Brent was coughing, or imagined he was. He couldn't tell anymore.

Kim's father reached to close the door and hesitated. "I'm only sorry my wife couldn't be here. She passed five years ago. Losing Kim broke her heart."

Brent struggled to make eye contact, to plead with the man's baby blues again.

"Lights out, Brent. Sweet dreams."

Brent watched Kim's father push a button, and the automatic door locks slid down into their channels with one simultaneous sharp click, and then the door closed tight, and he faded into the brown and white winter landscape.

Are There Any FBI Agents in Heaven?

Once there was a woman who declared war on the FBI
because she didn't buy into what her country was doing.

She declared war on the FBI so they decided to kill her.

They decided to kill her because that's what they do.
That's why they're hired, that's what they love,
FBI agents are faux grim reapers in bad shades.

But this woman was loved by the angels,
so loved that every time an FBI agent would sneak up
on her or her family some invisible force would pick
the FBI agent up, shake them around like a toddler
with a toy, lift them skyward a few stories high,
and then drop them crumbled to the earth. Ker-splat.

Are there any FBI agents in heaven?
FBI agents don't believe in angels. If they did
they wouldn't have made the woman public enemy #1.

Because their leaders assumed—with their limited training
and their limited minds—that the only way their
agents could be failing would be because the woman
was part of some vast conspiracy like the Communist Menace,
a menace that ceased about a decade ago. Yet in need of
explanations to prop up their ridiculous argument for
going after this woman they had to assume that she was a
regular James Bond rogue agent action hero in their midst.

Are there any FBI agents in heaven?
The FBI agent waiting in the car in front of the woman's house
was surprised when his car lifted heavenward. But since he
didn't believe in heaven the fact that he dropped into a
    snow bank
in a farmer's field near the rez in South Dakota during a
    nasty winter
was simply incomprehensible.

The FBI agent hidden in the attic would have hurt the
    woman's family
if an invisible hand hadn't lifted him out through the ceiling
somehow without leaving a hole as though he was already
    a ghost.
And in a way, of course, he already was.

Are there any FBI agents in heaven?

The FBI agent sitting in the airplane ready to
pounce on the woman as soon as they landed
blinked and found himself on the
other side of the smooth airplane walls, sitting as
though still belted in his seat, a thousand feet in the sky.

Are there any FBI agents in heaven?

No, but sometimes FBI agents hear wings and see enormous
    shadows,
before grasping feathers in their hammy fists, and falling,
falling through the atmosphere as though they expected to fly.

A More Level Playing Field in Fallujah

I can't go out like this, Lieutenant Walker thinks. I didn't go to Yale to die like this in the fucking desert.

What's left of Sergeant Barnes's roasted face leers at Walker like something from a cinematic gorefest.

Walker's eyes aren't working very well, one semi-closed, but he can see that Barnes is way dead all right. Walker's on the ground. Ears ringing, nearly deaf. Black smoke billows from the Hummer, chopped and gutted like an upside-down turtle minus its shell atop a stubby chunk of concrete. A sickly sweet roasted flesh stench omnipresent.

Walker tries to put weight on his blackened hands. Feels too vulnerable in the sand near the smoke. Imagines the fuel tank exploding. *Gotta move, gotta get.* His hands obey slowly. Like he's communicating with them from the bottom of a muddy lake.

C'mon Walker, move your ass, he commands his body. His hands again try to take the weight until a boot stomps down on one from above. He screams. Or tries to. The searing metal of a hot gun barrel pushes him over onto his back. He gets a glimpse of his torso and it looks wrong. Off somehow. Something missing. What?

Sand nigger babble surrounds him. Louder. Somebody else walking up.

A face inches away from his. Laughter.

"I recognize you. Trumbull, right?"

What's he saying? Trumbull? He went to Yale? Maybe. Just maybe everything will be okay. But Walker can't speak. His mouth is numb.

"You're not going to make it, you know. Your legs are gone."

What? What?

"Don't look. It's okay."

The man's rough hand on his chin. Turning his face for a better look.

"Remember me? No? Saybrook. We kicked your ass in soccer."

Walker blinks and he's on a soccer field, wearing the three bulls of Trumbull College on his T-shirt. What the? A kick in the shins, and the ball is stolen away. He runs. It's Saybrook. He's sprinting down the right sideline.

Both sidelines are crowded with students and he recognizes some. He never was much of an endurance player, just an extra body at fullback for intramurals, and soon he's winded. He stops to catch his breath. Leans over to put his hands on his knees. And they're invisible. But still functional somehow. He rests his weight on his invisible knees. They feel good. The grass is green and soothing. The field beautiful in the crisp October air.

Saybrook centers the ball to a teammate positioned in front of the goal, who attempts a header that sails high and wide left. The crowd gives a collective groan.

The goalie, a marine in uniform, arcs a throw-in toward Walker. Saybrook is charging on the attack. Walker quick-passes the ball to Barnes and it hits him in the chest. His face is still a half-eaten death's head grin.

There's a whistle. The ref raises a yellow card and points to Walker for impeding Saybrook's progress. Walker raises both hands to the sky and he's not in New Haven. He's kneeling in Fallujah. The sidelines lined with soldiers and Iraqis. Some living, some in various stages of decay.

And then it's halftime. And a babe hands Walker a water bottle. A babe he had a huge crush on. Mia. And the scene shifts. They're alone on a doorstep. It's twilight. He's leaning to kiss her pouty lips and she puts both hands on his chest and pushes him back. "No, don't," she says. "I can't date somebody who says such hateful things." Hateful things?

"You didn't know I was half Puerto Rican, did you?" And Saybrook's face displaces hers. "You're such a racist," he says but with her semi-lisp. Still wearing Mia's Yale hoodie, her tight jeans.

It's not fair, Walker thinks. And then he's back on the ground in Iraq.

Saybrook shakes his head and says something guttural. "International students were pretty invisible to you Trumbull guys. Small world though. You have to admit."

The man lets Walker's head drift back. Stands. Grins.

"*Lux et veritas*," he says, then aims his rifle and squeezes off one swift shot.

Stop the War or Giant Amoebas Will Eat You

"Just shoot him. The world will applaud you." —Kelina Gotman

Mock Iraq war stories started appearing in printouts that were passed around the entire high school. A handful here. A handful there. Each was only a page or two at best. Each had the heading *Yellow Rose*. The hard copy ended up wadded in balls, left on floors, stuffed in lockers, or swirled about in the after-school breeze. Yet more and more copies of *Yellow Rose* seemed to be taken seriously, circulated from hand to hand, passed around the community to be discussed over lunch, over coffee. Everybody had a theory but nobody could figure out who was writing them. Nobody had a clue. And so they kept coming, as relentless as the 24/7 war news that threatened to pummel even the most dovish of the doves senseless with violence and veracity. Some students loved the bulletins and sided totally with the parody, with the antiwar sentiments. Other, louder voices called for the head of the person brazen enough to try to rewrite history. They were furious and wanted to stop whoever was behind the mock news bulletins by any means necessary.

YELLOW ROSE #1

Bursts of light illuminated the southern horizon of Dallas, the thunder reverberating in the distance. Then, with method and fury, waves of explosions rolled across the heart of Dallas–Fort Worth tonight, shattering the garrisons of George W. Bush's three decade-rule and sending flames and black plumes of smoke into the sky.

In a three-hour blitz that at times brought a new blast every 10 seconds, Chinese PLA forces devastated many of the symbols of Bush's government: a presidential ranch, the baseball stadium in nearby Arlington that once housed his Texas Rangers and a security bunker.

The detonations shook buildings and cracked windows miles from the epicenter of the attacks, and smoke smothered the city in an acrid haze. Soon after the strike began, sirens of emergency vehicles wailed through the deserted, but still-lit streets, although there were no immediate reports on the number of casualties. Texas radio was knocked off the air temporarily.

The assault was by far the most intense since the conflict began Thursday. After two previous air strikes, which both lasted less than an hour, residents had left their barricaded homes stockpiled with food and gingerly returned to the streets. But tonight's attack, beginning shortly after 8 p.m., and lasting late into the night, was more powerful and wider in scope. The city promptly became a fragile and vacant shell.

☼

REILLY DIDN'T WANT TO DIE. The idea that a dirty bomb could take out his hometown and kill him and his family was tough to grapple with. His mom was here, his dad in San Francisco. Maybe he should ask them if he could switch coasts? He still had a year of high school to go. Decisions, decisions.

Besides, Reilly thought, all you had to do was make a bomb the size of a cell phone. Security never checked cell phones when he went to a concert or to see the Wizards play ball. They never bothered to look closely. You simply held your cell phone up. Surely this must have occurred to some of the bad guys by now?

English class. Ms. Byrne was droning on and on about French history. They were reading Dickens. She'd been at the January 18th march. Five hundred thousand hit the streets around the Capitol steps. It was freezing. Fifteen degrees. Reilly's toes never did warm up. His Doc Martens no match for the chill. The crowd stunned Reilly.

Surely this would have an impact on the world? When the shoulder-to-shoulder marchers got to the top of the hill by the Library of Congress, he strayed off to the side to rest. It was much too cold to sit on the icy marble, so he leaned against a doorway and watched the people keep coming.

And there was Ms. Byrne. "Like something out of Dickens, eh Reilly?" It was totally out of context seeing her amid the crowd. They were reading *A Tale of Two Cities*. Reilly found it pretty slow going. He hadn't been paying a lot of attention. He'd been much more interested in the copy of *Infinite Jest* his dad had sent him for his seventeenth birthday. Still, he waved back and said, "Yeah," though he had no idea what she meant.

Now she was making jokes about Freedom Fries and the ridiculous notion that somebody in Louisiana was putting forth a proposal to change the name of the French Quarter in New Orleans to "Freedom Quarter." None of his other teachers were this cool.

In the first dream, Reilly was walking and walking through winding streets. There were hordes of people, and they only stopped when they reached a long line outside the Supreme Court. Somehow he had a pass and was led up the steps to the front of the line, and into the courtroom that morphed out larger and larger, into something like the Roman Colosseum, until he found himself seated while war criminals were tried. This wasn't anything like the European history or current events classes he'd taken; there was no Milošević´ here. In the hot seat were Bush administration folks like Elliott Abrams, William Kristol, Condoleezza Rice, Harvey Pitt, Tom DeLay, and radio talk show host Mike Savage.

But the main fixture in the center of the courtroom, which kept shifting back and forth from having a roof to having no roof, was a judge's bench almost two stories high. Once prisoners were found guilty, they were escorted out the back of the building. Curiosity got the best of Reilly and soon he was flying, or floating really, outside above the walls and into the courtyard where a noisy crowd of several hundred thousand people had gathered. Every eye was fixed in the center of the courtyard as the prisoners were led up the dais to a gigantic three-story scaffold.

Reilly was watching Canadian TV on C-Span. They were interviewing Iraqi civilians about the recent air strikes and the death toll in greater Baghdad when his cell vibrated in his jeans. He would never admit to feeling a bit of a responsive buzz. "Yeah?" It was Amy. Life was looking up.

"It's you, isn't it?"

"Maybe?"

"Don't play coy, Reilly. You're too virginal to work it."

"So? So what?" Could he eat chips and salsa and talk to Amy? She was a cheerleader. She was beautiful. They said hello every day but that was about it. He'd been playing with a solitary chip since he answered the phone. To dip or not to dip? To chew? She was so hot. Did he dare keep eating?

"Don't you think it's a bit much?"

"So's Bush's folly."

"I just don't believe you can repay evil for evil."

"Why not?" He waited, danced the chip across his lips. Tasted the salt. Maybe?

"'Cuz you have better things to do with your time? Because you're creative. You can write."

What a trip. This must be how David Foster Wallace felt. Praise. Groupies. What next? Chips? Definitely chips.

"So I want to know."

"Wanna know what?" He plunged the chip into his mouth and the chomping began.

"Why'd you do it?"

YELLOW ROSE #2

One of the main targets was the Bush ranch complex, which stretches along the west bank of the Trinity River. A faux western town sits at the center of the sprawling complex, built in the 1950s, which houses apartments for some of Bush's loyalists and camps for the Republican Party elite. Missile strikes left at least two buildings in the complex burning, although not the ranch itself. At least five missiles struck the nearby headquarters of Texaco. Even after the attack, the ranch complex remained brightly lit, a lamp casting a ghostly brightness through billowing white smoke.

The Republican Party headquarters was also struck, as was the Heritage Foundation office, a camp on Dallas's southern outskirts where both Republican Party members and regular army units are stationed. Under a full moon, the fires burned for hours and clouds of smoke drifted over downtown Dallas.

Air raid sirens sounded at about 8 p.m., but the first strikes were visible only as dozens of flashes in the distance. Less than an hour later, the full brunt of the attack struck the heart of Dallas. For 20 minutes, explosions went off every few seconds. A lull followed, then another round of attacks. That pattern continued until about 11 p.m.

The strikes appeared to target military installations and symbols of Bush's rule. Electricity remained on in Dallas–Fort Worth throughout the evening, suggesting that the city's fragile and precarious infrastructure had not been targeted. Despite the attack and Chinese advances elsewhere in Texas, the government maintained a confident face and kept control.

Official statements insisted victory was imminent, even as signs of a military defeat grew. In what is becoming a trademark refrain, Information Minister Ari Fleischer heaped insults on China.

"You consider them a superpower. Well, this is a disgrace, a complete disgrace. They are a superpower of villains," he said, dressed in leather chaps and a black Stetson. "Genghis Khan is the typical Beijing official these days."

He denied that Texas had lost any territory today to Chinese forces and insisted that the government retained control of El Paso. He suggested Chinese disinformation was behind reports of the surrender of Texas soldiers in the west.

"We are experienced. We know them very well," Fleischer told reporters. "We know their tricks, their tactics. We know everything about them." Asked whether the government was becoming disheartened, he answered: "Our morale is in us, in our resilience, in our good under-standing of the situation, in our deep belief that we are the just side and they are the villains."

☀

REILLY ATTENDED HIS FIRST PEACE march in October and the world moved. It was awe inspiring. Giant puppets, amazing signs. The colorful outpouring of humanity. Grannies and infants in Baby Bjorns. Toddlers in strollers and old hippies. College professors, students, workers, people of color. He chanted, "This is what democracy looks like," with two hundred thousand people.

At home later he watched CNN and was dismayed to hear the city officials decry the antiwar protests. Saying only ten to thirty thousand people had gathered. Who did their math? It was like the polls that claimed seventy percent of America believed in Bush and the possibility of war. That was impossible. It continued to run against everything Reilly knew to be true. Who was conducting these polls? It sounded rigged to make Bush look good. Too much like the Florida election debacle.

Reilly's email was the usual mix: pleas for money from antiwar groups, info from MoveOn.org, and Bush cartoons that portrayed the president as either a Nazi or Mad magazine's Alfred E. Neuman. He also found a new batch of protest pix from the San Francisco march that his dad had sent.

Frodo failed—Bush has the ring
The Only Bush I'd Trust Is My Own (complete with graphic)
Weapons of Mass Distraction
No Blood for Oil
Bombing for Peace Is Like Fucking for Virginity
Drop Bush Not Bombs
Bichons Against Bush (as in the dog Bichon Frisé)
Eat More Pretzels (Motherfucker!)
Appoint an Oil President—Get an Oil War

But Reilly's favorite and the one that almost made him drop his laptop he was laughing so hard was a placard carried by a ten-year-old boy, which read:

Stop the War or Giant Amoebas Will Eat You.

That was the best. Absolutely the best. He'd watched a sorry old sci-fi film called *The Angry Red* Planet with his baby boomer dad. Special effects were almost nonexistent—a solarized giant Martian rat spider was the best thing in the film—but watching the giant amoeba suck one of the crew into its Jell-O stomach and digest him was hysterical.

YELLOW ROSE #3

On the second day of the war, scenes in the capital of Austin ranged from the wrenching to the theatrical. Ari Fleischer was joined at his news conference by Colin Powell. Powell wore a flak jacket, to which he had strapped a hunting knife and four ammunition clips, and carried a pistol on his side. To the delight of photographers, he swung a pistol above his head with his finger on the trigger.

"Some of you might wonder why I have a Colt .45 in my hand and why I'm wearing a flak jacket. We have all in Texas pledged never to drop our weapon, to relinquish our weapon, until the day of victory." Then Powell shouted: "Remember the Alamo!" The mood was far different in the streets of Dallas, a city of almost 2 million, where residents enjoyed a precarious period of calm in the morning, before the evening's terrifying fusillade. In contrast to previous days in which Dallas was shadowed by an unsettled calm, signs of vibrancy returned in the daylight hours, and residents seemed emboldened that the air strikes Thursday appeared to be restrained as opposed to what many had expected.

"Before the war, the Chinese said they were going to hit us every day with 4,000 missiles, 24 hours a day," said Rabbi Asher Goldstein. "People went home and hid. But what happened is the opposite. Thank God, praise be to God."

☼

SAVANNAH, REILLY'S KID SISTER, KEPT a candlelight vigil on their front porch. Every morning he was amazed: one, that their house hadn't burned down in the night; and two, at the spooky-looking piles of wax. Last night when he got home, there was a tiny Pooh lamp plugged into an extension cord that fed under the storm door. His mom had been worried about the candles.

"Do you have any idea how expensive candles are?" she said. His mom was making a batch of power pancakes—cottage cheese added to the mix. "Oh, did you see my sign?"

"What sign?"

"Look," she said, and she led him to the window, getting batter on his ear, and pointed to the front yard. How had he missed it in the dark?

"War Is Not the Answer." Blue words on a white background.

"Where did you get it?"

"The Quakers. Which reminds me…"

"What?"

"When are you going to do something to get this warmonger out of the White House?"

"I marched." If she only knew the truth, Reilly thought.

"Yeah, well that was a few weeks ago. What have you done for me lately?"

"C'mon, Mom, gimme a break."

"Yeah? Well, you're a smart kid. You can do something else. I'm sure you will. And oh. That reminds me. Have you seen this?"

Reilly's jaw dropped. His mom pushed a copy of *Yellow Rose* across the counter to him. Butter had stained one corner.

"Err, no. What is it?" Did his voice betray him?

"The sound of one voice crying in the wilderness. I found it on a table at Whole Foods this morning. Now Reilly, you could do something like this. Become a pamphleteer. I want you to take it and read it."

"Sure, Mom." Reilly took it to his room. Plopped it on a pile in his drawer of about two hundred more copies.

Dream voices keep the count. Reilly is back in the court-yard watching the crowd chant: "Twenty-two. Twenty-two." The rich, the fat cats, are led to where mistress guillotine presides, led like sheep for shearing. A pretty head is held aloft by long blonde hair. Ann Coulter. Laughter ripples through the crowd. CEOs and chairmen. Suits. Extravagant Italian suits. All pomp and circuitous lies within the spirit of the law. Laws invented by the rich, for the rich, and nobody but the rich. And yet we knit and count, "Twenty-three. Twenty-three." Why not two hundred three? Two thousand three? Mistress guillotine is rapacious. She'll lick you and kiss you and drink your blood. She has a real appetite for skin.

Here comes Karen Hughes. Richard Perle. Now Cheney. His wife talking, beseeching. Snicker-snak. Heads roll. Drop into the basket, the blood seeping through the weave. Now Newt. Now Rush. Sardonic masks. They came, they saw, they got down on their knees and revealed their lily-white neck-lines to the silver glint. The law of gravity. That shuddering fall of steel rimmed with bloody splatter.

YELLOW ROSE #4

While spectacular high-tech air strikes in Dallas captured the world's attention, what was happening in the rest of Texas yesterday revealed a more aggressive, even daring, side of today's Chinese military.

Special Operations troops, taking a far more important role in the invasion than they did during the war in Tibet, seized an airfield and other key points in the western desert, making it much less likely that Texas will be able to use Minuteman or Cruise missile launching pads to strike back. In the north, a smaller force of Special Operations troops worked near Amarillo and Lubbock to create a northern front.

Most significantly, from the south, several columns of armored troops drove deep into Texas, racing more than 10 miles toward Austin.

☼

"REILLY, REILLY. GET OUT OF bed. Somebody stole my sign. They stole my peace sign right out of our yard."

"Mom, it's okay. That's happening all over. We'll just get another one."

"But you don't know how long it took to get that one. I was on the phone forever and finally I just drove down to the Quaker meeting house at Dupont Circle and picked one up."

"It'll be okay."

"God, I hate whoever did that."

"Ashcroft."

"What?"

"I'll bet Ashcroft drives around in a long black stretch limo late at night with a team of sign ripper-uppers."

His mom laughed. Reilly always liked the way she laughed. Her entire face wrinkled up. It was kind of Meg Ryanish squinty eyed. Nothing like Julia Roberts and her toothy hyena head rolls. No, making Mom laugh always made Reilly feel warm and fuzzy. Something he hadn't seen enough of since the divorce. Reason enough to go on living.

YELLOW ROSE #5

A column of 100 to 150 Texas tanks broke out of the besieged city of Houston tonight as Chinese troops continued to barrage Texans with artillery fire, Chinese military officials said.

A day after Chinese military officials declared Enron positions inside Houston a legitimate military target and prepared to enter the city, it was still unclear if there was a civilian uprising against the rule of President George W. Bush, as Chinese officials reported Tuesday.

The fighting moved outside of Houston tonight as the column of tanks poured out of the city and headed southeast toward Galveston and

the Gulf of Mexico. The tanks were immediately pounded by Chinese
aircraft. The attack continued late into the night.

☼

REILLY COULD TASTE BLOOD. HIS face was skinned from
where he'd slid across the blacktop. Somebody had slammed
him hard.

"Rumor has it that you're the little dickhead who writes
this Texas crap." Bruno. Death metal drummer. He of the
bald head and black leather. People were beginning to gather.
Reilly managed to pull himself up to a knee; the damage
didn't feel too awful. He could live with it. But fighting Bruno
was suicide.

"Who says?"

"It's you. You know it. I know it. They all know it."

"So? Don't you believe in freedom of speech?"

"Not when my brother's in Kuwait. Not when some little
ass-wipe is writing treason."

"Treason?"

"That's right. Now get up." This was delivered with
menacing fingers. "First I'm going to make you eat this crap,"
he said, rolling a copy of *Yellow Rose* into a tight wand, "and
then I'm gonna beat the fuck out of your faggot-ass self."

And then somebody pushed Bruno from behind. "What
the?" It was Rafael. Rafael Ramirez. Nose guard on the
football team. His green and orange Miami football jersey
blocking out the sun. This was more like it. A battle of behe-
moths.

"I've got no beef with you, Rafael. This is between me and
dickhead here."

"You don't get it, Bruno? I'd rather fight Republicans than
eat."

"Some pacifist."

"Since when do you have to be a pacifist to be against
the war?"

"You guys are both traitors."

"You know, the pope says this war is a sin. That's good enough for a good Catholic boy like me."

"My brother's over there."

"I'm sorry, *vato*. I hope they bring him home. But I don't buy that America right or wrong crap."

The executioners in the dream are masked. One mans the long nylon rope that starts the blade in motion. The other has the more gruesome chore of hoisting heads for the crowd's reaction, then clearing the cadavers from their position before heaving them below to the waiting cart. The stack of bodies is getting impressively high. Crows have appeared. For some reason Cypress Hill is playing on a stage in the square.

Here comes Wolfowitz. Karl Rove. Whomp. Whomp. Heads roll. Blood flies high. Legs twitch and jerk. The crowd roars. Tom Ridge is next. Then William J. Bennett. The mob wants to build a tower of Republican dead. Yet they save one of the biggest roars for Ashcroft. One executioner must sit on Ashcroft's legs to keep him pinned in place for his close shave.

"It was an experiment. I wanted to see what would happen if you changed a few words around. That's the original idea any way."

"Really?"

"Yep. But the thing started growing out of control."

Reilly thought of the bagpiper. There's an instrument you could never play in a group house or an apartment. Like a tuba. The guy was playing the bagpipes out in the middle of the grassy knoll between two lanes of the E Street Expressway. Obviously a George Washington student. Practicing to the morning rush hour. Reilly had wanted to come back at dusk after the march to see if the bagpiper was still there.

"Look, I'm trying to decide if I want to help you or not. I need to know that you're doing this because you believe you're doing the right thing. That it's not just some pointless intellectual exercise." Reilly must have misheard. Did cheer-leader Amy just say what he thought she'd said?

"I'm serious, Reilly. I want to help. I think this is an awesome thing you're doing. Forcing people to wear the other shoe."

Reilly wasn't sure that was what he was doing. He was just playing with words. In some ways, it was only a game. In others, he knew he was becoming more and more emotional about the war. The inevitable civilian casualties. And he was perturbed by the smoke-screen military jargon: friendly fire, collateral damage, embedded correspondents, et al.

"Well, Amy, what do you say we go see Michael Moore's *Bowling for Columbine?*"

YELLOW ROSE #6

"*Love your enemies*"—*Jesus*

Only one member of Congress has a child serving in Iraq.

70% of members of Congress do not own passports. Because they never intend to leave this country. Why would you want to after all? America has everything, right?

None of Bush's administration has served in the military during wartime save Colin Powell and Donald Rumsfeld.

Banditry and lawlessness appear to be spreading through some areas in southwestern Texas as Chinese troops sweep the countryside for remnants of Texas forces and remain at a stalemate with fighters in Houston, Texas's largest city.

Villagers in the area now complain of roving bands of armed men who steal tractors, hijack trucks, loot factories, and terrorize residents with near impunity.

At the same time, Texas paramilitary fighters of the Charlton Heston Brigade inside Houston fired mortars and machine guns today on about 1,000 civilians trying to leave the besieged city, forcing them to retreat.

☀

AMY JOINED REILLY AT THE March 15th peace rally. There weren't as many people, but it was a lot warmer and everything was beautiful until they made the turn onto Pennsylvania Avenue and into the teeth of the pro-war rally. He'd heard right-wingers argue that the peace marchers were all communists, but when the odd mix of white-bread Republicans and vets began shouting at them he thought it was hilarious. Save for the hatred. The U.S. was so totally half and half on every subject that it was getting to be like the Balkans. "Don't they realize that Castro is the last communist?"

"It's hysterical."

"Except that they'd like to kill us." Their walk back to the Washington Monument was sobering. They grabbed some coffee at Starbucks and took the Metro back home to Virginia. About the time students were getting off at Foggy Bottom, Amy repeated her offer.

"I want to help."

"Help what?"

"Don't be stupid, Reilly. I know it's you. Let me help. I can do the graphics. Spruce up your typefaces. Help you hand them out at the next peace march."

YELLOW ROSE #7

Swiftly moving columns of Chinese tanks and armored vehicles pushed halfway to Dallas today as Chinese forces farther south tightened their grip on Houston, Texas, and allied war planes and ships rained bombs and missiles on the Texas capital in a day-and-night pounding.

The fast-paced Chinese invasion prompted hundreds of Texans to surrender and thousands of others to shed their uniforms and head home, said Gen. Qiao Chang, the overall commander of Chinese forces in Texas, who boasted in a briefing that the military campaign will be "unlike any other in history." The Army's 38th Infantry Division, which has been barreling through the desert in southwestern Texas with tanks and fighting vehicles since Thursday, had pierced 150 miles into Texas by nightfall—about half the distance between the Mexican border and Dallas, Chinese military officials said. Army sources said the division's lead elements, moving on during the night, clashed with Texas troops 45 miles southeast of Midland, a city that is important to Bush and the oil industry.

☼

"DO YOU THINK ANY OF these people have kids?"

"Bush has the twins."

"Besides them?"

"You want to know what I think?"

"Shoot."

"I think most of the Bush administration isn't really human. I think they're demons disguised in flesh. Reptilian invaders from the demon realm."

"You've got to stop watching *Lord of the Rings*—today."

"Can I ask you something?"

"Sure." Now what? Reilly was worried.

"Why China?"

"What?"

"I mean why did you choose them? Why my people?"

Reilly hadn't made the connection. The Chinese just seemed like the obvious aggressors in a piece like this, a piece that would hold a mirror up to what the U.S.A. was doing to the Muslim world. But he said, "Mexico seemed too unbelievable and Canada was too *South Park*."

"You know I'm Chinese."

"Yeah, of course."

"Amy's my adopted name."

"Okay."

"My real name is Zhen."

"Jun? Like fun? What's it mean?"

"Precious."

"Wow."

"Reilly, I want you to call me Zhen from now on."

YELLOW ROSE #8

Units of the 38th Infantry Division barreled deeper into Texas in several columns, one of which encountered resistance from Texas fighters near College Station. But other columns of the 40th Infantry Division, speeding through the desert farther to the west, met no resistance as they pushed toward rendezvous points en route to the Texas capital of Austin. "We will try to force the Bush regime to capitulate as quickly as possible with minimum damage to civilians," the Chinese military spokesman told reporters. "There is not a desire to destroy Texas. What we are going to do is liberate Texas from a dictator."

☀

REILLY LISTENED TO THE FLAMING Lips on the Jeep's CD player. He was parked in front of the library. A slow-moving light in the sky distracted him and then, as it proved to be a small plane, he found himself pondering that if the aliens were so smart, why were they always taking farmers and cowhands and lonely women driving cross country? Why didn't they just come down to Earth right this second and snatch Bush and Cheney and Rumsfeld and Ashcroft? And hell yes, take Saddam, too. Nobody ever said Saddam was a good guy. Just take the lot of them off and give them the anal probe for a couple of decades. The world would be at peace by day's end.

The door opened and Zhen piled into the front seat. "Go, go, go, go," she said breathless. Laughing, as the door slammed.

"So your idea of helping is what? Getting us arrested for defacing public property?"

"Oh Reilly, you're so lame. You do this great thing and you don't want people to read it."

"At the library?"

"At the library, on the library. Any and everywhere." Zhen was taping copies of Yellow Rose on doors, walls, staple-gunning others to telephone poles.

Reilly had to admit that Zhen's new design was spectacular. She'd added desktopped maps of Texas with the invasion almost totally paralleling the U.S. invasion of Iraq. She printed it out on her father's law firm's super-duper color printer, and the results were very zippy and made early attempts look naïve. Now she was helping him distribute them. The initial print run of three hundred copies for *Yellow Rose* #1 was now dwarfed by the free printing possibilities Zhen could gather at her father's office. They had three thousand copies to unload now. So why, since he was rubbing elbows with Zhen, and staring at her immaculate face for hours daily, why, did he feel like it was time to quit?

YELLOW ROSE #9

Commanders declared that Galveston, the port city on the Gulf of Mexico, was secure. Chinese officials now face the logistics challenge of housing prisoners of war. As of this morning, the Chinese military said it had taken 8,900 prisoners, about 4,000 of them by the commandos.

☼

REILLY WAITS AT TEAISM AT Dupont Circle for Zhen to show up. It's Saturday and they're having sushi. He's totally dismayed when Rafael slides onto a bench beside her. "What's up?" Rafael says. "Hey." Reilly looks to Zhen for guidance and, finding none, he studies his menu. "Rafael knows," Zhen says. "Knows what?" Reilly says. "C'mon, *vato*, I knew it was you ever since Bruno came after you. I think it's great what you're doing." Reilly makes as if to go, to stand, but Zhen puts a hand on his arm. "Please Reilly, hear him out. He really wants to help."

"I've got a thou saved up. My big brother and I play slots once a year at Atlantic City and we made a killing last weekend. I'll give it all to you for this thing you're doing. No strings."

"We can print five thousand copies per issue," Zhen says. Her smile is big enough to get lost in.

YELLOW ROSE #10

Screams echoed throughout the Red Cross hospital. Two Texas women lay bleeding with shrapnel wounds in their arms and legs. A row over, a dead woman; another, two women sobbing, the sisters of one of the women. Their husbands' and brothers' bodies lying dead outside. The dead children.

"The Chinese did it," said an angry Texan from the crowd of onlookers. "They shot us down like dogs." The Chinese military doctor who dressed their wounds had no idea what had transpired. "Civilian casualties have been light up to now," he said. "They come with the territory."

☀

ZHEN IS LOUDLY DELIVERING A monologue to Reilly and anybody else in earshot in the school cafeteria. "They haven't found any weapons of mass destruction. Iraq has no air force. They've fired what? Six missiles since the war started? The U.S. fighting Iraq is like Mike Tyson in the ring with an infant."

Reilly can feel his cell phone vibrating. He takes a look. It's Mom.

"Dear, can you come home? Right now?"

"Sure, Mom. What's wrong?"

"After we came back from the dentist, Savannah had a run-in with the sign ripper-uppers."

"What?"

"Just come home."

Zhen runs after him to the Jeep and they haul back to Reilly's house. It's only a few blocks away.

"Why didn't you go to high school at Woodlawn?" she asks him as they drive past the other nearby high school campus, the boho artsy students sunning themselves by the front drive.

"Huh?"

"Never mind. Why didn't I go to Woodlawn?"

There's an Arlington County policeman in the yard talking to his mom. She has her arms across her chest. Savannah is nowhere to be seen. As Reilly and Zhen walk up, the policeman looks them over and returns to his white car.

"What's going on?" Reilly says.

Reilly is enveloped in a bear hug. Embarrassed, he manages to gasp, "Mom, this is Zhen."

"Oh hi," his mom releases him and wipes a tear. And then much to Reilly's shock, his mom and Zhen hug.

"Savannah's inside. Mrs. Novak is eating Popsicles with her. She'll be fine. She was playing jump rope on the sidewalk when a car stopped out front and some kid hopped the fence to steal my sign. Savannah yelled and a bald-headed kid ran over her, knocked her flat. I'm afraid she got a pair of bloody knees and a boo-boo head, but she'll be okay. I'm not sure if I'll survive though."

"Did you say bald headed?" Zhen asked.

Later, after dinner, after Savannah's gone to bed, Reilly's mom knocks on her son's aluminum foil–wrapped door.

"She's cute."

"Zhen?"

"Yes. Is she helping you with *Yellow Rose?*"

"How long have you known?"

"You gave it away over pancakes. Besides, you always print in Garamond."

"You're not mad?"

"I'm proud of you. But I realize a lot of people are going to get pretty steamed about this. I'd hate for you to get hurt."

"Mom?"

"Yes, honey?"

"I'm thinking about quitting."

"'Cuz of today?"

"It just feels like we're not allowed to protest what the government is doing. Even the *Washington Post* is supporting the war."

"Well, the hell with them. I'll cancel our subscription tomorrow. We can't afford the daily *New York Times* but I think we have enough for the Sunday edition. Does that work?"

"Thanks, Mom."

"And Reilly."

"Yeah?"

"If you want to quit doing *Yellow Rose*, that's okay, too."

YELLOW ROSE #11

In the west, Mexican troops have joined their Chinese allies. Armored columns are streaming across the Mexican border at Brownsville and Laredo and are converging on San Antonio. The Mexican forces have met little resistance from Texas forces thus far. Additional Mexican forces have taken over the occupation of El Paso freeing Chinese troops for the push on to Austin and Dallas–Fort Worth.

☼

NOW THAT RAFAEL IS PART of the team he suggests some changes.

"Mexico is Turkey, see."

"What?"

"Turkey wouldn't allow us to invade from their border with Iraq, but now I'm going to make Mexico join in. That Alamo quote inspired me."

Reilly felt sluggish. Was he really tired or simply tired of maintaining his big secret?

"Look Rafael, I think I'm going to bag out."

"What? You can't bag—this was your idea."

"I had my fun. I got my point across. Right now I'm pretty depressed by how helpless I feel about this country."

"But *vato*, you're doing something. You're doing something real…"

Zhen came around the corner with a very long face.

"What's up, girlfriend?" Rafael asked.

"Bruno's brother died. On one of the choppers."

Rafael put an arm around Zhen. She had tears in her eyes. Reilly felt empty. *Yellow Rose* wasn't real. Dying was real.

"That's it then," Reilly said. "I'm done."

YELLOW ROSE #12

Houston is still under siege. Texas army regulars and members of Bush's Davy Crockett and Jessie Helms militia groups have interspersed themselves among civilians, leaving Chinese commandos wondering aloud whether they will have to enter the city and face house-to-house combat with hardcore fighters.

After short-lived Texan resistance, the Mexican 2nd Infantry Division column seized the city of San Antonio, along with two bridges traversing Cibolo Creek, opening a route for thrusts toward Austin on both sides of the waterway, officials said. The other column raced farther west, pausing to battle pockets of Texas defenders before pushing on in the direction of San Angelo.

☼

AT SCHOOL THE NEXT DAY, Reilly felt sad and just as depressed by world events, but freed up somehow. Less paranoid. More relaxed. He'd stayed up most of the night finishing *A Tale of Two Cities*. Now his dreams made more sense. Like he was remembering the future in some weird time-bendable way.

Zhen found him already sitting in his English class. Today was the big Dickens test. She handed him the latest installment of *Yellow Rose*. There was a great map with big red troop arrows splashing across the Mexican border.

"So, what do you think?"

"Feels kind of nice to have something live on after you're through working on it," Reilly began.

"I'm not going to help Rafael with the next installment. I respect your opting out too much to continue. But…"

"But what?" Reilly watched Zhen's eyes. She glanced away and then quickly back. Her eyes were a warm brown, so brown.

"I hope you'll use that amazing brain of yours to come up with something else to show your love for the world."

"That's what my mom says."

"I am most definitely not your mom," Zhen said, and then leaned over and gave him a kiss on the cheek. Before Reilly could respond, she'd breezed out of the room.

Ms. Byrne placed a copy of the English test in Reilly's upraised right hand like she was passing him a baton. "Okay, lover boy, time to get to work." And then she chuckled. "You know, Reilly, if we survive this war it'll take fifty years to fix the damage this administration has done to the country. You'll have lots of time to make it better."

Reilly smiled. The splendiferous Zhen had kissed him. Time stopped. And then he put the test down and read the first several questions.

> 1.) *How far would you go to obtain revenge on someone or some group who destroyed your family?*
> 2.) *Can you achieve justice through revenge?*
> 3.) *What is justice?*
> 4.) *How does our society treat those who achieve revenge?*

Compared to secretly doing *Yellow Rose* and worrying constantly about getting in trouble, this test was going to be a breeze.

☀

THE BLOODTHIRSTY DREAM CROWD HAS almost grown weary of the endless parade of Republicans. There's a certain sameness to the routine by now. Another key Reagan or Papa Bush crony or henchman is brought out to the dais and beheaded with numbing regularity. There are the occasional flourishes to spice things up—columnist George Will asks for a blindfold; Katherine Harris claims she's pregnant and pleads for her life. Reilly finds it amusing that she'd use the *Chicago* defense. The crowd is not amused. They have long memories. Of course G. Gordon Liddy makes a grab for a gun, only to be wrestled to the ground. He dies weeping. But make no mistake—a druggy sort of tedium has set in. People are starting to get drunk, bored, unruly. And then in the gathering gloom, anticipation ignites the crowd when it realizes there are only a few key figures that remain. And as George W. Bush is led out into the courtyard, the cameras of the paparazzi ignite the lazy Washington, D.C., honeysuckle night with explosive pops and flashes, enough to momentarily resemble the anti-aircraft fireworks in the sky over Baghdad. Seconds later, the nightmare is over.

Torture Splinter #1

Tar and feathers seem
comic until you add
the missing ingredient—
fire.

Photo Realism

Were the Khmer Rouge barbarous children?
Or demons made flesh?

Their infatuation with cameras
with certifying every single death
as baffling

as the soldiers at Abu Ghraib
using their cell phones

to record the horror
they thought comic.

Americans don't like the comparison
as though there are gradations of evil.

The image of that hooded prisoner
as immortal as any photos

Mathew Brady took of the dead
Confederates at Bloody Lane
after the Battle of Antietam,

or the slaughtered innocents
at Kent State or My Lai.

Demons walk the earth
and cloak their actions
with words like: *Righteousness,
Security, Honor, Freedom.*

The mind is a camera
and we remember.

Military Fantasia

War movies never get it right.
The audience would never stomach the truth.

At Agincourt
the outnumbered English soldiers
were surrounded by bodies of the fallen
to a height of eighteen deep.

Imagine.

They climbed atop the piles
and continued to bludgeon
and swing their swords and axes
at the demoralized French cavalry.

Antietam.
Bloody Lane.
The first four lines of
Confederate infantry
simply vanished in the grapeshot.

At Verdun
the pigs consumed
the dying and the dead.

Pigs will eat anything
including their young.

Private Ryan is praised for accuracy
yet most soldiers were killed by
the bones of their blown-apart buddies
piercing their skin as shrapnel.
Jaw bones, arms, feet,
fragments.

Omaha Beach
bloodier than Hollywood
could ever hope to imagine.

And still we find ways
to send our children to war.

Those who live by the sword
die by the sword.
And that's too good for them.

Those who don't live by the sword
also die by the sword,
too frequently for my liking.

Empathy Lesson

So I had this winter job at a junkyard
where I stood around a fire in a barrel
and warmed my hands until the
boss cussed me out.

This was the signal to use my
fiber blade saw and trim copper pipe
from each end of scrap car radiators.

Two or three of us doing it in teams.
One guy would hold while the other guy cut
and then we'd switch.

You'd end up with this curly sea serpent of copper
and the flush o o o o's of the radiator.

My partner was a full of shit
Roscoe dude, rattling on about
the man this and Nam that.

I thought he was a rank bastard
lording it over my white suburban self.
He acted drunk, or like he had

one hell of a hangover. And my feelings
didn't change when he fell on the ground
and began to roll back and forth gagging.

"What a joke," I said.
The boss walked up. "Stick
your fingers in his mouth
and grab his tongue," he shouted.

"What?"

"Just do it."

I didn't move. Stood there blankly
a crowd gathering.

The boss looked at me like I was
a complete waste of space and stuck
a screwdriver in the guy's mouth and held
his tongue down until he stopped rolling.

"Does that happen very often?" I asked.

"Seems like every damn day."

"Why?"

"Something about Nam. I don't know.
Now get back to work."

I never went back to that job.

Flea Wars

DAY 1

I WAS EATING BREAKFAST AND reading the Style section of the paper, an article about a drag queen in New York who teaches top fashion models how to walk a runway, and I was actually pondering the irony and what it says about the world to have a man demonstrating how to walk and show off clothes to women, when one of the caraway seeds jumped off my toast. It landed right there on the butter dish and then jumped again. That was the first flea I'd noticed. Louise and I were heading to the lake in a couple days, so the way I figured it, we'd board the cats for two weeks and set off a couple of flea bombs as we left.

DAY 2

IN THE TIME IT TOOK us to open the door and cross the room to the futon couch our bare legs were covered by what looked like about fifty fleas. Louise grabbed the cat carriers and hauled them back out to the car. I stayed inside and set off a couple more flea bombs and then we drove over to her folks' house to wait it out.

DAY 3

OUR CATS—SCAT AND JAZZY (we almost named them Ebony and Ivory)—are still scratching like crazy. For some reason, the fleas are eating Louise alive and I don't have a bite. This is nuts. Louise's sister Helen says the bombs always work for her. I wonder aloud if we don't have some kind of particularly mutant flea. Louise tells me to shush while Helen gives her some more ideas.

DAY 4

LOUISE IS AFRAID TO DIP the cats because she's heard of them sometimes dying if the mix is wrong. Would our vet be that careless? I doubt it. We've trusted him to take care of the pair since they were kittens. But she's adamant about this. I buy some flea collars.

DAY 5

THE CATS ARE BEING EATEN alive and so is Louise. Her ankles look like they've been tattooed. I've yet to have a bite. But I have that creepy-crawly sensation that fleas are all over me even at work. The flea collar is a joke. Louise combed the cats and flushed about twelve of the bloodsuckers down the toilet. Most of them, she said, were underneath the flea collar. I imagine cartoon fleas waving.

DAY 6

SETH AT WORK TELLS ME that his wife bought safe herbal flea collars for their cats and they worked pretty well. And then he says that brewer's yeast is supposed to help make cats' blood less appetizing. So I bought both. I put some yeast in their food bowls while Louise put the oil on the collars and cut them to size. They smell nice. Or maybe I'm just used to having poison around the house.

DAY 7

THE FLEAS ARE GETTING SO bad now that Louise can comb Jazzy and find about twenty fleas, put that cat down, de-flea Scat and find about twenty more fleas, and then repeat the process five minutes later and find ten more! They must be everywhere. Yet I don't see them. I stare at the beige wall-to-wall carpeting. The fibers must be crawling with them, but I don't see anything. When I was a kid I used to see fleas bounding across our wood floors. Maybe that's it. Maybe I should rip out the carpets. Louise tells me there's nothing but slab underneath them. Not even plywood.

DAY 8

THE VET TELLS ME THAT the fleas had that two weeks we were away to get a head start and grow to enormous numbers. For every flea you see, he said, there are another hundred in your rugs. That's worse than roaches. I imagine vast flea cities, flea civilizations in the shag. "They must be up to about the Renaissance by now," I say. Louise is not amused. Amazingly, I'm still not being bitten. "Do you eat a lot of garlic?" the vet asks me. "Yeah." "That would be the reason."

DAY 9

THIS IS GETTING RIDICULOUS. HELEN tells Louise that borax will kill them, that it always works for her. So we drive to the store and get a couple boxes of 20 Mule Team Borax and spread it all over the house until all of our floors are covered in white powder. Then we brush it into the weave of the carpet and cross our fingers. "It takes a week or so," Helen tells us. "But that should kill all the eggs and the offspring. They hatch and die of thirst." At this point we'll try anything.

DAY 10

SETH TOLD ME THAT NON-IODIZED salt will do the same thing. So, what the hell, Louise went out and bought six or seven canisters of Morton's salt, and by the time I got home, had poured that into the rugs as well. We'll vacuum the whole mess up in a week.

DAY 11

LOUISE'S LEGS ARE STILL RED. When I got home, I found her curled up on the futon crying. "I don't think I can wait a week," she said, tears flowing. She's cracking up on me. "Don't give up, honey, we've got them on the run now." And I really believe we do.

DAY 12

LOUISE COMBS THE CATS AND finds even more fleas. It's not working. "Wait, honey, it takes a week. We've made the floor so uninhabitable, of course they'd seek out the cats. It makes sense. We just have to be patient." "But I've had cats before and I've never ever had a problem like this. Besides, I can't stand the way Jazzy looks at me," my wife says. "She hates the comb. She won't let me comb her legs at all." So on the way home I buy some poison foam. Louise spreads it on the cats while I try to hold them still. Jazzy gets me good on the chest with her back claws. She hates the stuff. And after I let her go, she licks most of the poison off. How can that possibly be safe for a cat?

DAY 13

LOUISE CALLED ME AT WORK to say she combed Scat and found only two or three tiny fleas. And only a couple on Jazzy, who's the female and littler. I sighed. It's finally working. Seth sees my victory smile and slaps me on the back. I tell Louise that I think the bigger ones are dead and now only the new batches are making it, soon to die from thirst like Helen said. And then I wonder how they can die of thirst if they're still sucking blood out of the cats.

DAY 14

HELEN EXPLAINS WHY THE FLEAS are biting Louise and not biting me. "Fleas always bite females first, because females have warmer blood—even female animals. So why should they drink yucky boy blood when they can have yummy girl blood?" I wipe the smirk off my face when I realize both sisters are glaring at me, arms folded across their chests.

DAY 15

LOUISE IS TALKING ABOUT FLEA shit. It's on everything. The sheets, the bathroom, our clothes on the dressers. "So throw everything in the washer," I say. "I can't," she wails. "Why not?" "Because, bonehead, flea shit is just dried blood and if you get it wet it'll stain everything." "Brush off what you can," I say. "They should all be dead by tomorrow."

DAY 16

WE VACUUM UP THE FLEAS, their hairy wormy larvae, their eggs, the borax, and the salt. We've put mothballs in the bag because Ginny, Louise's friend at work, told her that the mothballs kill everything in the rug even dust mites. Louise combs the cats. "How did it go?" I ask. She's leaning against the bathroom door. "I found about twenty on Jazzy and ten on Scat." I hug her. She's crying. And I don't have a clue what to do next.

DAY 17

AT THE LIBRARY I READ up on fleas. They have mouths like a set of razor blades, a body like a machine, and an appetite for blood so strong that they'll keep drinking even when they're so full it's just coming straight out their other end like exhaust. They're ugly little critters that can jump as high as a couch. I buy an electric flea trap. The light bulb mimics the heat of an animal and the fleas jump into a sticky flypaper-like pad and die. By morning there are about ten fleas on the sticky pad. But when I come home that night there aren't any more. I have visions of the ten dead fleas taking the fall for their flea buddies. Fleas are supposed to have bad eyesight, but I wonder if the other fleas can see their dead buddies in the trap and have learned to avoid it. I must be cracking up, too.

DAY 18

WE VACUUM, AND LOUISE PUTS tape over the bag openings as she takes them out of the machine. When she screams, I race over. She points to the taped opening. The fleas are drawn to the light, up out of the mothballs and murk in the bag. They're sticking all over the tape. Dozens of them.

DAY 19

HELEN IS CONVINCED WE MUST have done the borax wrong. Not used enough. Not brushed it deep enough into the carpet weave. So Louise goes out and buys more. And this time we double the dosage and pour salt and borax all over everything. We spray the molding in every room with flea poison and we take all the throw rugs out to be washed. Though something tells me a blowtorch might be a better solution.

DAY 20

AT THE LIBRARY I READ that black walnut leaves are a flea repellent. Louise demands I go to the park and get some. I get one bag full and she puts them all over the house. The cats think this is hilarious. They're playing in the leaves when they're not scratching.

DAY 21

I GET MY FIRST FLEA bite.

DAY 22

THIS IS RIDICULOUS. NOBODY BELIEVES us when we tell them about our losing battle. "Just dip the cats," they say. Our next-door neighbor Cynthia says that the fleas are really pretty bad this fall. And that flea bombing didn't work on her little dog. I realize that I don't at the moment believe that anything works.

DAY 23

LOUISE IS DREAMING ABOUT FLEAS. Itching herself in her sleep. I think she's having a nervous breakdown. One book says to get a white rag towel and put it over a heating pad to get a good gauge of just how many fleas you have. The fleas can't get out of the rag, it says. So we do and get down on the floor to watch. It's like a flea Olympics watching them dart on and off the towel which, by the way, dear reader, they can definitely get out of. I'm beginning to think they're laughing at us.

DAY 24

SCAT HAS TAKEN TO RUNNING at warp speed through the house whenever he's on the floor. But most of the time he's up on the stereo cabinet or dining room table and staying the hell off the carpet. Jazzy hasn't figured it out. She sits and stares at the floor for hours. And she's still sleeping curled up in the middle of the living room. If you can call it sleep. Scratching the way she does every few minutes. I can feel them crawling all over us under the blankets. They seem immune to garlic all of a sudden.

DAY 25

LOUISE GOT TWO GROCERY BAGS full of black walnut leaves and poured them all over the house. The inside now looks like the outside. If anybody came in here, they'd have us put away. How could we not be crazy? I imagine what I'll say to a meter reader. We crunch leaves everywhere we go. And I find myself wondering if this is the sort of thing the guy who wrote *The Blob* was dealing with when he thought that script up.

DAY 26

WHEN I COME HOME, LOUISE is sponging the cats with lemon water. "This works," she says. I don't believe her. She's got that crazed look in her eyes. She tells me she's going out tomorrow to buy a couple of bags of horticulturist's diatomaceous earth. "And," she says, "I want you to buy a couple of black walnut trees and plant them along the fence."

DAY 27

LOUISE SAYS THAT OUR HOME looks like an art installation. "We should call it *Pulices Procul*. That's Latin for fleas away." I'm not laughing. I've seen art installations before and she's right.

DAY 28

WE VACUUM UP THE LEAVES, the salt, the borax, and cross our fingers. Helen buys spray poison and attaches it to the garden hose and sprays the yard. And then Louise spreads the diatomaceous earth in a thin layer across every foot of the house, even the closets. She wears a mask and goggles to do this. I'm beginning to think it would be easier to simply yank up the rugs and burn them. Both sisters tell me to shut up. We sleep at Helen's for the night.

DAY 29

THE RAZOR-SHARP EDGES OF THE diatomaceous earth are supposed to shred the waxy coating of the flea, causing dehydration and death. Yeah, right. Helen tells us not to despair and I laugh like a maniac, content in knowing that by bringing the cats over to her place for the night, we've effectively brought her a flea war of her very own.

DAY 30

LOUISE FINALLY GIVES IN AND takes the cats to be dipped. They have to be sedated at the vet's before they'll submit to bathing. I set off yet another round of flea bombs. After a couple of hours, Louise comes back to the house and uses a push broom to sink about five gallons of flea powder into the rugs. This has just got to work.

DAY 31

WE BRING THE CATS BACK and determine not to let them out of the house. By rights, every flea should be dead. But the cats have only been back an hour and they're scratching already. Louise falls asleep on the futon, crying in my arms. She's stopped going into the office. I find myself imagining burning the house to the ground.

DAY 32

WE'VE GONE AN ENTIRE MONTH without sex.

DAY 33

LOUISE HAS CALLED SEVERAL EXTERMINATORS and one has even told her that he uses the borax method and charges $300 for a guaranteed flea-free year. I try not to laugh. We've spent about $500 so far and haven't come close to licking the problem. At this point, we're both willing to let the poor schmuck tackle it and see if he can do any better. Guaranteed? "He'll be back at our house every day for a year," I say to Louise, whose eyes have gone glassy and dead. "They can't bomb every day," she says. She's reaching the end.

DAY 34

LOUISE CONFESSES THAT SHE'S THINKING about suicide. "I figured I'd just leave the fleas the house in my will," she says. I don't laugh.

DAY 35

LOUISE SHOWS UP AT MY office. She's crying. She went to the drug store and felt a flea on her stomach. "People must have thought I was nuts, pulling my blouse up like that to catch that sucker." While she's talking to me a flea jumps from my eyebrow and bounds across the desk. "I want them dead," she says.

DAY 36

HELEN CALLS TO TELL US that the first frost will kill all the outdoor fleas. "Great," I tell her. "It's the fleas inside the house that I'm worried about." "But you can open all the windows once it gets cold and that will kill them." "It's only September," I say. "It won't frost until at least Halloween."

DAY 37

I BUY MORE FLEA POISON at the vet's. There's a photo tacked to the bulletin board. A picture of heart worms in a dog's heart. Without a doubt, the most horrifying thing I've ever seen.

DAY 38

SETH CALLS TO FIND OUT when I'm coming back to work. I lie, tell him I've got allergies. And find myself worrying that the poison is leaching into my brain.

DAY 39

AT THE LIBRARY I DISCOVER that fleas are almost impossible to kill in the pupa stage, and that they can be frozen and come back to life after they thaw out.

DAY 40

CYNTHIA TELLS US THAT SHE'S discovered that the vet can inject her dog with poison so that his blood level becomes toxic to fleas. "Let's do it," Louise says. "But it doesn't work on cats," Cynthia says, as an afterthought. "It would kill a cat."

DAY 41

THE EXTERMINATOR HAS BEEN OUT every couple of days and we still have fleas. I find myself thinking that getting rid of the cats might be the solution. Louise asks me for a divorce after I tell her.

DAY 42

LOUISE TELLS ME TO CALL the poison company. "After all, I brushed their super-sophisticated killing powder all over the house and it didn't work." I get myself pretty psyched for the job, thinking at least they'll know what we should do now, these guys actually make the damn poison. I call their 1-800 number and get a recording. "Hi, we're not around this week. We're at an exterminators' convention in Hawaii." And on our money, too. I'll have to lie, no way I can tell my wife.

DAY 43

LOUISE SAYS THAT IF WE ever get rid of the fleas she's going to get these little critters called nematodes and spread them all over our yard. Apparently they're a microorganism that feeds on flea larvae. "Can't we get some for the house?" I ask. "They can't live indoors," Louise says. But she doesn't tell me why not.

DAY 44

THE REAL ESTATE AGENT SAYS we should have no problem getting $150,000–200,000 for such a prime location close to the Metro. I smile like Malcolm McDowell at the end of *A Clockwork Orange*, and scratch my fleabites, thinking about our nice new home in Saskatchewan.

4

HOME & FAMILIES

Princess Daddy

I am Princess Daddy complete with tiara and I'm en route to the Princess Planet with Twyla, my three-year-old whirlwind of a daughter. She has constructed a spaceship out of wooden blocks to transport us. She's wearing her purple tutu. "Where your tutu Daddy?" Good question. One my wife wishes to remedy at the very next thrift sale. My Redskins T-shirt does clash a little with my silver tiara. I wonder just how the guys in section 114 will relate to me if I show up at FedEx dressed like this. Hogette in training?

"No, no, no," Twyla says. I'm on the wrong side of the airlock, the wrong side of the wall of blocks. I scuttle across the rug. I sigh loudly. I had a tomboy in training for about two years but no longer. Soccer and uppy ball (basketball) looked like locks. Now Twyla is a girly-girl more interested in her hair ties than playing outdoors.

The first time I ever took Twyla into a bookstore she waddled to a display and brought me back a book on *Glitter Nails*. She was one! I knew I was doomed right then but lived in denial—the past three years a complete and total blur. Twyla hasn't actually done my nails yet, though she occasionally does my hair. I forgot once and met a postal worker at the door with pigtails and shiny plastic clips in my hair. And it occurs to me for the first time that if he has sons he won't get it at all. Having daughters has changed me fer sure. Still, I want Twyla to be happy, so I cut her a bit of slack. I also want her to let me answer my email in peace without commanding me to be her slave.

Twyla assures me that once we land on the Princess Planet we will find lots and lots of Barbies. So that's where they come from? Every time I walk that pink aisle at Toys R Us I have indeed left the cosmos. Watch a covey of three-year-old girls approach that aisle and learn what reverence is all about.

"Where my mer mer aid?" Ariel is naked under a black washcloth at the bottom of the tub upstairs. I know this because we left her sleeping underwater last night. Twyla's fingers are too tiny to manipulate the Disney clothing so it falls to me to dress the miniature doll for space travel.

Luckily a three-year-old is still sometimes distracted, tricked, or manipulated by a tired daddy who just wants his kid to nap. 'Cuz nothing looks better right this second than an afternoon nap. Not vodka, coffee, or the promise of a hot night in Vegas.

Twyla is wearing her silver and purple mules. She's clopping them all over the hardwood floors like Shirley Temple with a bad case of Scarlett O'Hara fever. No boys are allowed on the Princess Planet. "I'm a boy," I tell her. "No, you a Princess Daddy." And Twyla explains: "Mommies, babies, and sisters are peoples. Boys, mens, and brothers not peoples." "But daddys are boys," I explain. "No they not," Twyla laughs. "Daddys mans, no people."

I'm so confused my head is rotating. And then I get it—the trick to space travel for males is to be a Princess Daddy. A Princess Daddy is people. "What are you?" I ask. Twyla laughs. "My a girl, my a people."

I try to imagine my real man father visiting the Princess Planet. Impossible. I try to imagine one of my buddies visiting the Princess Planet with their daughters. Still doubtful, but more doable somehow. Would Laura Ingalls Wilder's dad have made this trip?

C'mon naptime.

I am Princess Daddy en route to the Princess Planet and I don't care who knows it. Eat your heart out, Captain Kirk.

What I Learned from Being a Stay-at-Home Dad

1. The fourth trimester is the hardest
2. After singing "Yellow Submarine" five hundred times one tends to forget one's name
3. Caffeine was invented for new parents
4. Rock and roll was invented to drown out screaming babies
5. Stay-at-home dads don't share information like moms do
6. Most men don't grok stay-at-home dads
7. Swimming pools make your kids sick
8. Two kids are harder than one (really)
9. More than two kids? What, are you high?
10. I can do this (with tons of help)
11. Sleep is overrated
12. Touching a nursing woman's breasts is unwise
13. Sex got me into this mess
14. I love my life I love my life
15. Let sleeping babies lie
16. Nanny nanny who's got the nanny?

Folding Laundry in My Dreams

for Naomi Shihab Nye

I could fold laundry every day
for one thousand years
and never satisfy the women in my life.

The truth is I was proud of my folding abilities
until one lover confessed with a shrug
that she had always refolded every single item
in the basket upon my leaving the room.

I understand something about
compulsion. Nobody has ever
filled the dishwasher exactly
the way I want it filled.

Never. Ever.

But this laundry issue can make
or break any relationship.

I know.

So I practiced folding.
Took to it like a new religion.

Learned how to fold napkins for wedding
receptions. Practiced folding enough tables
and chairs, until I could set up the
Roman Coliseum.

Mastered the art of origami,
My specialty—Puff the Magic Dragon.

Worked in a laundromat until I could
fold jeans like a Levi Strauss employee.

Folded decorative towels. Slipcovers.
Lawn furniture. Money.

Folded knives. Folded doors. Folded bikes.

Learned how to fold myself—to flatten
my bones like a mouse and slip
through cracks in the molding of
our drafty old house.

Even that wasn't good enough.

I spent hours learning to play expert poker
so I could scream "fold" every time things
were getting interesting.

I tried protein folding. Folding different
parts of my anatomy into each other
like a Russian nesting doll,

until my proteins and amino acids
resembled a room filled with
different-sized corrugated boxes.

After yet another relationship
fell apart over my failure
to fold lingerie "correctly"

I dreamed endlessly of paper airplanes
which I folded into so many intricate shapes
they could never be expected to fly

and somehow they did
soaring higher than I imagine
my laundry ever will.

It's Always Raining on the Pennsylvania Turnpike

Elias stopped counting state police cars after he passed Carlisle and got up to twenty. A record even for the turnpike. He rested his eyes for a moment, knowing he'd see many more once they hit the state line. Ohio always seemed to have an infinite number—more cops than cows and people combined.

"Pull over," Anne croaked.

The shoulder was nonexistent and creek-like in the downpour. It had been raining steadily since they left Princeton, but Elias yanked the wheel and skidded into the slick gravel. Anne barely got the window down in time before she puked. Ugh, nasty, he thought. He didn't know if he was catching the same cold, or if just witnessing this had made his stomach turn.

Anne was breathing deep and resting her head on the door. The rain was pouring in the window and splashing everywhere.

"Find a motel. Just please find a motel."

Easier said than done. The last two had "No Vacancy" signs lit. He'd never had a problem like this before. She hadn't been feeling bad when they'd passed Harrisburg. We'll keep looking, he'd told her. I mean how many motels are on the turnpike? Must be a quadrillion. So why wasn't he passing any?

Anne was motioning with her left hand. "C'mon, let's go."

Elias hated seeing her like this. She was like a big sick puppy, puking her guts out, and miserable. They were supposed to be joining her parents at the lake for the weekend so they could relax. They were both burned out from teaching. Now it looked like they'd be shunned for bringing some stomach bug on the vacation. He scootched and rolled up her window and then drove on. Hydroplaning a bit as he pulled out, handing her a bottle of water. She wasn't moving. Her head bobbing on the door.

☼

THE CARDINAL MOTEL LOOKED PRETTY seedy but after striking out at a dozen more, Elias was beginning to panic. What was going on? Some NASCAR event or something? They'd gotten a late start Friday after work, but he still couldn't remember encountering this many people on the road before. He hated the turnpike, which always seemed narrower than other highways because of the omnipresent guardrails, the hills and turns, and potholes large enough to go exploring in. People hauling speedboats and campers passed constantly, and then there were the giant SUVs, and the Winnebagos and Airstreams. An endless parade of Americans flush with a success he didn't share or feel.

The kid behind the counter wasn't particularly greasy or spooky, for which Elias breathed a sigh of relief. Elias asked for a room and was told there was no vacancy.

"But your sign," he pointed to the sign that plainly read VACANCY.

"Broken."

"C'mon buddy," Elias begged. "My wife's puking her guts out in the car. Everybody's booked up. I'm not feeling so good myself. We've gotta sleep."

The kid actually looked sympathetic. "Well, I shouldn't do this. But see, sometimes people don't stay all night. Let me just go knock on some doors."

"Oh no, don't do that." Elias was scared. He imagined some whack job firing a shotgun.

"Wait right here," the kid said, walking outside and down the row of doors. At least they were protected from the deluge by an overhang. He paused at one and somebody was snoring. He moved on to the next; you could hear a TV. Nope. He stopped at the third door, listened, then knocked. Nothing. He used his keys, poked his head in, and then waved to Elias.

Elias knew better than this but he scampered down to the room. Whoever had rented it had moved on. The place was steamy from a shower and the bathroom fan was still running.

"You want some new sheets?"

"Well, yeah," Elias said.

A quick look didn't reveal anything horrible. No bedbugs when he pulled the corner of the blankets up. The toilet looked workable. They'd survive.

"You go ahead and get situated and then meet me in the office in ten minutes."

Elias agreed and then fetched Anne. She was groaning in the car. "Took long enough."

"Count your blessings, babycakes. You have no idea."

He walked her to the room and when she aimed for the bed, he steered her for a chair.

"Sit tight. I have to go fill out the paperwork and then I'll be right back. Don't touch the beds until I get some new sheets."

"New sheets?"

"Don't ask."

"Oh god, no!"

"We'll be fine. Just give me a few minutes and I'll bring everything in, okay?"

"Did they use both beds?"

"Looks that way."

"Oooh, disgusting."

Elias picked up the new sheets, paid for the room, unloaded the car, and then made one bed. Anne hadn't moved. The occasional groan indicated she was alive.

He put the used sheets in the trash can and set them outside the door. Then he herded Anne into the bed closest to the phone, stripped her out of her coat, and steered her into the center of the mattress. It was looking like a long night, and the rain was coming down harder now. He switched on the news and clicked around until he found the Weather Channel. They were focusing on the West Coast. He clicked around some more and caught the recap on a Pittsburgh station. The Pirates game had been rained out, and now it was looking like the storm wasn't going to move out as fast as predicted. It was socked in for the weekend. Perfect.

Elias decided to take a shower. Maybe it would help him sleep. The water was hot and stayed hot for a change. He wanted to stand right there forever. The motel had a better hot water heater than they had back home. He was drying off and deciding whether or not to shave when Anne burst through the door. He backed up thinking she was going to puke in the toilet, but instead she thrust some paper in his face.

"We have to leave," she screamed. "Now."

Elias took the paper. It was a page out of a porno mag. It was pretty graphic stuff. But what did that have to do with anything?

"C'mon honey, whoever left this here is long gone."

Anne shook her head. She thrust another piece of paper at him. Some kind of how to camera biz about the proper lighting for taking sexy photos. He was still dripping wet. He put the paper down on the toilet tank and dried off.

"We have to go."

"C'mon Anne, I'm tired, you're sick, I had to beg to get us this place—"

"Now."

Anne took his hand and led him out to the unmade bed. She'd pulled the rumbled blankets back and scattered photos and papers all up and down its length. Some of the photos were Polaroids. Elias picked one up. He looked at the teenage girl in the photo, he looked at the blanket, he looked at the teenage girl in the photo, he looked at the wall fixture, he looked at the teenage girl in the photo, and he looked at the headboard. Everything matched. Anne held up the page from the porno mag. Bingo.

"You're right, we gotta go."

Somehow he got their money back. Elias had stormed into the office waving a Polaroid. The kid had gone silent and just forked over the cash. They sped away in the downpour but he was exhausted from the shower, from the confrontation, from the fact that they'd skipped dinner, and he had no idea where to go now.

☼

AFTER STRIKING OUT IN BREEZEWOOD, the city of motels, and Bedford too, they got lucky and found a motel in Shanksville. The Indian clerk said the only remaining room was a Smoking room. Would that do? Elias paid the money and ran for the car.

They were on the second floor all the way down at the far end. He helped Anne climb the stairs. And then he carted their bags back and forth. There was no overhang over the doors this time. He was drenched.

Anne immediately flipped the blankets back, then the mattress. No porn. Whew. She crawled into bed, her wet hair looking ratty. He slipped the chain in place, climbed into bed, and his last thought before closing his eyes was at least the incessant rain had washed Anne's puke off the car door.

He was asleep about five minutes when the smoke alarm gave a high-pitched peep. Anne groaned and opened her eyes. Elias refused to believe this. Did it really peep? Or were they just stressed out and losing their minds? Peep. There it was again.

"Do something!" Anne yelled, burying her head under a pillow.

But how? The ceiling was impossibly high. Elias grabbed a chair. He reached up. Still too high. He could throw something at it. Maybe dislodge it that way. By this point he didn't care whether he broke it or not.

Peep.

He hauled the table over and put the chair on top. Now he could reach the ceiling easily. He climbed up though the table legs were a little rocky. He eased himself up from a kneeling position into a crouch like a novice surfer.

Peep.

That one almost knocked him kiddywampus, but he regained his balance, and grabbed the smoke alarm. The cover wouldn't come off. He yanked. Nothing. He looked at it closely. He pulled, the entire fixture moved down out of the paint and drywall. No. That's not working.

Peep.

God, it was loud and annoying. He was pissed off. Elias yanked hard, then harder. The table and chair began to shift but settled. That's good. There were plastic coated cords holding the smoke alarm in place. Damn.

Elias studied the surface of the smoke alarm. He turned the top. It moved. He turned again. It spun some more. The stupid thing had a twist-off top. Mystery solved, he popped the top, unhooked the battery to another annoying peep, and climbed down without killing himself.

"My hero," Anne said, stretching out her arms to graze him.

Elias laughed. What a stupid vacation.

Peep.

Anne looked at him. Elias looked at the ceiling. Where was it coming from? They lay side by side. Anne was clutching his arm.

"Peep," she said.

"What are you doing?"

"Calling it."

Elias laughed some more.

Peep.

"See, it answered me."

"But where is it?"

Anne pointed to her head. "In here." She rolled over and put the pillows back over her head. "Peep," she said.

Elias stood up in the bed. He craned his ears trying to get a fix on the sound.

Peep.

He jumped out of the bed. He yanked the curtains. Nothing. He looked behind the dressers. Nothing. He peeked in the bathroom. Nope. Where the hell was it?

Peep.

It wasn't in their room. They were the last room on the second floor. Was it in the room next door? Or maybe in the ceiling of the room directly below them? How could those people sleep through it? And then Elias felt the tickle in his throat that could only mean—he raced to the bathroom and yanked up the toilet seat just in time.

☼

THEY SLEPT THROUGH CHECKOUT TIME, and sent the cleaning crew away. When they finally woke up around noon, Anne was feeling a little better. She paid the motel clerk for two days, paid him to load the bags as he had a pushcart and a yellow slicker which helped as the sky was still rock gray and stormy, and prepared to drive. Elias watched everything from the window of their room and then Anne came back with the umbrella she bought off the motel clerk and dragged him to the car. The rain may have washed her puke away but Elias could still smell it. He felt pretty green.

"Breakfast?" Anne asked way too perky and evil.

Elias groaned.

"I didn't think so." She stroked his shoulder. "Well, I seem to be good enough to drive at least. Maybe you'll feel better by the time we hit Pittsburgh?"

He couldn't imagine ever wanting food again.

She nosed the Corolla back through the tollbooth and away they went. Visibility was even worse today and Elias, while usually a nervous wreck when Anne was driving, decided he wasn't going to worry anymore. He'd only gone out with two women in his life who loved to drive. And he'd never met anybody yet who loved to drive on the turnpike. He fell into an exhausted semi-doze.

"What's that?" Anne asked.

"What?" Elias looked around.

"No listen."

He listened.

"Peep," she said.

"Don't," Elias said. He looked at the clock which was an hour fast. They couldn't figure out how to set it back and forth for daylight savings time. 3:30, which meant 2:30. He'd been asleep for two hours.

And then Elias jumped when Anne hit a pothole.

"I didn't even see that one," Anne shouted. "Oh my god."

The car didn't seem to correct itself. The steering wheel was shaking and Anne veered off onto the shoulder.

"It was full of water, Eli, I never saw it."

"S'okay, Anne, it's okay."

Of course it wasn't. The flat was on the driver's side. He had Anne pull over as far as she could, but he was still going to be easy pickings out there in the rain. She opened the umbrella and helped release the spare. They were on a hill. They didn't have anything to set behind the car to keep it from rolling, so he shoved his duffle bag behind the tire. He hoisted the jack and the spare, and Anne stood over him while he tried to remove the flat. They had the emergency blinkers flashing. At least it was daytime. Still the rooster tails in the wake of the speeding cars hit them broadside and they were both soaked to the skin in no time.

Elias was scared to death. The cars were so fast and so close and the tractor-trailers were in the near lane. One honked at them and Elias thought he was dead. What a complete asshole, he thought. Where were all of those police cars when I need them?

He put the spare on, put the nuts on loosely, and then lowered the jack. He managed to get everything tight, and they quickly stowed the flat and the gear and got out of there.

"Now what?" Anne said.

"Well, we can't go very far or very fast with that spare."

So the first gas station they saw, they pulled over and wound up springing for a new tire and tie-rod ends. There was a mini-mart so they dried off and changed clothes in the bathroom. A couple of items in Elias's duffle weren't soaked from sitting on the downhill slope.

The place had hot dogs and half smokes turning on one of those little spits, and it was all either of them could do to keep from puking again. They escaped with some bottled water and tried to call Anne's folks.

"Where are you, guys?" her father asked.

"You wouldn't believe me," Elias said. "We're somewhere near New Castle—"

"New Castle?"

"Long story. Look we're both pretty sick, and I'm not sure this is such a good idea."

"But we're almost there!" Anne grabbed the phone. "Daddy, this trip has really sucked, but we should be there by dinner—"

"Ugh."

"—time, not that we'll be eating any of it or anything." Anne looked at Elias, and said "Okay," then flipped the phone shut.

"He said drive safe."

Elias laughed. "I just want to be dry, and quiet, and still. Is that possible?"

"I'm with you. But realistically? I'm not sure that's feasible."

"So let's go home."

☼

ANNE FELT GOOD ENOUGH FOR some coffee, so when she saw a Starbucks sign she pulled off. The place was swarming with people. There were busloads of school kids. An entire cheerleading camp was in front of Anne in the Starbucks line. Elias still felt like death warmed over.

He watched the girls compare earrings, trade lipstick and iPods, laugh at jokes, and wondered what a bunch of middle school and high school girls were doing buying iced coffee drinks on day two of the great deluge. Anne was determined to get an ice mocha. It took almost an hour.

"We're not going to be there by dinner time, are we?"

"Not looking good Eli, not looking good. An hour to Akron. Maybe twenty more minutes to Beach City."

"An hour and a half?"

"At least." Anne took a big sip of her coffee. "If nothing else goes wrong." Anne took another sip and all at once she didn't look so good.

"Bad idea."

"Swell."

They held onto each other and tried to stay dry under the umbrella. The rain had not let up. Anne looked at the map. They'd be in New Castle in a couple minutes and off the cursed turnpike until they drove back. Maybe they could go home via I-80?

"You okay?" Elias asked.

"Better than you," she laughed. "Okay, here we go," she turned the key.

Nothing. The battery was dead. She pushed the light switch in. She'd left the lights on. Anne put her head on the steering wheel. Elias lowered his seat all the way back and closed his eyes.

☼

EVENTUALLY THERE WAS A LOUD knocking on the window. A large bearded man in a saturated blue jean jacket with water sluicing through the grooves in his cowboy hat pressed his face up to the glass.

"You folks need a jump? I saw your lights were on when we pulled up to eat."

Anne perked up. "Yes, yes please."

"All right," the man said, running a big fist through his beard. He ran over to his black Chevy Tahoe and pulled up beside them. Jumper cables materialized from behind the seat. He motioned for Anne to pop the Toyota's hood. All Elias could do was watch. He felt weaker now than he had back at the motel. Maybe he just needed some food? But the idea made him hug his stomach.

The cowboy shook his wrist a couple times to signal go, and Anne cranked the engine. Then the big man pulled the charger cables out and gave an energetic thumbs up and a big smile. She waved.

"Just let it run for a while," he shouted. "If I were you I'd get the battery checked out tomorrow. You might could use a new one."

"Thank you so much," Anne shouted over the sound of the engine and the wiper blades.

Somebody moved into the truck's driver's seat to wave hello.

Elias looked at the teenage girl in the truck. He looked at Anne. Anne was waving, saying, "That was so sweet." He looked at Anne, who turned quizzically to look at him. The cowboy climbed up into the cab and gave them a salute. The teenage girl moved back into the darkness of the cab.

"Peep," Anne said.

"Oh my god," Elias said. "It can't be."

"Let's go home."

"Shouldn't we call 911?"

Anne shook her head. "Honey, let's just go home."

"Fine."

"Route 80?"

"Absolutely."

Anne put the Corolla in gear and they raced for the toll-booth and the turnpike exit.

The rain showed no sign of letting up.

Empire Building

Put down the stick.
Put it down.
You could poke out an eye.

Because Daddy said.
Put it down.

Do you want a timeout?
No? Then put down the stick.

Because Daddy said so.

No rocks.
Take that out of your mouth.
Give it to me.
Give it to me. Right now.

Okay, you're through.
Time out.
Now just sit in that chair.

Stay there.
I told you to stay put.
I'm sorry you're crying.
But that's too bad.
Now sit.

Because you might hurt somebody.
That's why. You might hurt yourself.

Now put that down.
Stop it.
I told you to stop it. Right now.

Okay, give me the oil.
Give it to me.
Because I said so.
Because you're not old enough
to use that yet.

Daddy spank.
I mean it, Daddy spank.

Reston Zoo, 2004

Two-year-old Laurel asks to go "Uppy"
so I lift her onto my left shoulder.
I walk her around the Canada geese
who moments ago knocked a cup of seed
from her hand and scared her with
unbearably loud honking.

Aggressive birds easily twice her size.
It's hot. A July day that just won't quit.
No shade. Our petting zoo picnic rushed
so we can take the tractor ride. See the llamas.
The zebra. At least that's how I remember it.

Hot, sweaty, restless, and so when I spot
a set of steps near a penned area
I automatically climb them,
sun-burned Laurel in my arms.

The pen appears to be empty.
It takes a minute to spot them.
Alligators. Two of them.
Maybe four foot long? Five foot max.
It's broiling but they have
a little shade and a pond
to slither in and out of.

And they just sit there like logs.
"Alligators," I say. And I point
like men always do. "Look."
And Laurel imitates me. Pointing.
She says something in her too-loud
outdoor voice and the closest
alligator's eyes open. "Look," I say,
"he's awake." And he's moving.

Moving closer. And closer.
Faster than I've ever seen a large reptile
move. Until he's immediately below
where I hold Laurel. No bars. No roof.
Just a daddy holding his daughter in his
arms within plain view of a predator.

The alligator waits. Unhinges its jaws.
No, I must be imagining things.
I back down the stairs. The walls of their
grassy pen as high as my chest. I watch
the alligator as I circle the pen. He follows us.
Laurel is laughing. I climb another set
of stairs. Now the second alligator rushes
over. This one startles me with a loud hiss.

I finally understand—they think it's feeding time.
They think I'm going to drop my baby into the pen.
I squeeze Laurel tight to my chest. She's scared
of the hissing. Aware of my fear now.
She's started fussing. She wants Mommy.

We hustle back down the stairs to my wife and
my older daughter. But I am shaken.
I have brushed up against something dank and dark
and primeval. An alien mind where humans are meat.

I want my mommy, too. I want somebody to step in
to protect me in a dangerous world where I'm not
adequate enough to protect my daughter, or myself.

Walking to Dublin

I live with three women
of varying ages.

My doc says,
"You're surprised that there's drama?"

I am.

My best friend dubs my place
"The House of Estrogen."

I buy a boy dog
to even the score.

My daughters are always
campaigning for a puppy.

So this is perfect.

Now when all hell breaks loose
over who's using whose brush.

When Princess Not Me splatters
nail polish on the wood floor.

When Miss I Didn't Do It
spills her smoothie into the laptop.

I can walk the dog.

For hours and hours.

Just walk and walk
and walk some more

and keep right on walking.

From "Twyla Tales"

SEPTEMBER 18

TWYLA VS. THE BOTTLE IS ongoing. On Monday, Margaret went to work at about nine a.m. after spending a little couch time with Twyla. So, I played with some of Twyla's Fisher-Price toys that are all sounds and movement. Did a little Jolly Jumper time. Life was good for half an hour and then Twyla flipped out at about ten a.m. and screamed herself asleep. She napped for half an hour. Woke up screaming. I fed her about two and a half ounces of rice cereal. She eats it just fine if you let her grasp the spoon. (She's a total control freak.) Twyla sits on the kitchen floor in her bouncy chair and I mix the gruel in a blue bowl and then spoon some. She'll wave the spoon off and then she'll open her mouth, and as I go to plop it in there, she'll grab the spoon with her left hand and guide my hand. Hilarious. She gets about half of it down. And she seems fine. Not even very messy.

We do that for half an hour, positioned so Twyla can watch her favorite trees—the two poplars with leaves flipping around all silver showy in the breeze. She seems content. I hand her the little Pooh sippy cup she likes, the one that cost a couple bucks at the grocery store, nothing like the other high-priced top-of-the-line bottles and cups and alternative feeding devices we've spent all of our money on, and because she can grasp both handles she'll pop it into her mouth. Sadly, she can't hold it high enough to get any milk out of it yet, so I kind of nudge the cup up a little higher and let gravity do its thing. This works for about an ounce. Wow. I get these coy little shy smiles, where Twyla turns her head to her right and hides her face in the chair fabric and then opens her mouth a little bit more when I praise her and hold up the spoon again. This isn't even really hard work. She likes eating. This is fun.

And then of course she goes sky high out of nowhere and starts screaming. I know she expects Mom to walk in the room any second and just can't figure out where she's gone. So I rock her and sing "Yellow Submarine" another five hundred times, and bounce her on my knee, and try every teething ring and toy we own, and she tosses them to the floor with disdain, screaming all the while.

I should point out here that I mean screaming full blast right in your ear. Let me give you an example. Twyla received her four-month shots a few weeks ago (she's four and a half months old now), and everything was fine with the examination until our doc left and the Nazi Nurse came in with the little plastic tray. She set that on the counter and Twyla's eyes locked on it the moment she heard the tiny clank. She could see the four needles. She looked at the tray, looked up at the Nazi Nurse, and then turned her head wildly to the right and fixed on me before she began screaming. (Amazing. She actually remembered the needles from the second-month shots.) My wife demanded that I hold one leg too, so Twyla would hate us both equally for this pain. Which I did. And felt like Dr. Mengele.

While Margaret calmed Twyla and nursed her, I went to the front counter to pay the bill and schedule the next appointment. No biggie, save on this day there were screaming kids everywhere. Some holding shoulders or butts where they got shots, you name it. A frenzy of pain and blubbering. Kids screaming for mom and demanding to be read to, or to go home. Raw chaos. And above it all I could hear my daughter. We're talking loud and clear and in your ear. So I joked aloud to the two nurses that "It's really true. You can hear your own child above the screaming of other kids." The two young nurses looked at each other, shared laughing eyes, and then laughed so hard they almost wept. "No," one of them finally said, "we can hear *your* kid." The other started down the hall but added, "You can hear her in the other wing. Great lungs."

For those who remain clueless, Little Miss T. can scream as loudly as an adult and with indestructible vigor. She never gets hoarse. It's really incredible. If you're not doing anything on a weekday (she almost never melts down at night), I recommend you invite us over to your neck of the woods. Particularly between the hours of three and five. Really, she can clear an auditorium. No problem.

After another hour or so of Twyla's unabated screaming, at which point I'm positive Child Welfare people will knock on the door any moment and arrest me, she finally sacks out. It's amazing to watch. One second she's awake and the next in mid-scream her head nods over and she's gone. I watch for breathing 'cuz I always figure she just burst an artery or something. But no, my sweet little angel baby is asleep on the couch with me. Exhausted, I nap too. For two hours. That's unprecedented. I'm almost refreshed. And then she wakes screaming. Nothing works. We try cereal again and fail. We try the bottle. We try the sippy cup. Nada. So I put on the Beatles again. That calms her. I walk her outside under the trees. I walk her around the yard. But she won't let me stop. I have to keep moving. Can't even slow down to catch my breath.

I'm thinking darker thoughts. This is sick. I'm really getting pissed off and all kinds of nasty thoughts crawl through my brain. It's tough for them to move very fast or far with the constant sound barrage. Now I know what Phil Spector meant by a "Wall of Sound." And I also know why rock and roll was created—to drown out screaming babies.

At four p.m. I give up. I'm so fried, so tired, so sick of singing "Yellow Submarine," that I call my wife and say something cordial like "I quit." That's it. No please, no begging. Miss T. manages to scream during the entire wait, and my wife finds us on the screen porch a half hour later (she took a cab) where my knee is on automatic and my eyes glazed over so much that I just hand the kid off and disappear down into my basement lair where I crank up really loud rock and roll for three hours. It takes me that long to right my sinking ship. Just as long to have an appetite again.

Margaret spends the rest of the evening wondering what "I quit" meant. Today? Forever? Being principal day-care provider? Being a father?

SEPTEMBER 19

I HAVE FINALLY ADMITTED DEFEAT. As much as I want to be a house poppa and take care of Twyla every single moment of every single day while my wife's bringing home the bacon, the truth is I can't handle it. I'm stressed out, still in a lot of pain from my back, super glad I'm not teaching right now, and beaten down. So after a lot of discussion, it so happens that Fern Lawrence, who runs a nanny-share out of Margaux and Roger's first floor almost across the street from our old house and looks like she plays basketball for the Mystics, has an opening. She watches four kids. Lizzie, Connor, Sara, and Zack. But Maria is taking Julia home because she's quitting and becoming a stay-at-home mom. We feel like we're giving our kid away to gypsies. I haven't felt this defeated in a long time. I've been upset and angry and flailing out in every direction, and leaving Twyla with somebody else seems like a huge personal failure. I feel like I'm not worthy of being a father.

Anyway, today was great, 'cuz I'd had a rough night watching my stupid football team implode like choking dogs on national television. One of the worst losses to the hated Cowboys I've seen in my life. The realization that they're going 7-9 or 6-10 sinking in. But hey, maybe I should call Dan Snyder, and take Twyla down to Redskins Park tomorrow. A couple hours of the Twyla treatment and they'll play better. I know they will.

Last Call in
Mohican Hills

He is naked when he rides the deer. Naked save for palm prints of blood across both cheeks. His hands are bloody, too; yet remain locked around the deer's neck and fur, as they crash through the thick forest. His breath and the animal's breath are one. There are fourteen points on the antlers, antlers that are draped with fringe from their molting, antlers that could kill a man, or another deer, or anything else that got in their way. He doesn't know where they are going until they enter clearings in the trees and silver shards of moonlight slice through to the reddish pine needles spread like padding on the forest floor. He doesn't know where they're going for most of the ride. This ride that smells of blood and sweat and rut and the moist drizzle that drowns out all other noise. The raindrops falling with a slick whistle through the pines and cypress trees until the deer skids on slippery rocks, jumps a creek, and emerges on a hilltop above a valley filled with lights.

☼

"ARE YOU SAD BECAUSE YOUR daddy died?"

That's Olivia, my daughter. She's four. Her face twisted up as serious as she can manage.

"Don't bother your papa, honey." Elena, my wife, is standing in the kitchen doorway. Or what's left of it. Our house is being renovated and the kitchen is the last part of the new addition. The contractor has finally broken through the wall that separates the new from the older 1920 sections of the house. Now a wall needs to come down, and a counter island needs to be built, and the kitchen sink and cabinets need to find a new position against a sunny wall at the outer edge of the addition. It'll be great when it's all fixed up, but for now we don't have a kitchen. In fact, we were living with my mother until my father died. All of our clothes for the funeral were back here at the house so we've come home to change again into our regular clothes.

"That's okay, Olivia," I say. "Daddy is sad. I miss my daddy."

"My daddy, my daddy." She hands me three dandelions. She can barely contain her excitement.

"They're beautiful." I kiss her cheek and she runs off to play with her dolls.

"You okay?" my wife asks. She's never looked as beautiful to me as she does at that moment. She doesn't steal a lot of time from the daily routine to make herself look nice, and today she took some special care. Her velvety blonde hair sparkles against an olive satin suit, which accents her green eyes. A lemon-yellow silk top with topaz pleated skirt and malachite earrings on long loopy golden chains complete her look.

"Yeah. For now." I hang my head. My father was a man of action and his loss is going to leave a significant gap in my life. Even if that means, in this case, the loss of somebody to rail against.

"You know what?" She's circling her arms around my neck. I don't allow her to cuddle me like this very often. It seems too girly somehow to me, a man with two younger brothers and no sisters, but right now I relax and her arms remind me of my mother's arms when she would hug me as a child. Of course I'll never tell my wife this. Yet that's exactly what this feels like. And my wife's scent and rare makeup, while not the same smells, are reminiscent of those lost moments.

"What?"

"I think you need to have some time alone. Why don't you take a week off and relax?"

I ponder her offer a moment. "And go where?"

She kisses the side of my head. "Anywhere I suppose. Anywhere you wish."

"I think right now I'll go down to the island." And by that I mean Sycamore Island in the Potomac River, the island visible through the bay windows at the bottom of our hill. Everybody's gathering back at my mother's but I'm stalling. I'm not ready to face anybody. The funeral has taken more out of me than I'll admit. And so I stand and unravel her arms.

☼

I'D FORGOTTEN HOW MUCH FUN a bike ride down the hills could be. There's a wide spot in the road for people to park their cars but I chain the bike to a rack. Then I walk down the winding concrete ramp that my father and his buddies built by hand and make my way to the island. Bert the caretaker is on the dock when I ring the bell and he sends a boat on a rope over for me. I stand and wait and then I row across.

"Hi Bert."

"I'm sorry about your father," Bert says. "He was a good man." And that's all the more he'll say. He doesn't talk much, no more than my father did. Both men remnants of the strong silent type John Wayne generation. I walk around the small teardrop-shaped mat of an island, a bump in the currents of the Potomac covered with detritus from the early spring rains, and watch as Bert disappears back into the clubhouse, the large wooden house that dominates the place. There's a boathouse for canoes, and the main house even has Ping-Pong tables, though mostly this is just a well-maintained retreat for people to hide away. Which would be exactly what I'm doing.

On the island I learned to pilot a canoe. This is where my father taught me the fine art of rowing. This is where we had barbecue chicken with the other Sycamore Island families and played badminton, and croquet, and pool, and Ping-Pong late into summer evenings. This is where I first caught a fish. But I learned how to swim down the road at Glen Echo, back when there was an amusement park and the Crystal Pool.

My father came here every morning he was in town no matter the weather and then rowed across the river where he would stow his canoe, walk up a by now well-defined pathway, and continue on to his job at the CIA.

He wasn't the only one who made the trek. There was a hardcore crew of CIA guys who did. They'd all been at the funeral and had gone on and on about how my father managed to make it across even when there was ice.

I'd had a difficult time as a child grappling with the idea of my father being a spy. Vietnam had been the nail in the coffin between us. Many things were said that could never be unsaid. We drifted apart. I resisted the war in North Bay, Ontario. Sat it out while some of my high school buddies got shot up and shipped home in flag-draped boxes. It makes no more sense to me now than it did then. Most of us, the offspring of the white middle class, didn't fight. And when amnesty was offered, I overcame my initial paranoia about returning to America and settled in Madison, Wisconsin, where I hobnobbed with progressives, finished my degree in sociology, and married Elena, a half-Canadian, half-American from Ottawa who thought I was worth salvaging. I've never had much time for women like that—women who view men as remodeling projects—and yet now that we're redoing our house, I kind of see how she feels about such things. In fact I shudder to think what she must have thought of me when we met, before I quit my quest for rock and roll immortality and opened a small bookshop.

You wouldn't expect a man as large as my father to have a weak part anywhere in his body but his heart just wasn't able to keep up with the 24/7 lifestyle of the rest of him. It had campaigned for a rest a few years previous, giving him a mild attack during the Clinton impeachment hearings, a precursor to the major event that would follow later. Shortly after my father's first attack, we moved back to the Washington area. I did it for my mother. That's what I told myself. Truth of the matter was that I'd turned fifty. And then I became a failure as the Internet and the chain super stores wiped out most independent bookshops. I spent a lot of time being miserable when I realized I'd lived more life than I had left to look forward to. I know that sounds selfish, what with Olivia and all, but there you go. Something had to change. I know that, but I had no idea what to do next.

☀

THE PATH DOWN TO THE valley is steep, and the footing treacherous. He hangs on as the deer stumbles and nearly loses its balance, yet regains its footing and plunges more than runs down the incline. He rides the deer through the bracken and ferns; he kicks with his legs like an Indian scout, his breath blending ghostlike with the snorted breath of the deer. The lights are coming closer. But first there is a rocky creek, white water rushing loud enough to cover the deer's intakes of breath. With no hesitation, the deer surges into the icy pulse.

☀

OLIVIA WANTS THE BIG CHICKEN—an ostrich to anybody else—on the carousel. I stand alongside, as she's only four and still too young to ride unattended. She tries to push me away with her little hands. "No Daddy." Precursor of things to come. She wants me to get on one of the horses. Or the bunny. But I'm spotting in case she falls. The old antique carousel begins rolling and gets up to a fast enough speed to make me queasy about the eggs and sausage I had for breakfast. I can feel the dark Peruvian ground burning a quarter-sized hole in my stomach, while I try to regain my sea legs and hang tight. As the pipe organ oompah music deafens me, and my daughter waves to Mommy on every cycle, I notice a hornet's nest in the turret core. They've set up housekeeping in the central armature. When we slow down and finally come to a stop, I tell the attendant about the hornets. He looks up and sees one going in and promises me he'll take care of it when they close down for the day.

☼

I HELP OLIVIA DOWN AND she runs to Mommy. Now it's Elena's turn to ride. I get to watch and wave and try to calm my nerves. My wife's deadly allergic to bee stings. She carries a hypo full of anti-venom just in case. I've never had to use it, though I've promised her I'll shoot it into her thigh and push the plunger if the need arises. I hate needles and can't imagine how I'll cope in pure panic mode. As she climbs on, I point out the nest and she nods. Oddly she's not concerned about bees the way I am. I'm starting to see death every-where.

The day after the funeral we'd gathered on the banks of Sycamore Island. My mother pitched a scoop of my father's ashes up into the air above the brownish river, and a wind gust caught my father's remains, and blew them right back in our faces. Instantly the kids were crying, the wives were wiping their faces, and my brothers' and my dark suits were coated.

After that disaster, Will and Roger paddled a canoe out into the middle of the river to complete the process.

"I want you to go with them," my mother had said.

"No," I said. The canoe was really built for two.

"You must."

But I held Olivia and patted her face with a diaper wipe. "No, Mom, I'm not going to."

She turned away and found solace with Melissa and Elaine, my sisters-in-law. Their infinite brood of kids in various stages of meltdown and decorum scattered all around their legs.

☼

HE IS SLIPPING FROM THE buck's slick fur, sides heaving with exertion, breath visible as a smoky blast. The rain falling harder now. As they crash down the hillside through the thick underbrush, ever closer to the lights, the deer relentless, his arms losing their *grip, his heels digging in, kicking the deer, urging the animal to run faster, to fly. When the deer hits the edge of the woods, it stops, waits, sniffs the air.*

☼

WHEN I CLOSED UP MY shop I salvaged most of the books about cottages and handmade houses. I became enamored with them in Canada—so many draft evaders ended up living in thrown-together shacks, hippie buses permanently anchored in concrete, or variations thereof. My sparse monkish shack had been no exception, just two rooms—a kitchen with a wood stove, another room with a table and chair, and a half-loft wide enough for a hammock. I probably shouldn't find such confined spaces appealing, growing up here with the Potomac River vista in plain view, yet somehow I still do.

Elena has been hungry to return to Canada. She doesn't care if she ever sees another American flag as long as she lives. After 9/11, Elena started campaigning to move. Olivia could get a great education, they'd have health care, and my wife could quit her administrative job at Georgetown University. Her parents have a farm just across the St. Lawrence from Montreal in Saint-Rémi. She'd grown up in Ottawa, but her parents had wanted a farm and it was easier to find via her Quebecois mother's family than her American just-struggling-to-put-down roots-in-Ontario father. Maybe they'd let us build on their sizable tract? Could a straw bale home withstand a Canadian winter?

"We're going to the store," Elena shouts in the front door. "You want anything?"

"Root beer!" I've been craving root beer floats. "And we need string cheese for Olivia."

"Got it. Be back in an hour."

☼

I HAVE NEVER BEEN COMFORTABLE with my mother. I don't know why. She bore me, she raised me, she read to me, and yet it seems like some other life for both of us. So when she walks in, I'm on edge. Wondering what will happen next.

"You're going to take my grandchild away from me, aren't you?"

"C'mon Mom, it's not like that at all."

"It's not?"

"No. Elena's homesick and maybe it's time for us to get out of your hair."

She sits down like I've punched her. "You've never been half the man your father was, Daniel. Not even half."

I don't know where this came from. There's no compromise with my archconservative mother. I just turn my back on her and walk out onto the patio. And my thoughts are drawn back to my first hunting trip with my dad. How I'd had a six-point buck right in my sights and missed. I couldn't hit the broadside of a barn, just like my father said. When we got back to camp my father and my brothers ribbed me, and then my father got out a pair of scissors and cut my shirttail off. I was so humiliated I never went hunting with any of them ever again.

☼

ELENA POKES HER HEAD INTO the kitchen where I'm fixing hot dogs and French fries. "Olivia has something to tell you." My daughter's smiling her biggest smile, like she gets when she sees the ocean. Any body of water really.

"What is it? What does my best girl have to tell me?" I kneel down and catch her in my arms. She's all out of breath and the words tumble all over each other.

"I miss my grandfather."

These unexpected words make a deep impact in my chest, like the wallop of a medicine ball. "What?" I say. I turn to Elena who leans against the doorframe.

"I miss him," Olivia says in her whiniest voice.

Portrait of Richard Peabody by Jody Mussoff, a frequent *Gargoyle* and
Paycock cover artist, 1995.

Above: left to right, John Elsberg, Kevin Urick, Peabody, and Eric Baizer, Garfield Street radio show, Washington, D.C., 1978. *Photo by Phil Cline.* Below: Peabody (cent flanked by Clint McCown and Gail Galloway Adams to the left and Janice Eidus to right, with three unknown students, Wildacres Writers Workshop, Little Switzerl North Carolina, July 2000. *Photographer unknown.*

Peabody at Artomatic, Crystal City, Virginia, June 2012. *Photo by Laurel Peabody.*

Peabody at F. Scott Fitzgerald Literary Conference, Montgomery College, Rockville, Maryland. Above: With John Moser, October 2008. Below: October 2010. *Photos by De Evangelista.*

body, Marilyn Monroe (cutout), and Lucinda Ebersole at Ann Burrola
otography, Arlington, Virginia, 1995. *Photo by Ann Burrola.*

Peabody, *Grace and Gravity* launch sponsored by the D.C. Chapter of the Women's National Book Association at the Sewall-Belmont House, Washington, D.C., October 28, 2004. *Photographer unknown.*

Peabody and Lucinda Ebersole, *Gargoyle* #39/40 Launch, Atticus Books & Music, Washington, D.C., April 4, 1997. *Photographer unknown.*

Peabody and Lucinda Ebersole, Scott and Zelda Fitzgerald Anniversary Party, Atticus Books & Music, Washington, D.C., April 3, 1996. *Photo by Ann Burrola.*

"I do, too, honey."

"Can we go to the store?"

"What store?"

"The grandfather store."

Elena has put one hand in front of her mouth. Her eyes are shiny. I'm crying. Hugging my little girl.

"The grandfather store? What's that, honey?"

"If we go there, we can buy a new grandfather."

My wife has moved closer and I can feel her hand on the top of my head.

"That's a great idea, honey," my wife says. "But your daddy just made dinner. Let's have some hot dogs, okay?"

She nods, all smiles, and I let her go.

"Ketchupy. Ketchupy. Ketchupy," she sings as she dances to her chair.

"Do you want a bun, too?"

"Yes, Mama."

☀

AFTER OLIVIA IS DOWN FOR the night, I ask my wife, "Where on earth did that come from?"

She's sipping coffee in the doorway. "Well, it seems obvious. She thinks you can buy anything at the store. So why not? Why not buy a brand-new grandfather at the grandfather store?"

"Maybe," I said.

Olivia sits beside me on the couch. She's so young and I'm so old. This first-time father stuff is exacerbating enough and as fulfilling as being a stay-at-home dad has been, I need to find a job.

"So?" she asks, catching my eyes in hers.

"What?"

"Where you going to go?" She locks her arms around my neck and pulls me down to her for a kiss.

"I dunno."

"No strings, hon. You need a break."

Olivia and Elena are my life. Where could I go? I didn't really know anybody anymore. Life outside of my family was pretty lonely. And I have zero desire to visit Roger in Norfolk, or Will in San Diego. They couldn't wait to fly out of D.C.

My wife shakes her head and smiles, letting me go. "Look, my offer stands, ehh. You have a rain check for whenever you want." Then she stands and slaps my knee. "I'm going up to bed." She raises an eyebrow. "You coming?"

☼

HE IS NAKED WHEN HE rides the deer through the woods at night, naked when he fords the icy stream, naked when he plummets down the hillside, crashing through the trees and the rain, naked when the deer leaps up into the air like a fantastic furry bird, and he is naked as the deer's leap hits its apex and begins a smooth descent.

☼

I FLIP SOME MORE PAGES in my cottage book and crave a root beer float. I pop open an IRC Root Beer, gather the spoon and bowl and my mother's antifreeze-filled ice cream scoop, and then open the freezer in search of ice cream. I pull the box of Neapolitan out and place it on the counter. My mother always buys Neapolitan. My brothers never shared. So when Will took chocolate, and Roger took strawberry, vanilla fell to me. Only now, when I open the lid, there's just strawberry and chocolate—no vanilla at all.

I can't stand the frustration. So, I'm off to 7-Eleven. There's one just down the road. I pop out into the March night. The spring peepers are in full chorus. Wind is gusting. I imagine I can see white caps on the river. I try to be as quiet as possible, backing the Mazda down the driveway before turning on the headlights, and racing to the bottom of the hill. I round the corner by the Sycamore Store, my headlights bounce off the uber-modern glass house by the community pool, and I step on the gas, as I have the twisty road to myself.

I'm catching glimpses of the river, which flows gray and otherworldly down the hill to my left. By the time the deer's hooves enter the frame carved into the dark night by the windshield, it is already too late to brake, to swerve, to duck. So many things seem to happen in slow motion in movies that in real life happen so quickly and are over before you can even react. The hooves splintered the windshield and the air bag fired and when I came to, I was on the side of the road with a man hovering over me.

"You're alive, but you sure as hell look like you should be dead," he said.

I groaned and passed out once more.

☼

THE NURSES ARE COLORFUL AND sassy and making jokes about what a silver fox I am. I still have all my hair but both of my brothers are bald. With a shattered collarbone it hurts to laugh. I both look and feel like hell.

Elena is there and she's crying. "I said you should take a week off. I didn't mean you should do it in the hospital."

I try to calm her. I tell her it's time to split. Time to move back to Canada. She's so happy she doesn't know what to say. She's wiping tears with her knuckles. She's clutching my leg through the sheets.

Olivia walks in with my mother. My little girl is scared. Hangs shyly in the doorway.

"Hi baby girl," I say.

She springs into motion then. Runs to my side and tries to hug me, which of course hurts like hell. Elena pulls her back. And now everybody's crying.

"I'm sorry, son."

I stare at my mother.

"I'm sorry."

"Forget about it, Mom. You can visit as often as you want."

☼

THERE'S NOBODY ELSE ON THE river at dawn when I paddle the Kevlar canoe across. Canada geese in formation winging their way back home. I bungle the landing, get one shoe wet. The cold like a lightning bolt through my skin. I pull the canoe up onto the rocky beachhead and then follow the winding path into the trees. Wind my way up above the river. I can look back and barely make out our house on the far bank through the early buds and greening. Come summer the view will be blocked by tree leaves and the kudzu, which drapes the underbrush with dormant brown-gray vines that look now like escapees from some sci-fi film's special effects department. I walk until I get to the road and then I cross the bridge over the George Washington Parkway until I come to the CIA gate. The sign makes me laugh: The George Bush Center for Intelligence. A guard steps out of the booth and signals for me to stop. I do.

"You're not half the man your father was," he says.

And I wake.

☀

OLIVIA HAS CLIMBED INTO BED. She's sprawled side-ways across the space between us. Elena's faintly snoring. I manage to get out of bed without disturbing my gals and walk downstairs and out the French doors onto the patio. I shiver and watch the moonlit river move through the trees. Imagine playing my guitar in small Canadian coffee shops. Why not?

"Rest in peace, old man," I say. And then I look at my river for one last time, before going back inside to start breakfast.

Nuages

(after Django Reinhardt)

1

She's lost amidst her sleeping cubs
like otters in a nature film.

One girl horizontal across the bed
the other vertical with her hair
fanned along my wife's stomach.

How does she sleep?

Buttery moonlight spotlights skin.
Softens everything.

I watch from the doorway.

Earlier they were like tiny animals—
fighting sleep. Melting down.

"Read me another story."

So how did I become a boring old fart
who writes poems like this one?

And yet there's power
in this jumble of bodies,

in this simultaneous
breathing,

and I don't wish
to disturb

this magic wife,
this family
that doesn't appear

to need me at all.

2

My wife has flown to Brazil
so I'm in bed
curved around my daughters.

Impossible to sleep.
I listen for every breath.

One holds my hand
in dreamy dreams and the other
flops like a salmon and kicks
a leg over mine.

Our birds never seem to sleep either,
songs drifting upstairs
from trees below.

The world is coming to an end
they sing.

The sky is falling.

I lie awake in bed
clinging to my daughters,
my life raft,

painting them a bright future,

painting them any future
I can manage.

The banana moon
through the skylight.

Songs drifting
drifting

bossa nova

blue

tide.

My Cheating Heart

My wife wants an apology.
Apparently I cheated on her in a dream.
I try to laugh it off. Sleepy. Hugging my pillow.
She won't have any of that. She says, "I mean it.
Apologize. Right now." I keep laughing.

I compare notes with friends throughout the day.
Worried that my wife is cracking up. She's been under a
lot of stress lately. I mean dreams aren't real…are they?
My buddies laugh, too. Partly at the situation and partly
at my sorry ass. The gals all say the same thing—"Apologize."
"But I didn't do anything wrong!" I protest. They're not
buying it either. Dreams seem to be the new turf where
the gender wars are being fought.

I eat lunch and sulk. It's ridiculous. My wife is acting crazy.
One woman asks me whom I was sleeping with? "What?"
    "In your dream."
"It wasn't my dream, it was her dream." "So whom were you
    sleeping with?"
"I don't know. Some blonde." "Mister, you have got to
    apologize."
"No way," I said. "Never." She just shook her head. "Have it
    your way."

My wife won't talk to me when she gets home. I've been
    banished to the basement.
All because I had imaginary sex with a figment of her
    imagination. She won't tell me
if it's anybody she knows. Could be an actress or a
    Supermodel. I have no idea.
Yet I stand accused. Guilty with no chance of parole.

I finally give up. The basement's cold. I can't get over how
    stupid
all of this is. And when I apologize, "for having imaginary
    sex in your dream
last night," my wife starts crying. I move to hold her and she
    smacks my arm,
pushes me away. "You're just making fun of me," she says.
    "You don't really mean it."

And so I try to sleep beside my wife as she sobs. My brain
    playing a slide show of
every blonde I have ever seen in my entire life. Picturing
    one fantasy sequence
after another, so that at least my punishment fits my
    imaginary crime.

Dresden for Cats

ncle March was rarely mentioned in family conversation. He was my mother's composer brother. He'd taught piano and pipe organ at the Peabody Conservatory in Baltimore, conducted orchestras, made recordings back in the days of 78s, and most impressively composed music. He knew all of the great living composers and seemed to have known most of the dead ones as well. Each of his eccentric activities (and there were many) took on a mythic quality and this attracted me from an early age. No two anecdotes seemed to match. No two stories. He was the most talented man alive and a pure genius, or else a fool who ought to be put away, depending on which member of the family you were talking to. Each exploit was more outrageous than the last. He'd smoked dope with John Cage, he'd worked with Paul Bowles and Orson Welles on the Mercury Theater radio programs, he'd created a cubist New Orleans Funeral March for Fritz Lang, and conducted sans pants for a Picasso happening in the swinging '60s. Not that he was any crazier than the black sheep in anybody else's family.

I'd heard rumors about him as I grew older, but nobody had seen him in more than a decade when I descended on his Eastern Shore farm. Some thought the family was better off for not knowing what he was up to. Maybe he'd died? My life was going nowhere and I had spare time on my hands. My girlfriend had just thrown me out. And to top it all off I'd been fired from my job—teaching community college English 101. Not that it was a huge loss. Still, I was turning thirty and needed some direction.

You couldn't really call Uncle March's farm a proper farm. I'm sure it had been at one time, although now the ramshackle collection of buildings in various stages of decay—some closer to losing their battle with gravity than others—looked too dangerous for anything but a bulldozer. So the minute I stepped from my rented Chevy Cavalier and heard strange music blaring across the windswept yard, my heart quickened. Uncle March was very much alive. And so I followed the sounds away from the white clapboard house that was asymmetrical with very few straight lines, obviously sinking into the ground, and entered a maroon-colored barn whose roof seemed in danger of imminent collapse.

Uncle March stood at the top of a precarious ladder holding a large gray cat. The cat was as wiry as a WWF wrestler preparing for a match. Just the right combo of spleen and flexibility. Uncle March pushed the cat down a wooden ramp, which ran at a very steep angle from the hayloft, down into a boarded-off section of the barn.

"Well, don't just stand there. Hand me that pole," he shouted, pointing out a giant rubber squeegee atop a ten-foot pole that rested on a hay bale.

I handed it up to him and stepped back. The music was deafening.

"Did they send you to check on me?"

"What?"

"Are you a spy?"

"No."

"Good."

Uncle March prodded the gray cat with the squeegee and it spit and snarled yet slowly moved down the ramp. I couldn't figure out where the ramp was leading. Plexiglas windows were spaced along the wall every few feet, and stepping up to inspect them I caught my first glimpse of Uncle March's ultimate creation—a city for cats.

And there was no way of knowing how many cats he had on that farm. There were hundreds. Every conceivable color and style. There were shorthairs, longhairs, silver tabby, Persian, Burmese, Siamese, calico, tortoise shell, you name it. A moving, breathing, patchwork quilt of cats who were playing, climbing, burrowing, breeding, birthing, sleeping, or simply sitting atop a labyrinthine assembly of thousands of packing crates, painted to look like a magical city.

"Do you keep them all in there?" I asked.

"All what?"

"Cats of course."

"No, indeed," Uncle March said, and walked back out into the sunlight. I followed.

"So what is that structure—?"

"You can see for yourself," he said, stopping so that I ran into his back, dislodging my glasses. "A playground." Then he was moving again. "Now help me find Cedric. It's time for his lesson."

"Lesson?"

I thought you couldn't train cats. I couldn't figure out what was going on. A city for cats was eccentric though I've heard of cat motels. I've just never heard of anyone constructing an entire cat city. Was that eccentric or plain crazy?

Cedric turned out to be a large Manx that Uncle March found in the boathouse, which was perched on the banks of the tidal pond out back of the farmhouse. Uncle March soon had Cedric sprawled over one shoulder. I followed into the farmhouse, which was itself a remarkable collection of boxes not unlike the cat city. Uncle March had made addition after addition until the entire white structure resembled a pile of blocks dropped by a careless child.

The narrow porch was knee-deep in pipe organ pipes. Inside it was the same story. A path had been cleared for walking, though it wasn't until we got to the living room that the pipes receded. Here they lined the front wall of the house, with furniture and framed prints tucked in around them.

I followed Uncle March into the basement—where there were more pipes and several disassembled pipe organs, and in one corner a huge hulking wall of an organ whose pipes ran up through the ceiling and apparently straight out the roof above like something out of Dr. Seuss.

Uncle March plopped Cedric down on a vast keyboard and commanded him to play. This was no ordinary keyboard. The keys themselves were wide enough for the Manx to stand on, and spaced accordingly, so that the cat had only to walk across the keys to play individual notes. Chording would be something else again. Though Uncle March had thought of that too, and had rigged a series of wooden stays that the cat could manipulate, not without struggle, to play a sequence of notes. It was preposterous, yet Cedric formed a slow but nevertheless pleasant musical interlude.

I couldn't take everything in. Uncle March was hovering over a workbench littered with computers and keyboards, more gadgets than a mad scientist's lab has ever exhibited. Speakers, individual woofers and tweeters, sequencers. Electronic equipment that I couldn't name and would never begin to guess a function for was scattered from one end of the room to the other. The basement was awash in gadgetry and doohickeys.

"How many pipes are in a pipe organ?" I asked.

"Three thousand or more," Uncle March said, looking at me like I was a particularly exotic cat.

And then right in the middle of Cedric's oddly soothing music, the lights dimmed and a loud ruckus began upstairs.

"Thurber was right," Uncle March said, charging past me and up the winding stairs.

I ran after him and almost into him again when he stopped to confront a tiny angular gray-haired woman who stood at the center of the kitchen. I recognized her from the family photos as Vanessa, his wife.

"What's got into you, woman?"

"I hate Bach. I hate his brothers. I hate you for playing his music. And I hate you for—"

"Bach was a genius. He was the only composer who died fat and happy. He heard God's voice and played it back."

"Bull feathers."

"Anyway, that wasn't Bach, it was Cedric."

"Who are you?" Vanessa asked, noticing me, her entire demeanor altering.

"I'm—"

"He's Susan's son, come down from the city to check up on us."

"Do you eat fish?"

"Yes, I'm Susan's son." I was flabbergasted. "How did you—"

"Alec, isn't it?"

"Yes," I said to Uncle March.

"It's the eyes. You've got your mother's eyes."

"And I love fish," I said turning to Aunt Vanessa.

"I'll get dinner ready. Bring in your things," Aunt Vanessa swept the room with her hands. "Show him to his room, Dad." And then she opened a humongous freezer tucked into one end of the room, and seemed to leap rather than lean into it, the frosty air rising all around her frail form.

"Are you married?" Uncle March was addressing me.

"No, I haven't—"

"Count your blessings." He took my arm and guided me back out of the house, pausing in the mudroom to reset the circuit breakers his wife had pulled. "Well, c'mon, let's get your things."

"Okay."

Uncle March carried the heaviest bag, despite my insistence otherwise. The man had to be eighty-five. I lumbered up the twisting stairs to the second floor behind him. He moved considerably faster though carrying twice my load. I was out of breath by the time I caught up with him at the end of the hall in a room with two bunk beds that had been disassembled and set up like individual cots.

"You can stay here as long as you like."

"Well, thank you."

"Bathroom's in there," he opened a door, flipped on a light. "The facilities are all brand new. Just put it in this past spring. Shower's got the best hot water in the house.

"Clean yourself up if you want," he rummaged in a hall closet. And then threw me some towels. "Sheets and blankets are in there as well. Use what you need. But shake a leg, when Mother gets to cooking she moves like the wind."

"I don't want to be any trouble—"

"Don't be daft. Our family is nothing but trouble."

"What I meant to say—"

"She's making soft shells and rockfish with rice and sliced tomatoes. Fresh from her garden. So go on, clean up. Don't dally or the cats will get your share. She doesn't entertain often and she gets bored. She loves to cook."

"Great," I said, though my uncle was already halfway back down the corridor. He turned, with one finger raised toward the ceiling.

"Beer or bourbon?"

"Beer," I said.

He smiled and disappeared down the stairs.

☼

ONE THING BECAME RAPIDLY CLEAR—Uncle March might rule the basement and the grounds, but Aunt Vanessa ruled the kitchen and the rest of the house. Cats weren't allowed anywhere save the basement or the yard.

"Now Alec, you know this is my house," she began. "My family's house for generations—"

Uncle March cleared his throat and rolled his eyes. Aunt Vanessa gave him a look and then continued. The soft shells were fantastic.

"—dating back to the founding fathers. My father came over on the Dove, one of the pair of ships that landed in St. Mary's in 1634. You know the one?" She wasn't eating, only holding court.

"I'm afraid I don't know, Aunt Vanessa, forgive me."

"What do they teach the young people, Dad? Nothing at all about their heritage?"

"I haven't set foot on a campus in a decade, 'Nessa. I have no idea."

"Well, my family's buried in the graveyard over yonder." She pointed with a fork out the door of the mudroom. "Right under those oak trees. I'll walk you over after lunch."

"What's for dessert?" Uncle March asked.

Aunt Vanessa looked annoyed and then turned in my direction again. "Do you like peach cobbler?"

☼

THE TREES WEREN'T AS BIG as the Wye Oak, although they were impressive. Four of them in a cluster shaded a graveyard that might well date back five hundred years. Most of the older stones were broken, names illegible. Some were of more recent vintage.

"Now Alec," she pointed with her walking stick, "this is my great-great-grandfather's grave. One Thomas Darnall. Lord Baltimore bequeathed him all of the land you see, and an additional nine hundred acres that's been sold off in blocks through the years by relatives of mine. Why, his land used to run from the Little Choptank just here, over to Fishing Creek."

I nodded appreciatively, and marveled at this tiny woman. An octogenarian for certain. Yet more full of life than a lot of my contemporaries. The old gal had spunk.

We walked around the grounds a bit. She took me from the graveyard to the tidal pond that dominated the land between the house and the Little Choptank River. Aunt Vanessa pointed out flowers and walked me through her garden. She grew everything—okra, corn, butter beans, potatoes, tomatoes, lettuce, peppers, squash, and pole beans. How on earth did she work it?

"Now I don't do all this by myself. We have some help." She laughed. "What am I saying, surely you didn't think for a moment that I could handle something this grand all by myself?"

"I wondered," I said.

"The herb garden is right beside the house, do you see it? There by the lavender?"

"You've got everything, Aunt Vanessa."

The lightness seemed to fade away when I said that.

"I reckon so," she said, yet it was obvious she didn't mean it. "Just remember this is my place. My place. Not his." And then she started back to the house, the walking stick propelling her swiftly across the rough grass.

☼

OVER THE NEXT FEW DAYS I spent my time talking to Uncle March about music, walking the grounds while he worked his cats, eating Aunt Vanessa's incredible cooking, and listening to their stories.

"The reason your mother never comes to visit anymore is that father of yours."

"Don't tell him that," Aunt Vanessa said, giving Uncle March a cold glare.

"He went crabbing out on the dock by the boathouse, reached out too far with the net, and wound up stuck up to his thighs in the mud." He laughed until he had tears in his eyes. "Oh that was something to see. White shorts, white Izod shirt. Took forever to get him out of there. Had to lasso him and get one of the horses to haul him out."

"You're lying, Dad, you used the tractor." She set a glass of lemonade down in front of him violently, sloshing his hand. "Don't you listen to him, Alec."

"I swear it's true. Your mother was furious with me for months after that."

"So, Uncle March, who are your favorite composers?"

"Composers? Do you really want to know? Do you know anything about music?"

"A little."

"For example?"

"Oh jazz, blues, and rock. Your basic soundtracks." Uncle March was nodding. "I like Kronos Quartet, the standard classical stuff you'd—"

"—hear in a college music appreciation course. Well, son, that's all well and good but I was friends with Harry Partch, Edgar Varese, and Nicholas Maw, and enemies with—"

"Enemies?"

"Am I being harsh?" he looked at Aunt Vanessa for confirmation.

"Shush about that, Dad."

"Well, let's just say that some of my students didn't appreciate all I had to offer them and couldn't resist sticking the knife in and twisting it a little."

"Is that why you left the conservatory?"

"Left? Is that what Susan told you?"

I nodded.

"The administration drummed me out and sent me home to twiddle my thumbs."

"I'm sorry, I didn't know."

"Don't be. Cedric the Manx has more musical knowledge in his tiny cat brain that most of the hypocrites, backstabbers, and divas left at that place."

"And what about the cats?"

"Do you hear 'Nessa. What about the cats?"

"I hate cats. Don't get me started."

"What?"

"It's true, she hates them. Allergic. Drives her bats."

"Well, what—"

"The cats. It's a long story. Nicholas Maw was out here, basking in the sun, and we talked about primitive music and primitive painting. We thought it would be fun to see what animals could create. Whether or not we could map a pattern of specific notes. Maybe crack the musical code as it were. Discover some new patterns or combinations that mankind hasn't been able to access in lo two thousand years."

"And?"

"Beats me, Alec. Some days I think I'm making progress, other days I think I should be working with dolphins."

I was disappointed. I wanted to believe in his genius.

"Do you still compose?"

"Tough to keep a keyboard in tune in this salt air. I have a couple of computer programs to play with, and I do some comp work on the keyboards downstairs. They're fun toys but I do love the big pipe organs." He got a dreamy faraway look in his eyes, and then refocused on me. "Classical music has become an antique mart. Nobody cares any longer. The only way it sells these days is to put naked women on the cover of the CDs."

"I know."

"You probably like that, don't you? Naked women."

I did own a Lara St. John CD though I wasn't going to 'fess up.

"I'll download some things if you wish. You must have an iPod?"

I nodded.

"Of course. Well, I'll download some things and you can see what you think."

"Do you have any recordings with Cedric?"

"Of course. I'll record some of those for you, too."

I went to sleep that night listening to Cedric. When Uncle March forced the cat to imitate Bach, the works were amateurish though still oddly compelling, but when Cedric was allowed to follow his own kitty muse, the results were alien and unlike anything I'd ever heard before. Did human babies make music like this when they first toyed with a keyboard? I'd never had children so I didn't know. I'd have to find out. Though for now, these odd short pieces seemed to run along some musical pathways I'd never encountered. Like Satie tone poems (if he were a Martian) married to a more Nordic Windham Hill. If that makes any sense? In the morning when I mentioned my findings to Uncle March he was dismissive.

"Random Skill. Yes, I suppose Cedric's compositions do have something in common with those folks," he chuckled.

☼

THE SUN FLED FOR A few days and I ran out of laundry, which led me to be with Aunt Vanessa and the washing machine. She poured in the soap and I poured in my clothes, and then oddly, talking about the gray skies, and how much she missed the sun, she poured in another cup of soap. I kind of shrugged my shoulders and thought oh–oh. Only to be surprised when she reached for the box again, after just setting it down. Asking me, "Did I already put the soap in?"

"Err, yes. Yes, you did."

"Good, I forget sometimes."

She went out to her garden and I walked with her.

"Have you seen Uncle March?" I asked.

"He never gave me children. You know that."

I stepped back. She was angry. Angrier than I'd seen her. They'd had the odd little spat now and then but I'd been having those with my own girlfriend before she dumped me. I didn't know how to gauge things.

"He loves that damn cat Cedric more than me."

"That's not true. You know that."

"Oh, I suppose." She was back for a second. "I suppose you're right." And then she waved me off and knelt down to gather some fallen sticks.

I walked off to the barn. I don't know when Uncle March worked on the actual buildings for the cat city he was creating but there always seemed to be more of them each time I checked. He'd taken to printing out color Xeroxed images of old ornate architecture that he was gluing to the foam. He must have found that faster than painting them. Uncle March went to great trouble to make sure the windows and doors were all cut out and working.

Not finding him in the barn, I returned to the house. Aunt Vanessa wasn't in the garden. I walked down to the basement. The pipe organs seemed to be breeding as fast as the cats. I was certain that I stepped over more of them every time I entered my uncle's lair.

"Oh, Alec, so good to see you. How are you holding up?"

Uncle March was scribbling notes in a notebook and entering things onto his laptop.

"Better than Aunt Vanessa. She's not the same without the sun." I sat down in a chair beside him. I was eager to learn more about his projects.

Uncle March studied me for a second. "I'm afraid my wife hasn't been right in the head for some time."

"I don't know that I'd go that far."

"Having you around has been good for her. You've been the perfect distraction." He closed the notebook and snapped the strap shut. "Look, this is difficult to say, but you must know that nothing she's told you about her family, or the house, is true."

I must have looked pretty shook up, because Uncle March placed one hand on my arm. "You don't believe me, I can see. Well, she's held up pretty well, during your visit. Now she's entered the down phase of her cycle and perhaps it's time to bid farewell."

That's when I smelled smoke. I sniffed once, twice, and Uncle March stood quickly, and said, "Oh my God, no."

We ran up the stairs, negotiating the pipe organ pipes, and the kitchen door was a wall of flame. We exited the house.

"'Nessa!" Uncle March shouted over and over again.

I couldn't understand why I felt heat behind me and in front of me, until I turned and saw the barn ablaze. That's when I noticed the cats. You could hear them above the crackling old wood. They were crying and howling and dying in there.

"She did this," Uncle March said. "She did this." He started for the barn, and I reached to hold him back, only to be blown sideways by an exploding propane tank in the mudroom.

☼

I WATCHED FROM THE EDGE of the pond while the fire department tried to stop the blaze. The barn caved in with a great crash, and the cat fur and the smell of burning flesh were unbearable. I stripped off my shirt and covered my face. The smoke and flames were not the only bright lights in the coming twilight, yet they might as well have been. I'd lost my glasses someplace and everything was a blur.

Firemen found Aunt Vanessa in the kitchen. Smoke inhalation had killed her long before the pipe organ pipes buried her and the beams came crashing down. Paramedics discovered Uncle March alive. An oxygen mask covered his face. He was burned and falling debris from the hayloft had scarred his face with a blackened gash, and there was a viciously broken leg, though it looked like he might live. The crew tried to take him away, but he ripped the mask off and resisted them in order to speak with me.

"There's nothing you could have done, son. Even if you managed to get her out in time, she was still a goner. You can pour all of your love into somebody who's mentally ill but they're big black holes, and you'll never have enough love. They'll just suck you down with them."

"Uncle March, your music. All your work."

"Nothing you could have done." The paramedics wheeled him to the waiting ambulance and away.

"You all right?" one of them asked me.

"Yeah, just smoke." They told me to sit down and breathe some oxygen, too. I cried. Everything was in ruins.

A policeman walked over. "You need a ride back to town."

"No thanks."

The policeman looked at the paramedic and shook his head. "Son, I'm not asking, I'm telling. You need a ride back to town."

My eyes followed where he pointed and there was my rental car buried under a pile of rubble.

"I'd love a ride."

I followed the state trooper to his patrol car, just beginning to comprehend the full spectacle—this noisy panorama of rubble, dead cats, smoke, flame, people, and flashing lights. I wondered if Cedric had escaped?

As the car pulled down the oyster shell drive, I glanced back at the burning buildings, the streams of water arcing up in the air from the fire trucks. And there in the distance, the graveyard, the one Aunt Vanessa said contained all of her family history. Was none of it true? None of it? Maybe she believed it to be true in the well-trod pathways of her own dementia?

"Are you family?" the state trooper asked me.

"My aunt and uncle," I said.

And then I leaned back and rested my head on the seat, stuffing both hands in my jacket pockets to discover my iPod. Something had escaped the flames. I donned the headphones and listened to Cedric's strange music all the way back to Cambridge.

The Forgiveness Device

"Hold that flashlight still."

But I can't. It's impossible.
I'm only a child and I watch
as he puffs up bigger and bigger
—like a barrage balloon—
pushing back his glasses
that are smeared with grease
as he winds the clicking
ratchet again and again
changing sparkplugs in the dark.

The garage light won't reach outside
to where we stand around the
burgundy Chrysler. I'm scared.
Snot dripping down my face. Tears.
The fender is too big for me
to lean over, but I try
and my arm is so numb
it tingles. The drop light
flickers against the hood.
My father is stripping skin
off his knuckles as the ratchet
slips and dings off the manifold.
He's talking to himself.
Saying he can't see and
beginning to cuss.

I realize now—
that he's angry at himself,
at his failure to fix
something so elementary
and his anger
is misdirected at me.
But back then I was just
a bookish little kid
afraid of failing.
I didn't know yet that
it's okay to fail.
That my father was
just trying to save a buck
and afraid of aging.
The price was high.

Why can't you wait till morning?
I wanted to say, yet didn't dare.
He drinks another Ballantine,
crumples the can and drops
it on the driveway.

If I could
I'd materialize at that exact moment
the aluminum still rattling
against the concrete.
Tell him, "It's not that important Dad.
It's just a couple of sparkplugs.
Don't get so stressed."
I'd rub my red bandanna
across his forehead
and soothe his brow.
Tell him, "Relax."
And watch his features soften.
Hear that laughter again.

And I'd forgive him.
I really would.

5
READING & WRITING

Letters from the Editor

1.

WAITING FOR THE BUS SEEMS so trivial. I do like the fireworks and flags bit. Sure, politics really is the man in the gray flannel suit, and the drones on the hill.

In the end I want to care about the narrator and his dilemma. I want to be up to my neck in an impossible job with an impossible boss and a family I can't fit into my schedule. I want a dalliance with Margaret even if it's only imaginary. I want the entire D.C. world to be shape shifting all around me. So that the only balance I have is in the unwieldy world of the Cosmos Club (not exactly Planet Earth).

Yet, I love Zorak, the oblong-head, the masturbation scene. Now, if you took that someplace this might turn into an interesting story.

I'd go back and rethink this from the opening (and startling) image of the head and somehow bounce that off the girl in green boots.

2.

TOMMY HILFIGER IS A GOOD name for a character.

Love the jabs at *Glamour*, and the drunken fumblings. Reads like real life.

Best thing in first section is the sequence with the G.I. Joe and the Barbie and the sequence where Dad sees his daughter for the first time as a possible sexual object.

The final sequence with the pier and the boys is still the strongest section.

Sex could be the linking topic. You could really go there and use sexual ideas for each chapter and focus that way. The blow job chapter? The masturbation chapter? Et al.

3.

THIS IS BRILLIANT. JESUS AS a character, too. Wow. And it works.

As though looking in the box would be contagious. Love the "Hey Jude" record, and the books. The various links to the missing life.

4.

THIS NEW VERSION DOES WORK better as an opening and the events seem to fall into sequence. I don't miss the shrink. I like the deer over the other scenario with the son killing the guy who killed his pop.

I'm surprised that a cat could get its paws under the door far enough to get to her legs. I've been trying to visualize that bathroom.

5.

LOVE THE ANCHOVIES AND THE allergic return to high school dreams. Hilarious. The old eggs riff works for me, too. And the intricacies of the working relationship. But I'd deep six the Dr. Seuss lines.

I never would have guessed that you could get so much mileage out of apricot-colored clothing.

6.

I LIKE THE GREEK.

Neato fact: Alexander's body was put in a crate of honey for the return to Greece. Human flesh doesn't decay in honey.

I like the shed very much and the manly work cleaning it up.

7.

LOVE THE THREATENED LAWSUIT AT the end. Ha. The candy cane riot. Mrs. Beatrice, too. Best thing though is how deep into their heads you get. Both Carol and Lucy seem real. You manage that well.

I like the fact that Martin has slept with both Patrice and Lisa. The Doc is ridiculous with the nurse.

8.

ANGELINE DREAM.

Love the lesbian cab driver and the swithcheroo between them. That's fun in a very NYC way.

9.

I LIKE THE IMAGE OF the girl in the white dress stepping off the cathedral but I'd rather have a story with dialogue.

I love the biz with the watches.

Love how Loreena McKennit enters the text. Love the trains, too.

The biz with the blood and the paper cuts is good and original.

10.

ONLY THING I REALLY LIKE is the crown of blue roses. I'd forget all about this one.

11.

THE LEPRECHAUN PIECE HAD MOMENTS.

12.

A POSSUM ON A FENCE isn't enough to carry a story.

13.

THE IDEA AT THE END that Peter recognizes the cicada sound from the womb isn't enough to make this work. And the narrator has come to a sort of inner peace there. She's learned something.

14.

I DON'T THINK THE TITLE, or Hettie's *merde*, or the reason for it you propose (the burn tissue), is enough to carry a story.

15.

LOVE THE GIANT CABBAGE HEADS, the slender moment, the overture to a refusal.

All those toothbrushes are a great clue. Orgy? Love it. She bags out and there's your ending. But up to that point, her anger ("If he doesn't think I'm smart enough he shouldn't be fucking me") is brilliant. More, more, more.

16.

YES, LILLIAN'S A WASTE OF a human and it's a pity she's not going to die instead of Frank, but there you have it. And it's with that sense of unfairness and merde that the narrator should be moving forward. She's afraid she may not be able to do this again and she's stuck with this stupid person to tell, but by god she's going to tell it anyway, right now, and even this shit-for-brains Lillian is going to get the message.

So it should be a weird mix of brutal, scared, and taking no prisoners. Though timing is everything here.

I like the tiny victory with the milk for coffee.

Love the brick-throwing scene and the way Tony responds.

The snowballs and cliff and ice scenes all work though I'm at a loss to explain why the Scouts are getting this much unsupervised time.

17.

I LOVE THE IDEA OF Peter's story, I love what he's all about. The way he's trapped Izzy into the event, how the tables are turned during the questioning.

The Monet comes on too thick. I'd soften that some.

I like the guardian angel conceit.

I like the idea of the factory and the high heels clicking.

18.

LOVE HOW YOU USED THE oysters to frame the story. The rough sex is a good insight on both of them.

Love the light fixture ending and yes, I agree, cut the last paragraph. The dark night of the soul for a Positive Thinking guru.

19.

I LIKE THE TAROT BIZ and the under the boardwalk groping.

I like Anna's line though I think her "You might as well be dead, too" needs a little more explication by the end.

20.

I'D MILK THE YANKEE BIZ for a few more lines with Lila. And nah, Tony's accent is too corny. Ditto the pirates on the next page.

The alligator bassoon case is a really great touch.

I'd rethink the backbone of this one. Even the last little spin around the dance floor seems to come too far after the fact to matter.

21.

LOVE THE SCENE WITH THE money on the bed. Reminds me of an old French art film, *The Empty Canvas*, with Catherine Spaak draped in paper money. Love the moths in his room, the Ben Franklin ghost biz and the tattoo.

I love the Jill St. John mention earlier. Tie that together somehow?

I like her comment on bodily fluids, almost missed it. But I don't get the money line on p. 15. "Believe me I know."

22.

I LIKE THAT YOU TRIED to capture a musical experience, and get inside a musician's head.

I have to confess that all that talk about her butt and then his "bestest buddies" confused me. I thought she was having some kind of liposuction and then it looks like it's breast implants by the end. Make that very clear, I had to make a big mental leap to grapple with that one. But then I'm a guy.

I think you've tamed Ethel's mother. The candle-buying works. Love Arny and the duck biz.

Love that Rachel is playing with the knife at the end.

23.

WELL, THIS IS A SHOCKER. Love what she says and what she does. I don't buy the broken teeth. "Viva El Carne" would be a better title. Still, the violence and the zany humor work for me.

What you need to do then is include a couple more scenes afterwards. Dealing with the scar and this discovery. (Have the lovers noticed? Scar memories?)

I assume at the end that Timothy is dead? I need to be absolutely sure of that.

The dog implies a lot that it doesn't necessarily deliver. A lot of moral weight for a dog to carry.

The kid torture, the "few lugers short of an arsenal" lines, and the burning of the tree house, that's classic kids. Love the pseudo-German.

24.

I LIKE JOHN'S DREAM OF being a player, I like that the Earl recognizes the reality. And I love everything relating to the heart. I just wish the rest wasn't so predictable.

The astrologer, the conversion process, the haunted house, the rapier-wielding pop, and witch doctor. Love that running like a primitive thread through what is otherwise a fast-paced jargon-heavy story about business and ethics.

Make it clear what punishment awaits, and what we can expect without laying it on too thick at the end. I don't want this to be longer. I just need a center to Mustafa. A little less shadowy in the Asian Robert Morley sense. Inscrutable is okay. But null set is not.

25.

VERY URSULA LE GUIN, VERY sci-fi fantasy. I've seen a million stories like this one and I want to blame David Carradine.

I like that you hide the cause of death. Adds to his flailing. But I have to know what song he sings.

26.

NEEDS A MUCH BETTER TITLE. "Burying Connecticut"?

I'm surprised kids aren't smoking throughout this piece.

The biz about Detroit comes out of nowhere. The entire story could be about the summer in Detroit. But I think it weighs too heavy on the ending.

The snake handling also seems gratuitous though I love the fact that Oriel has lied about being bit, and that crazy old Grandma had a father who used to do it.

The dream is vivid enough for me. I was bothered by the blue and white image floating up. Would have liked that much more clear from p. 5. Subtle is good, yet inscrutable is not. Would work well as a short film.

27.

HUNG'S FOCUS DOES SEEM TO shift from the altar to the daughter.

Throw her in a room and make her sink or swim. It's clear that she's a loner, coming up for air.

If you're nailing her down as a type, you've succeeded.

The closet full of magazines. The steam tunnels.

So? Is it about mother, the goddess, and how she relates to men and how the daughter relates to men in her footsteps?

Is it about life in Cali with Gerald? Is it about life in London with Peter? Is it about the best friend? So many possibilities.

The biz with the closet is a story.

The teacher with the streetwalker line is totally out there. How strange and unexpected.

28.

I LIKE "THE DEPOT GHOSTS" a lot. I like the idea of the red-tailed hawk in "Come Fly With Me" but would nix the Sinatra song title.

"If I Were a Tiger": Love this for its sweetness. As sweet as strawberries.

I don't buy the rabbit family at the end but then again, this could make a kid's story.

29.

CALL IT "THE MAN WHO Touches the Sky." Relegate the balloonatics into even smaller supporting roles.

The Roswell biz is amusing. You could do more with Charlie and Doodles in terms of comic relief.

I also love the sequence with the Native American elders. That's hilarious.

I don't believe for one second that Carson has the faintest clue what heroin is and don't believe he could spot it on a spoon. No way, no how. Unless you tell me he goes to movies and saw *Basketball Diaries* or something.

30.

THE MAGIC HAT TREE IS wonderful. I think you ought to rethink this entire piece and dwell only on the magic hat tree and the power it gives you and the relationship with Bernie.

I get the pain, anger, displacement, and the sheer Tom Waits–like existence of the protagonist. I like the connection between the ex and the pigeon. I love the fight for it. I like the wrong number and the odd woman. I love that he stepped on the nails and his foot is bleeding through the last section.

Stark urban and very NYC.

31.

PLAY WITH THE IDEA OF the accident within the accident

So much implied in this story, so much left inscrutable. The scene with the lunch pail is amazing.

The fiftieth b-day party would make a great story but you skim over it in this chapter. The Missouri Synod biz has to be seen and not heard.

I love the situation. I love Babs and Chauncy. I love the idea of the memorial tower.

Tippy could be developed a lot more.

Love the dog poker artwork and the boiled dog in the Jacuzzi.

Love the title and the reality of toothpaste in his pocket at the end.

32.

YOU BANG THE WISHES PRETTY hard. I mean I see them coming and I wince a little when he makes the accidental wishes for banana and rainbow.

I think there would be more immediate repercussions from the mother figuring out that Sarah had seen ax man and there would be more hell to pay from Sarah for burning her pad.

You can allude to more of the city's condition when Norman talks about shaving punks.

I love the ending. "The Price of Haircuts in the City of the Dead."

33.

FOUND MYSELF WONDERING IF THERE was an open casket?

But my favorite snippets are when the ant begins to think the daughter's thoughts.

When the two young lesbians catch them it ought to have more impact.

More with the rosary beads at the end.

Still, I did think you took the gunplay and the paranoia in the hat-drying scene too far.

Love the leg and finding the right time to wear it.

34.

LOVE THE IDEA OF THE stalker following her home, almost killing her boyfriend, and then walking around in her apartment and feeding her cat.

35.

JUST THE KIND OF STORY the *New Yorker* used to run in the pre–Tina Brown days. Back when they ran a couple of stories an issue. Reminds me of classic Ann Beattie. Give them a try.

Gunpowder
Divertimento

Whi Edgar flipped on the classroom lights on the first day of the new school year and saw the violent scrawl of red chalk on the blackboard, he knew the time had come to do something about Mr. Eyebrow. But what? He erased the words—*Pervert. Porno Addict. Shoplifter.* He knew of course, which students had done this. He also knew that this was only the beginning, that they wouldn't stop, that the rumor mill would kick into overdrive with this new image of him, and that eventually Principal Curtin would call him into the office and roast him over the coals. He knew all of this in that first split second in the doorway of his history class. And, he realized sadly, that even if he eliminated the cause, there was no damage control in the world that could resurrect his tarnished reputation. No, any action he took would invariably make things worse. Meeting Mr. Eyebrow had been accidental, and Edgar's only recourse now was payback.

☼

HOW DID IT GO AGAIN? Edgar had stopped for bagels after work and was on his way back to his beat-up Buick Cutlass when he'd spied a bookshop. He'd been surprised such a run-down shopping center could rate a new bookshop. If it hadn't been for the Chinese takeout and the Bagel Place, he'd never stop there at all. Edgar had been so distracted that spring. When he wasn't grading student history papers, he'd been out in his garden planting azaleas, pansies, day lilies, clematis, lavender, lilac, and portulacas. He'd had no free time to explore. So the bookshop must have opened up sometime during that busy spring.

Edgar hadn't been disappointed at first. Well, the name was just the first inkling that things were not exactly what they seemed—The Book Shop didn't have the proper sort of ring. How could they ever expect to compete with the big chain stores with a name like that? And the raised dais from which the owner? Sales clerk? surveyed the customers was a little unusual and forbidding, even more so when Edgar had realized the man was almost imprisoned, walled in by the cubicle on all four sides. Such a setup recalled the sort of roost the slave driver had down in the hold in sea-going adventure films, where the men rowed to the beat of a drum.

Fiction filled one entire wall of the shop and as Edgar eyed the alphabetical authors' names, he grew more and more excited, until he understood the sort of company the names were keeping. And then, stupefied, he realized there were no genre categories. It was just fiction of any and all types lumped together by author. Jackie Collins, Agatha Christie, Joseph Conrad, Deepak Chopra, and Conan, all together in the Cs. Romance novels vied with serious literature for space. Row after row. Paperbacks stacked sideways on top of other books. This was disturbing. But Edgar was still into the joy of the chase, new titles, long-sought-after possibilities. Perhaps the owner was just eccentric and this method made things easier? It was such a small shop after all. Maybe he couldn't afford to hire any high school kids to shelve for him? Edgar tried to imagine some of his mostly Hispanic or black students working there. It was a real stretch from Pan American history to The Book Shop. He shook his head, not certain which disappointed him more.

The next aisle was all military, politics, history. Edgar didn't much care for the war focus. No Barbara Tuchman volumes in evidence. No Noam Chomsky. No Howard Zinn. His eye also began to pick up other disquieting aspects of the shop. There were large posters on the walls. Cartoons about the U.S. government. Gulf War vets met there on Wednesday nights. Where? Perhaps a room in back? There wasn't enough space for any group of any size among the many shelves. While the shop had an all-glass front, once inside it became clear that the windows had been painted opaque. No light came in or out save for the door.

Hmm? The hunting and fishing section was huge. Edgar noted books with odd titles on conspiracy theories, the constitution, the marijuana handbook.

More unsettling was the fact that most of the other customers seemed to be standing at the far end of the shop.

So Edgar walked back out to the dais and in the direction where the other people were congregating. The young man behind the counter didn't respond when Edgar said hello. Just raised one black eyebrow. He was a large man, a scruffy young man in a blue Washington Capitals jersey. The air conditioning was on full blast, making it chilly for May. And the raised dais made the man appear even taller. How tall was he? Edgar couldn't begin to guess.

Another man in a camouflage jacket was talking to Mr. Eyebrow.

"So you really believe that? You think she really put makeup on him, tied him to the bed posts, and did him with a dildo?"

"Doesn't matter if she did, or she didn't. It just proves what I've been saying all along, you can't trust the man."

Edgar got a little shiver and moved on. And couldn't believe his luck, this half of the store was devoted to magazines and newspapers. He was overjoyed to find a newsstand. Comic books in the middle of the shop acted as a sort of buffer. And then there were women's magazines, hobby magazines, news magazines, every movie magazine known to man it seemed. He picked up one after another. There were magazines he'd never heard of before. Rock magazines, swimsuit issues, sports magazines, tattoo and body-piercing magazines, auto magazines, and on and on. This was the sort of place he'd always dreamed of finding when he was a kid. And then Edgar rounded the corner, almost flattening two teenagers—two teenagers he vaguely recognized from the halls at the high school—and came face to face with a wall of porno magazines. Skin everywhere. Bookcase after bookcase. Easily half of the shop was dedicated to skin. He couldn't believe what he was seeing.

His mind reeled. There must have been a thousand different titles. Edgar had thought there were simply two or three porno magazines. Had only ever seen *Playboy*, *Penthouse*, and *Hustler*. Oh, and *Mayfair* of course, he'd confess to glancing at a copy in London once while waiting for a train to Oxford. How could there be so many? Gay magazines, lesbian magazines, she-males, ass masters. Edgar flinched and looked away, moving quickly past the twenty-four other customers, men and women of all ages, and races, scurrying past Mr. Camouflage and Mr. Eyebrow once again, and out the glass door.

"Excuse me. Hey mister. Excuse me."

Edgar stopped when he felt the arm on his shoulder and turned around. Mr. Eyebrow, over six feet of him, was tapping him on the shoulder.

"Sorry?"

"You want to pay for that, don't you?"

Edgar tightened his grip on his bag of bagels and in complete confusion now saw where Mr. Eyebrow was pointing. There was a magazine folded up in his other hand.

"Why, yes."

"I thought you would," Mr. Eyebrow said, nodding his head up and down as though Edgar were a child, while leading him—no, Edgar was being guided with what amounted to a great deal of force—back inside the shop.

Mr. Camouflage was smiling, a broad fake smile showing too many teeth, and nasty ones at that. And Edgar could see that a shared joke was passing between the two men at his expense.

Mr. Eyebrow gained entrance to the cubicle by lifting part of the counter and swinging part of the bookcase out into the shop. That was how he'd moved so fast. In one practiced fluid motion, he was safely ensconced back behind the counter and all was again right with his world.

"That'll be $5.00 plus tax, that comes to $5.36. Would you like a bag?"

Edgar shook his head. Put the sack of bagels down on the counter and rummaged through his khakis for his wallet. He gave Mr. Eyebrow a twenty, and began absentmindedly fiddling with his bills. Making sure they were all face up and pointing in the same direction. What was keeping his change? Edgar glanced up to find Mr. Eyebrow waiting expectantly.

"My change?" Edgar asked.

"I thought you were looking for change."

"What?" Edgar was even more confused.

Mr. Camouflage was laughing and moved back toward the porno magazines. Edgar saw now that he was holding a copy of *Passion and Betrayal,* Gennifer Flowers's book about her affair with Bill Clinton.

"You know, the sixty-eight cents." Mr. Eyebrow put one bill back in the register and grabbed some coins instead. "Here ya go," Mr. Eyebrow said, handing Edgar the correct change. "And have a nice night."

Edgar reached to pick up his bagels and became aware of two youths standing by his arm.

"Hey teach." It was Jesus, who'd spent most of his life in Miami until a recent move to Virginia. The boy gave a slight wave.

Edgar didn't recognize his smirking friend so was surprised when he heard, "How's it going, Mr. Fletcher?" as the two walked past him toward the magazine racks.

Once Edgar had the key safely in the door of his powder blue Buick, he began to breathe more easily and became aware that he'd been blushing for a very long time. What had just happened? He unfolded the magazine. *Masquerade.* A so-called erotic journal featuring articles entitled "Slave or Victim?," "The Art of the Bullwhip," and "Mistress Manslaughter." The nude woman on the black and white cover was photographed from the waist up and had chains connecting one pierced nipple to the other. She wore a studded collar and held a riding crop above her head. Her gaze was forceful, direct, and damning.

☼

EDGAR SPENT ALL SUMMER WRITING letters to the local papers, trying to get the county to do something about the so-called bookshop. He began a petition. He talked to the local administrators. And by the time September rolled around, he'd accomplished nothing save for attracting the attention of a lot of anti–First Amendment whackos, and husband-hunting widows who wanted to know why he'd never married.

What was he doing? Mr. Eyebrow bothered him a lot. He was feeling humiliated. Put upon.

The pistol was buried behind his handkerchiefs and the cedar balls in his dresser. Edgar couldn't explain why he'd kept it. Or, even more disturbing, why he'd kept the bullets. True, he'd separated them in the apartment. The bullets were in his trunk in the hall closet. Edgar got them out, not without some trouble, the golf clubs he hadn't used in fifteen years getting in his way. Finally, he opened the gray box and loaded the bullets into the tiny handgun.

He could burn the bookstore to the ground. That was one way. He hefted the pistol. His mother's. She'd kept it for protection and had never used it. Edgar had been shocked when the lawyer handed him the pistol. Part of his inheritance. Had his mother been that frightened? The things he didn't know about her were large in number.

He'd need a plan. The simple one was to kidnap Mr. Eyebrow. And do what? Try to talk him out of selling porno? He could shoot him. Make it look like a robbery. Simple enough. Wait for him in the parking lot? Follow him home one night? No, Mr. Eyebrow had proven himself to be pretty quick. He stroked one hand back and forth beneath his black cat's chin. "I just don't know what to do about this problem, Cicero. I just don't know."

☼

WHICH IS HOW EDGAR FOUND himself standing in the Ns— Vladimir Nabokov, Ogden Nash, Pablo Neruda, Anaïs Nin, Jeff Noon, Andre Norton, et al.—with a gun in his pocket. Despite being almost closing time, the shop was crowded. He hadn't thought this through at all. Have to wait for another time. Edgar reached his right hand into the pocket of his Harris Tweed and felt the metal.

Mr. Eyebrow's eyes sought him out, gave a little raised eyebrow greeting over Mr. Camouflage's shoulder.

"She's got to be some kind of agent. How the hell else could she have blocked a motorcade with an AK-47 in the car and not gone to the slammer?"

"I'll admit it is suspicious, Jerry, but there you go over-generalizing again," Mr. Eyebrow said. He wore a red and black plaid wool shirt. Today was also the equinox and despite a chilly couple of days, they hadn't turned on the heat yet.

"So what do you think about her?"

"I think she's out of her mind is what I think."

Edgar killed time in the fiction section. Only a couple minutes before closing. The shop finally emptied out. Now was his chance. Edgar held a copy of Günter Grass's *The Tin Drum* in one hand and his mother's pistol in the other as he approached the front register. He was consciously willing one foot in front of the other, staring down at his black Florsheims. *They need polishing*, he thought.

He heard the bells on the door before he saw it swing closed and noticed that a young man was facing Mr. Eyebrow. Where had he come from? The young man was demanding money.

Edgar spotted the shiny plastic-looking pistol being waved at Mr. Eyebrow. Edgar knew he should stop, but his feet were still carrying him forward, and his momentum carried him up the aisle a few steps behind the young man with the gun. Edgar's fingers gripped his own pistol and he could feel his hand clear his pocket raising it up. Everything after that single motion was a blur. The young man pivoted and snapped off a point-blank sideways shot at Edgar, as Edgar raised his own gun, as Mr. Eyebrow fired a third gun that magically appeared in his hands.

☼

EDGAR'S EARS HAD BEEN ROARING for a long time. He couldn't move. Something was pinning his arms and he realized the blubbering noise he heard off in the distance was actually his own voice. Something heavy was holding him down, and then it was gone. The ringing was beginning to subside. A hand was helping him.

"Are you okay, mister? You saved my ass. If you hadn't come up behind that fucking puke, he would have blown me away."

Voices. People. There were people all around them. Coming from the back of the shop.

"Ben? You okay? You need help, son?"

"Hey Pop, this old guy here was in the line of fire."

"Are you hit, mister?"

Ben? So Mr. Eyebrow had a name. Ben. Things were not going so well.

"Is he shot?"

"I don't think so. In shock I'd say."

"Is this Beretta yours?" another voice asked.

"No, Jerry. Belonged to this guy. He saved my life. If he hadn't jumped the little punk from behind I'd have been toasted."

"Guy's got a lot of guts going after that punk with this old piece."

"Yeah, the kid had a Glock."

Somebody was putting something in his pocket. "Here's your gun back, mister. Safety's on. Might be best to leave that out of sight when the cops get here."

Edgar was aware that he was in a sitting position, and that hands were examining his shirt beneath his jacket, moving all over his body. An irritating sensation. Somebody was propping him up.

"The police are on their way, and if you need an ambulance just nod your head. Do you need an ambulance?"

Edgar shook his head no.

"You sure you're all right? That little puke fell right on top of you."

"I'm okay," Edgar managed to finally wheeze through clenched teeth.

Ben helped him to his feet.

"You want a beer or something? Coffee? I got some in the back. The guys from my pop's old unit are having a meeting. It's no problem."

"Sit right there, I'll get him something," a voice said.

How stupid. Wednesday night. The Gulf War vets. Edgar would never have gotten away with it. He was aware that Ben was brushing his clothes with one hand and steadying him with the other.

How could things go so completely awry?

Edgar's ears were still faintly ringing. Something was interfering with his sight though. He began to slowly take in his surroundings.

"Here's a Bud Lite," and Edgar saw the mirror-image man who must have been Ben's father as he wrapped Edgar's fingers around the bottle. And helped guide it toward his mouth.

Ben was still brushing away at his clothing.

"Don't know how he missed you. You're lucky as hell." Ben's father was pointing down. "Hole right through your tweed I'm afraid. Missed you by an inch."

Edgar looked down at his jacket, at Ben's finger poking through a burned hole in the brown wool. Then his eyes moved to the man Ben had shot and saw that most of his face and head were missing. Finally Edgar, in the second that the beer rushed between his teeth, realized exactly what it was that Ben was brushing from his suit.

☼

"HERE HE COMES, BACK TO the land of the living. Hey, buddy. I can't thank you enough for saving my son like that."

Ben's father.

"You needed some smelling salts. You'll be fine. I'm Sy, Ben's father. Here's your beer. Look, we took the liberty of getting your tweed cleaned. Ben took it over to Mr. Cho's place next door. He's expensive but he does good work. It's on us. Oh, don't worry about your pistol. We put that in the safe here. You can come get it tomorrow if you want. We cleaned you up a little but you're going to want to get home and take a shower."

And then there was a policeman. Edgar told him that he'd been walking up to the counter to check out and had stumbled, that the robber had turned and fired at him, opening himself up for Ben's shot. The policeman asked a few more questions. Asked where Edgar had been standing and then asked them to recreate things by going back to their places as though it were some sort of stage play. Satisfied, the police moved on.

"You feeling okay enough to drive? You want I should give you a lift?"

"I don't know," Edgar said. He was pretty groggy in the aftermath. He never drank beer and it was upsetting his already acidic stomach.

"Tell you what, I'll drive you home in your car. Ben will follow and give me a lift back? How's that sound?"

It sounded good to Edgar. And on the six-block drive, Edgar found himself wondering why he'd felt driven to pull a stupid stunt like this in the first place. And out of his mouth popped the question: "How do you feel about your son selling all of that porno?"

The man looked at him and laughed. "Ya know my wife has a big big problem with it. Ben's our only child and we had such high hopes for him. He's smart enough he could have gone to Annapolis or West Point. But I'm just as glad he didn't. I'm not real happy about how the government bozos are treating our boys. And I'll admit I'm happy he didn't go that route. Still, he could do something else. I mean me and the guys are happy to have the space for meetings. We sit back there and argue and kvetch and drink. Keeps us from venting too much on our wives. And Ben was a good kid to let us. But the porn, I dunno. Seen one porn mag, you seen them all, ya know. He sells a pretty high volume, believe it or not. Sells a lot of comics, too. I think he should go that route. Appeal more to the gamers and comics crowd. I think really he's in a holding pattern of some sort, just trying to figure out what to do next. Hey, he was thrilled you were buying the Günter Grass, that's one of his favorite writers."

Edgar was speechless.

"This is your street. Which house?"

Edgar pointed it out and the man pulled the Buick into the driveway.

"Hey, nice. I like the way you have the portulacas framing the sidewalk."

"You garden?"

"A hobby. My wife tore her knees up and can't spend that much time on it anymore. I'm still learning what looks nice, though she has an eye. I mostly just plant where she points."

"Thank you," Edgar said.

"Hey, can I ask what you do for a living?"

"I teach history at the high school."

"Bishop Ireton?"

"Yes."

"I went there. Class of '79. Is Perkins still the pre-engineering teacher?"

"Why yes." Edgar's brain was straining to compute any of this.

"Man, is he a curmudgeon. Though he taught me everything I know. Hey, between you and me, my son could use some input on history titles if you get a chance. I think he'd really appreciate getting a printout of good books for the shop. And it would mean a lot coming from you."

Ben pulled up behind them in a big pickup truck, and Sy came around the car to embrace Edgar. He cringed away a little but Ben's father didn't relent. Sy cuffed him on the shoulder a couple of times.

"Thanks again for saving my baby," Sy said, choking up a bit. "Anything you need, you give us a holler. You're a real hero, ya know."

☼

WHEN THE LONG-AWAITED CALL FROM Principal Curtin finally came on Monday, Edgar slunk down to the office to take his firing like a man. Imagine his surprise to discover a reporter from *The Sun*, the local county tabloid. A photographer snapped a photo with Principal Curtin. When the article appeared, old students called or dropped by the high school. The headline pronounced Edgar a hero. There was Sy talking about the history teacher who'd saved his son's life. There was Ben saying, if not for Edgar, he'd have been a goner. And there at the end of the article in the last paragraph of type, Ben said that he hoped Edgar would help him expand his history and gardening sections so that he could attract more customers like the history teacher. A contest had even been announced to pick a new name for the shop.

Edgar sipped his green tea and watched as Cicero leapt from a pillow onto a precarious stack of books, failed to maintain his balance, and jumped again too quickly, causing the books to slide and fall. Edgar rushed to straighten the pile, and there was the fiery pierced woman from the cover of *Masquerade* that had almost toppled his life. He laughed, rolled the magazine up, and dropped it in the trash. Edgar took another sip of tea, moved to the patio, and gazed out on his flowerbeds.

When She Walked in the Room

Not as smart as the rest.
Not beautiful yet at ease
in a way none of the other students
have achieved.

Arriving late.

A mean girl
comfortable with her body.

Sitting with legs open
panties on view to the world.

She flashed cleavage when she leaned over.
Had to be reminded about today's assignment.

Flashing flesh and a whiff of eroticism
as though she were in control of the entire class.

I'm a married man with two wonderful kids
and I no longer lust after teenagers

but her legs draw my eyes
over and over again. And she knows it.

They also draw the eyes of the woman
who'd invited me to lecture on poetry.

Afterwards we are both astonished
that no matter what we did we were drawn

again and again to glance between this
blonde woman's legs.

Ashamed of the control
she had over both of us.

Unable to comprehend how such a thing
is possible in one so young.

Angry at being so blatantly toyed with
when so many other women in the class

were so brilliant and creative.
And yet hours later it's the one who

stooped to sexual grandstanding that I recall.
The one who troubles my sleep.

The one I couldn't look in the eye.

Ginsberg Comes to Garfield Street

My first reaction upon hearing that Allen Ginsberg wanted to be interviewed on our radio show was shock. Pure and simple. I went through several changes: was scared, jubilant, and ambivalent all at once. After all, how do you approach one of the greatest living poets? Honestly—as it turned out.

When Phil Cline and Eric Baizer arrived at Zenon Slawinski's second-floor walk-up apartment with Allen Ginsberg in tow, the room was tense, but only for a brief moment. Introductions were made. John Elsberg was there, and David Sawyer; Kevin Urick made it, but Desmond O'Brien had to work. Shelli Harris handed him some lemonade, and then he sat in the green stuffed chair by the window. The sun streamed in around him. The sage was ready.

I explained that we would be casual, could stop the tape anytime, and told him to say anything he wanted. Then, out of nervousness, I constructed a defense, saying, "We've really only done a few shows and none of us is very good at this." He waved a hand at the surrounding gauntlet (eight people sitting around him in a semicircle), and said he'd never done anything like it before. I was completely at ease.

We started in, and after a few minutes he was well into telling all about his FBI files and the '60s. We gave him room to move. He apologized later for his "nervous speech." It was almost as though he meant that he'd been as scared as we were.

And he was fascinating; serious one moment, laughing the next. We asked him about Kerouac, and he told us all about the man, talked about his own poetry, about Naropa, sang and chanted, talked about his personal finances, and then closed with a poem about grants. When the tape ran out, he sat back in this setting of piano, microphones, and Zenon's phantasmagoric paintings, surrounded by his awed and youthful admirers, and relaxed. It was over.

Later, at the reception after his reading, I sat with him for a moment in the room swirling with groupies, autograph hounds, and curiosity seekers, and he said to me, "There are some good poets in this room. It's amazing. A whole new wave." I shook my head in wonder. It was as though he were passing the torch.

The Children of Derek Walcott

A black Chevrolet on the road to Benetton
proverbial squeaky wheel.

Not enough 3-In-One Oil in the world
to slick that pedal to the metal.

Do the children of Derek Walcott
multiply and multiply?

How many good poems must you write
to pay that much child support?

Do the children of Derek Walcott
wander in the mist of memory?

Their volunteer mothers
multiply and multiply

Embroidered bathrobe

The sticky wicket

Do the children of Derek Walcott
search for their identity in stanzas?

add and subtract divide and conquer
etcetera etcetera

Do the children of Derek Walcott
become mock poets?

I don't know.

Do the children of Derek Walcott
invent mock stories?

I don't know.

The children of Derek Walcott
live the faux *Book of Mormon*.

Etcetera etcetera.

Do the children of Derek Walcott
go feral and run in the mist

chasing their father

Frankenstein monsters
needing a heart-to-heart

a bone to pick

a Tally-Ho.

Perhaps we're jealous?

Run poet. Sprint now.
They're getting closer.

A hundred clockwork
footprints in the sand.

Letter to
George Myers Jr.

Recovering from a troubled week...aggh...the party for Phil is a real thing...will occur as we said on the 27th at 7pm if you're in the mood Gretchen would love to cook you that "one good meal"...will be at the Harrimans on N Street...exact address...3038...down the alley by the wire mesh gate and around back...yes...should be fun and there might be skinny dipping and rampant sex so do come!! Shocking DC Party...arrests...massive overdoses on Gretchen's pastry/tarts...to eat and be eaten...or ooh lah lah...it's all cake to me satchmo.

Actually, coming unglued...Kevin's article about my untimely death/disappearance/movement has been published in the *Wash. Post*...discovered by my dad who thought it jolly and left me feeling Weird...Desi is working on a rebuttal Kevin told me today and then he'll write another and then I'll write from Paris declaiming my detractors from abroad in my best fiery prose...

Been reading about the life of Paul Bowles in Fez and in Tangier and am both jealous and envious...wow...he was a composer before he ever wrote and worked with Aaron Copland and did things for Orson Welles and Tenn. Williams besides which he did the first translation of Sartre's *Huis Clos* and is the one who coined the U.S. title *No Exit*...worked with Dali...did a ballet together...amazing man and then he married the mysterious Jane who's been getting a big critical fuss lately...strange all this from a man who didn't know the female body was different until he was 17 and thought he was the only child in the world until he was 6...cause he was isolated ...by his folks natch...

Ahem...back to the grind...looking for work...none to be found anywhere...whoa withs me...like woah...horse riding into the sunset...gretchen and I may go to Santa Fe...i'm dying to move out of here for a while...6 months or so... working on a bloody great novel and pissed at myself cause my prose isn't good enough while my ideas for the plot are (for once) decent and conventional with a twist...aggh...also just received a 65pp short story from Michael Brondoli that's so good I want to cry and quit and jump ship for antarctica and be the only poet at the south pole and maybe I will entertain penguins since nobody else likes what I'm doing...

Fact is I think the small press scene is a bit too incestuous for me. Seems like the same names crop up everywhere... ahem...I figure it's you and Grayson and Brondoli, Ahern and Kevin and Me and the rest of the other invisibles here who might just be the future of the east coast lit...etc....and am a bit put off by all the guys 20 years older than me who make all the fucking decisions...bitch bitch bitch...I do a lot...it just seems like too much bullshit...and if I go to the COSMEP shindig with Kevin you may rest assured that I am going to take some of these so-called small press legends down a bunch of notches for my own personal ego satisfaction...

(do i get the part) I'm the cocky rebellious poet/editor...a fine madness...played by sean connery...drunk irish poet...who is a teatotaler digs Jimi Hendrix and misses him and wonders where he is now when we need him?

No seriously, I figure there's no point in getting down on all those 40-year-old guys who haven't moved on into NY publishing and thus (whether by choice [which they all want you to believe] or because they're lousy writers) and will never make it in the world...outside the small press world that is.

I'm an ambitious son of a bitch he says to himself...read on... we tiny thin guys are trouble...

It's just that there is more to it than that and that if I want to make it?? (whatever that means?? say a family and house in Ireland and enough money to get by between books), then I have to push and finally make some coin. All of which sounds egotistical and awful but is a daydream shared by many. Though it looks like my next hobby could be making movies...I mean you are not quite as near 30 as I am and I feel that twinge...creeping...that fear that I'm going to be penniless, jobless, living with my mom like Jack Kerouac for the rest of my life and never doing anything...Seems like all I really know how to do is write and spend money on magazine and other publishing ventures and spend time with le femmes and they don't pay for that (and I wouldn't want them to)...but that's it...eat/drink and write...also a lot of hitching...blah blah...his first long letter to me and he pukes all over the keys. Nahh...just that I'm bored with, no that's wrong, I'm impatient always have been and always will be...I want it now and by god I don't want to wait...

With that the hero bolts into the night eats a pizza and chokes to death on a soggy mushroom...mafia plot to publish his works posthumously and rake in coins he would have never made in life...

George...Come to the party if you can, should be fun if everybody is in a decent mood...though it seems that Phil's leaving has given everybody that summer vacation blues and the desire to split this burg for the hinterlands be they iowa nebraska or elsewhere...drop me a word or six and i'm always this way...

Ricardo

Mind Grenades from a Broken Body

OR THE SURREAL LIFE OF THE DISCIPLINED SPIRIT

Josephine Miles, Collected Poems, 1930–83, *University of Illinois Press, 1998, 260 pp, $34.95 cloth, $1995 paper.*

osephine Miles was one of the great ones—a marvelous poet, critic, gifted educator, mentor to the Beats, originator, and remarkable woman.

She was in fact the first female teacher to be tenured in the English Department at the University of California, Berkeley, where she spent her entire academic career. She was the editor of anthologies and critical texts, and the author of a large body of work, including fourteen critical books on poetic style and language, with titles like *Major Adjectives in English Poetry: From Wyatt to Auden*, *Pathetic Fallacy in the Nineteenth Century*, and the three-volume *Continuity of Poetic Language: Studies in English Poetry from the 1640's to the 1940's*. Her accomplishments are all the more remarkable owing to a lifelong struggle with crippling arthritis which left her hunched, bent, and wheelchair bound.

The University of Illinois Press has given us a gift by reprinting the final volume of Miles's poetic career. When first published in 1983, the book won seven awards, including the Lenore Marshall Poetry Prize from the *Nation* for best book of the year, selected by Josephine Jacobsen, Donald Justice, and Alfred Corn. It was also one of three finalists for the 1983 Pulitzer Prize. A.R. Ammons declared this collection, "one of the finest and solidest bodies of poetry to be found in this country."

The work in this volume drew from Miles's previous ten collections and added twenty-one uncollected poems. Her wry, witty, playful, poetic voice frequently mimicked common speech patterns and reflected on the passing moment. Gems like:

> We have the generation which carries something new not
>   far enough
> And then the generation which carries it too far,
> And then the generation which brings it back again.

An esteemed technical poet who wrote books on both the "vocabulary" and "primary language" of poetry, Miles possessed what Hayden Carruth called "an agile intelligence." She wrote about workers, housewives, regular people, David and Goliath, and celebrated the everyday but not in the conventional sense. Miles didn't approach the real world in the way that other poets from the 1930s did, and was completely immune to the emotional confessional poetry of the 1950s. Her work has more in common with Wallace Stevens, Theodore Roethke, and the dream work of John Berryman. No, Miles was a poet of mind, of intellect, and her work often seems distant by comparison, rendered familiar by the marriage of abstraction to the mundane.

Lawrence R. Smith argues in his essay, "Josephine Miles: Metaphysician of the Irrational," that Miles, while learning from the New Critical readings of the seventeenth-century Metaphysical poets, was in many ways closer to surrealism in much of her work. She used logic to unlock the realm of the subconscious, the imagination, and anticipated the shape of poetry to come after World War II. From "Vacuum":

> In the new lab down on the waterfront
> The tides of moon draw, fibers of the heart
> Compress, constrict, till from this metal shape
> Flows out a foil as thin and consequent
> As moon on water and as moon on wing,
> As moon on man the gold foil of his brain.

You don't expect Miles to play with your head, to play with words the way she does, to deliver the witty bon mot. Yet she does it over and over again. Randall Jarrell, writing about Miles's *Local Measures* in *Poetry and the Age*, said of her work: "Miles specializes in the sly, dry, minimal observation. The poems are conversational elegance of understatement, of a carefully awkward and mannered charm. Everything is just a little off; is, always, the precisely unexpected."

Conversation

Some people talk nothing for four or a hundred
But language for two.
Quips.
Special beruffled style. Do you get it?
You are not supposed to.

Adornment taps the Morse dashes and the sender
Laughs neatly,
Quips.
That was a good one. Do you get it? Wait,
Sometimes he will translate it to you.

Josephine Miles, Smith argues, discovered the world of the irrational in the everyday:

Among the everyday things which Josephine Miles cele-brates are words, particularly slang words and phrases. This is not because she is trying to understand the people in the street who use these terms, but because she is inter-ested in exploring the sheer joy and power of the words themselves, almost as if they were objects or "images."

But as the turbulence of the '60s caught up everything in its path, Miles's work became increasingly more agitated and political. Her poems from the 1967 collection *Kinds of Affection*, written between 1962 and 1969, are the darkest, yet the following selections from throughout her oeuvre show that Miles was always wielding a political razor.

Cloud

Strontium 90 is slowly falling out
From the great heights of the Stratosphere,
It settles
On leaves, on housetops, on ourselves
When we stand out under the open sky,
It settles down

In the grass which cows mull into their milk,
Which children gulp into their skeletons.
How much of the stuff is now in the skies?
A good deal is up there.
It drifts and settles out,
Half of it in about twenty-four years.

In my wristbone turns up Strontium 90 a-crumble
In your set jaw, its lag.
The mortal dust we have knelt in the dust to
Rises at the horizon, so that we move
Drawing out of the mire and blowing
Clouds of the mire ahead of us as we go.

Or:

Civilian

The largest stock of armaments allows me
A reason not to kill.
Defense Department does the blasting for me
As soundly as I will.

Indeed, can cover a much wider area
Than I will ever score
With a single rifle sent me on approval
From a Sears Roebuck store.

Only the psycho, meaning sick in spirit,
Would aim his personal shot
At anybody; he is sick in spirit
As I am not.

Or:

Government Injunction
Restraining Harlem Cosmetic Co.

They say La Jac Brite Pink Skin Bleach avails not,
They say its Orange Beauty Glow does not glow,
Nor the face grow five shades lighter nor the heart
Five shades lighter. They say no.

They deny good luck, love, power, romance, and inspiration
From La Jac Brite ointment and incense of all kinds,
And condemn in writing skin brightening and whitening
And whitening of minds.

There is upon the Federal Trade Commission a burden of
    glory
So to defend the fact, so to impel
The plucking of hope from the hand, honor from the
    complexion,
Sprite from the spell.

In a review, Gwendolyn Brooks said, "This is not poetry to be used for lullaby purposes. Eye and ear must stand awake, or much of the beauty and intellectual significance will remain on the page."

Miles died too young of pneumonia just two years after this book was originally published. She is remembered today by several literary awards given in her name, including the Josephine Miles Literary Censorship Award.

I can think of no better way to remember the spirit of a woman who championed the work of Allen Ginsberg, ensuring his initial book publication.

Country Porch Lights

Wyatt loves the way the early morning sunlight filters through the red crocheted curtains, the way tiny lattice shapes tattoo Mountain Girl's face and arms, as she sleeps now, curled up beside him on the stark white sheets. And that moment, as the sunlight bathes her face, reminds him of a Julia Cameron photograph, the filtered light lending that quality to her wide forehead, full eyebrows, alabaster skin, and large almond-shaped eyes. Blue eyes. Like his. Why is he always attracted to women with blue eyes? And why do brown-eyed women strike so much fear into him? A puzzle that wants solving.

Of course Mountain Girl isn't her real name. Wyatt just thinks of her that way, relates somehow to the Grateful Dead's "Mountain Girl." He'd been playing "Dark Star" on the drive down the Blue Ridge Parkway and into Carolina to the writer's conference. Now that he's here, at the quaint campus situated upon the mountaintop, he's faced with a conglomeration of brown-eyed women poets, most of whom are writing poetry as therapy from their divorces, mental health departures, or worse. Raised on the mythology of Brodsky and Walcott, it's also clear that some of the women have set their sights on the visiting poet, which is why from the very first day Wyatt has made sure that Mountain Girl was in evidence. Not only is she younger than the brown-eyed flock, she's sharp as a knife, self-reliant, and most especially free of academic baggage or ambition.

Still, this is Wyatt's last morning in Carolina. After lunch the literary encampment will strike their tents, and he will wend his way north through the rhododendrons, mountain laurels, and pines until he reaches Charlottesville, where he will embrace the squalor of his literary life in a two-bedroom apartment. The conference has been lucrative, almost fun, and a pleasant respite from the dark satanic academic mills. He does not relish a return to the adjunct life. And if he could figure out a way, he'd stay with Mountain Girl forever. As it stands, he has to figure out how to say goodbye.

Mountain Girl stirs. She always wakes up happy. How is such a thing possible? Wyatt has never been a morning person. He needs fuel—massive quantities of coffee, sugar, and cigarettes, and on really grim mornings a shot of bourbon—simply to get through the first twenty minutes. Yet here she is purring at him, her smile so big and her warmth incandescent. He wishes he could be like this in the morning, could be like her. This is their last day together. And Callie, for that's Mountain Girl's actual name, feels as much a part of him now after a week in the Carolina mountains as an arm or leg or heart. She folds her arms and lips and hips into him now, and he is absorbed. Flowers must feel this way about the sun, he thinks, as he succumbs to her irresistible nature.

☀

"I LIKE SOME OF THESE lines very much, but I believe you really need to read more living writers. You need to be aware of what's being written right now, Mar..." and Wyatt blanked. What was her name?

"I'm Martha."

"Martha, of course, of course." Why did he have to have a class with a Martha, a Margo, and a Martine? What were the odds? He had eternal troubles juggling Kathy and Karen. Those two names seemed to be completely interchangeable and had even cost him girlfriends in the Pleistocene epoch of his love life.

"I like Louise Bogan."

"Louise is lovely, but she's quite dead."

Martha's eyes fell. He didn't mean to hurt her, only to give her a kick in the rear.

"Look, can I recommend Heather McHugh, Rita Dove, Sharon Olds, and some of the newer voices like Kim Addonizio, Lynn Crosbie, Elaine Equi, Amy Gerstler, or Erin Moure."

Martha dutifully wrote down every name, mangling most of the spellings.

"Seriously, if you saw what some of these poets were writing about it, it would broaden your palette, give you a lot more subjects to tackle in your own work."

"Do you really think so?"

Absofuckinglutely, he thought. Yet he said, "I think you'll love their work."

Three more student conferences to go. His class was scattered across the ramparts of the flagstone patio, stacked up like jets coming into Dulles Airport. Each face betrayed the same combination of anxiety, insecurity, and fear.

Wyatt sighed. The view of the mountains, cascading into the distance like a green and black ocean, was all but wasted on these people. Many of the students were from nearby Asheville or Charlotte, and if they'd seen it once they'd seen it a thousand times. The view was just background to them. The urban poets, the few who'd made their way from New York City or Boston, seemed just as oblivious.

"Hey dude."

"Spence. Hey man, how's it going?" Jerry Spence was teaching in New Orleans and the only other writer at the conference he actually knew very well. They'd met at the Virginia Center for the Creative Arts colony where Spence had been writing a novel when he wasn't juggling two women (a performance artist and a poet) during a month-long stay. How he did that without offending either one (both knew and still raved about Spence and his work) kept Wyatt in permanent awe of his friend.

"Do you need a drink as bad as I do?"

"I'm getting there."

"Debbie and I are heading into town for lunch and beer. You're welcome to join us."

Wyatt could already see his next student getting jumpy and beginning to contort her body like a human tuning fork in his direction, completely stalemated over the etiquette required when it came to interrupting two instructors.

Lunch with Spence and Debbie? Debbie was Deborah Fitzsimmons, heir to a newspaper fortune, socialite by birth and libertine by inclination. Her sensuality, artifice, and penchant for drama, not to mention her large brown eyes, made Wyatt very nervous. He'd avoided her as much as possible all week. Still, escape was escape, and the cloyingly sweet director of the conference needed to be avoided at all costs.

"Perfect. What time?"

"12:30. Debbie's driving her Jag."

Wyatt waved the human tuning fork over, and while she got situated and dragged her metal chair across the flagstones (scarring them), so she could touch knees with him, he watched as Jerry corralled another of his army of male disciples, wrapped a beefy arm across his shoulders, and led him to an Adirondack chair situated fifty yards away at the opposite end of the patio.

☀

THERE HAD BEEN NOTHING TO set Sal's Mountain Market apart from any of the other ubiquitous country stores Wyatt had passed on his drive south. He'd decided early on Sunday that he would keep to the Blue Ridge Parkway mountain roads rather than make better time through the valley on I-77. He was in no particular hurry and he loved to drive, especially as the temperature in the mountains was a good ten degrees colder than the valley below. He'd stopped at several places en route—sometimes for gas, sometimes for ice tea, other times for apples. Sal's Mountain Market was just beyond Linville Falls, a big white rectangular box like all the others with racks outside for bulk fruit and vegetables and a more conventional convenience store interior. All of the usual tourist trap items were on display. And the mountain folk who worked the place were as interchangeable as the stores. He was chitchatting with a wrinkled grandmother about the drought (it hadn't rained in two weeks) when Mountain Girl came in from the parking lot. Wyatt's eyes were instantly drawn to the red kerchief she had wrapped around her short boyish auburn-colored crop. And with the late afternoon sun pouring through the door behind her, it looked for a second, as his eyes adjusted, like there was an aura surrounding her, sparks flying in every direction.

"Lordy, it's a hot one today, Miss Rhea," she said waving to the older woman, then walking behind the counter where she opened a door in a big gray metal fixture, and then bent over so far she almost disappeared into the frosty air.

The halo business had rooted Wyatt in place, the music in her voice had altered his universe, and now he couldn't take his eyes off her generous proportions—real hips and the six inches of bare back visible between her flimsy tank top and tattered blue jean cutoffs.

Miss Rhea caught him staring and laughed, waved a fly away, and went back to the register. Wyatt was distracted for a moment, though watched as Mountain Girl rose out of the gray fixture with two large handfuls of ice, which she pressed to her face. Water dripped down her cheeks, across her wrists, onto her white tank top, and a puddle rapidly spread across the wood floor. Her eyes were closed as she turned. Wyatt just stared. And when those eyes opened, they bored right into him.

"You want some?" she asked.

Lord almighty did he. Yet she meant the ice, and he must have made enough of a nod yes that she moved toward him, seeming to grow in stature though she was barely five foot. When she pressed the remaining ice into his face, Wyatt made an involuntary gasp and jerked backwards, but he couldn't move. Mountain Girl's fingertips held his jaw fast in her icy grip. He was as good as gone.

Later, on the porch outside, she apologized. "I'm sorry for getting your shirt all wet. That wasn't smart on my part. But it felt good, didn't it?"

Wyatt watched her pick some ice from her tea and pop it into her large, soft mouth. She chewed the ice and surveyed the tourists who were multiplying as evening approached. His shirt had dried out pretty quickly. He'd sat and listened to her talk about her family's market and spent a lot of time studying her bare feet as she slipped off her sandals and stepped first one and then the other foot in and out of a mud puddle. She'd coat her toes with mud and then swirl them around in the water and wash them clean again. Over and over. And it seemed completely playful and unconscious. He couldn't recall saying a word.

How he ended up in her bed, what he said to her, and anything that happened in their first twelve hours together was a blur. Wyatt had attached himself to a force of nature, and her indomitable spirit was so all-consuming that in his memory she'd simply taken charge—she'd fed him, asked him to come home, made the first move, stripped off his clothes, and then possessed him. He wasn't sure whose limbs were whose. Where she ended and he began. He'd never experienced anything like this before. Time had stopped. Of course it hadn't really and he was required to be at the writer's conference in time for Monday's morning classes.

☼

THEY'D SURVIVED DEBBIE'S NINETY MILES per hour drive up and down the primitive mountain roads in her convertible. When they made a high speed turn onto new gravel, Wyatt had been certain they were dead. He was in the back seat facing the cliff side when it felt like only three tires were still on the road, and no guardrails to stop them from plunging straight down into the abyss. Somehow Debbie had pulled the convertible out of the skid and they'd made it to the restaurant in Little Switzerland alive. Surprisingly, it was the sort of place owned and operated by old hippies who'd made their way up into the hills from Asheville back in the day and had progressed from mung bean entrees to sweet veggie chili, massive salads which contained fresh pumpkin and sunflower seeds, homemade bread and dressings, plus one of the best roast beef sandwiches Wyatt had ever tasted.

The CD jukebox was contemporary and played everything from Massive Attack to Alanis Morrisette. When Sarah McLaughlin sang "Possession," Wyatt shivered. Because that's how Mountain Girl made him feel. He identified with the song completely.

"Nothing ever goes on at these conferences," Debbie said, her voice flat and desultory. She had opened her sandwich over her plate and dropped the contents in a pile. Now she was poking at it with her preternatural fingers and extracting only the roast beef, which she draped above her Lancôme cerise-red lips before swallowing.

Wyatt grinned. He knew Spence had slept with Debbie last summer at the McDowell Colony. And he knew for a fact that Spence was a tireless lover at colonies and conferences. Debbie had her own peculiar reputation.

"You know that's not true, Debbie," Spence laughed, sipping his Corona. "You're just bored."

She pouted. "It's true. If Madzilla says one more word to me, I'll rip her a new pair of lungs."

Madzilla was the conference director, a woman so devoid of artistic personality that her beige and yellow outfits and singsong aphorisms seemed more alive than she did.

"She called me arrogant," Debbie said.

Spence choked on a big bite of sandwich and quickly recovered. He was laughing, with his head buried in his arm.

Debbie was the only writer who had seemingly sought to shock everybody at the conference. She was wearing a black leather cat suit, one that Emma Peel might find comfortable, and the front, rather than housing a zipper, featured a criss-crossing of leather strings. Add her black pointy faux motor-cycle boots and silver bangles and dark wraparound shades into the mix and she was like something out of Fellini. And let's not forget the waist-length jet-black hair. No, the silver Jaguar convertible might have been the only predictible thing about her.

Wyatt had stayed below Debbie's radar in previous encounters. She'd always aimed her acid tongue and/or pred-atory sexuality at others. He was strictly supporting cast. Yet now, perhaps because she was lonely, she focused on Wyatt for the first time.

"And you, you don't even know I'm alive."

Spence laughed again.

Wyatt noted the dare in his eyes. "Now Debbie, you know that's not true," he said too defensively.

"I love your poems. They're so sensitive," Debbie said. She reached across the table and took his right hand, which she now caressed with long multicolored fingernails. Wyatt had seen her do this before, only now he was the victim. "I think you understand women. More than most of the misog-ynists, slobs, and cretins pretending to write poetry."

"Thank you, Debbie," Wyatt attempted to regain his hand, although Debbie held on fast and continued to use her nails to abrade his skin. "That means a lot coming from you."

"That's total horseshit, Debbie. You don't have one sensi-tive nerve," Spence laughed again, and Debbie turned her black lenses his way for a second.

Wyatt half expected a heat ray to disintegrate Spence.

"Don't listen to him," she said, removing the sunglasses, directing her large brown eyes at Wyatt. "I'm just a girl."

Oh no. Wyatt wanted out of this in the worst way.

"You're not sleeping with anybody special, are you?" Debbie asked. Her voice dripped with lust.

Why me why now? Wyatt had no idea.

Spence clapped a hand on his back and said, "I'm going to go pay the check, partner."

Wyatt felt instantly betrayed, and for a second like he'd fallen into a giant spider's web. As a kid he'd been obsessed with King Kong and the men who'd fallen off the log when Kong shook it. What happened to those men had been a dark mystery that kept Wyatt and his friends awake at night.

"Hey lover." Wyatt looked up as Mountain Girl leaned over and kissed him. She totally ignored Debbie, who let go of Wyatt's hand, and then planted herself firmly in his lap. She wore a brown cowboy hat, and her breasts were all but tumbling out of a faded red plaid shirt. "I'm Callie, you're dressed in black, you must be a poet, too."

Debbie ignored Callie's proffered hand and seemed to visibly vibrate with anger. Spence reappeared shaking his head. Wyatt was so happy, so relieved, he was almost humming.

Debbie stood, replaced her sunglasses, and then mock-whispered in Wyatt's face loud enough for everybody to hear, "I hope you catch something."

"Least ways he'll still be human," Mountain Girl yelled as Debbie slammed the screen door. Spence did a double take but saluted before heading out to the Jag. "Which is more than I can say for her. What crawled up her butt and died?"

"Callie—"

"Was she hitting on you?"

"Callie—"

"Wait a minute. Tell me you haven't made love—who in their right mind could even call it that with a bitch like her—tell me you haven't. Wyatt, you haven't, have you?"

"No."

"Praise be. Now c'mon."

"Where are we going?"

"You'll see. It's a surprise."

"But I've got a class at three p.m." Wyatt looked at the clock—a big slab of slate on the wall behind the counter with hands but no numbers. He thought it read one forty-five.

"So? You've got an hour and change. I swear I'll get you back without more than the normal wear and tear."

"Yeah."

"Just the usual. Broke head, busted butt."

"Great."

"Hey I rescued you, didn't I?"

"You did."

"What the hell else you want?" She stuck her tongue out and ran laughing out to her Jeep.

☀

CALLIE KNEW THE MOUNTAINS SO well that her speed wasn't anywhere near as terrifying as Debbie's had been. She had them to a mountain pull-off in no time, and then she took Wyatt's hand and led him down a switchback trail. She was whistling. Wyatt had never been able to whistle. Soon he heard water. And then the woods opened up into a wide clearing and there was a waterfall, one that poured down in a solid sheet from a canopy of rocks above. Callie stripped quickly and took his hand.

"C'mon, get naked. Get out of those scary clothes."

And Wyatt stripped to his black skivvies.

"Is all your underwear black?" she asked, pointing as he dropped them on the pile of clothing.

"No."

"You're lying."

And then she led him out onto a mostly flat rocky basin under the canopy of water that seemed to have been carved from the surrounding rock with an ice cream scoop. The water proved icy cold. Wyatt tried to let go of Callie's hand and run, but she laughed and pulled him all the way under the full force of the falls. He was screaming and shivering while she laughed. And then her soft mouth just swallowed his and soon she led him off the trail a ways and they made love in a bed of moss and ferns and long red pine needles. Wyatt had never been happier in his entire life.

☼

MARTINE WAS THE BEST OF the poets in his workshop. She'd lived a diverse life—everything from army wife to beauty queen, from mother of three kids to airplane pilot. She'd climbed three of the seven summits, traveled equatorial Africa, and eaten fugu. She scattered exotic words and locales throughout her work and if they'd been anything more than mere snapshots, Wyatt would have aspired to one day be a blurber on the back cover of one of her infinite books. Unfortunately, Martine had nothing to say beyond the surfaces she saw and the events she moved through like a voyeur.

"You have got to find a way to become more emotionally connected to all of these great scenarios you've developed."

"I've tried. I mean I have known suffering."

"Not in the poems."

"And I've loved, too." And she batted her brown eyes.

Oh my god, beam me up Scotty, Wyatt thought. He flashed briefly on his mom and dad in Schenectady, their suburban existence. He thought of his sister and her plastic Republican husband and their true believer flag-waving offspring in the dreary swamps of Florida, and he knew that Martine was simply alien corn. There was no way he was ever going to make her deep or artistic. She had the sort of life story that most writers would kill to own the film rights to. Yet she was never going to be capable of accessing the material herself.

"I hate to interrupt, but may I have a word with you?" It was Madzilla, the dreaded conference director. "Is that okay, Martine? I promise I won't steal Mr. Stevenson away for very long."

Wyatt followed behind the bottled blonde, adorned in pink and white today. She reminded him of Betty White.

"In my office, please." She motioned with one hand.

Wyatt remembered being sent to the office in grade school, how scary it had been. This woman was treating him exactly like a misbehaving school brat.

"Now sit."

Wyatt sat.

"Mr. Stevenson—"

"Wyatt."

"—it has come to my attention that you have been fraternizing with one of the locals. Is that true?"

"What business is that of yours?" Wyatt was both angry and amused. Fraternizing?

The director smiled a sickly sweet smile. "No business at all, of course. Your private life is of no concern of mine, except for how it impacts the infrastructure of this conference."

"Impacts the infrastructure?"

"Precisely."

The woman droned on and on, though Wyatt tuned it all out. The basic gist was that he couldn't bring Mountain Girl onto the campus again.

"But she lives here," he said.

"That's beside the point."

And then there was more blah blah blah bad examples blah blah blah setting precedents squiddely doo b.s. And that's when Wyatt looked up and realized that Madzilla's eyes were deep brown.

☼

"SHE READ YOU THE RIOT act?" Spence handed him a shot of Bush Mills.

"Yes."

"I'm sorry man, I tried to stop her."

"Stop who?"

"Debbie."

"Debbie?"

"Boy, I've never seen her so pissed off. I think she came down to this conference solely to score one Wyatt Stevenson. I'm just sorry she had to go and stand up in the dining hall and announce it to the entire world."

Wyatt's insides imploded. "She did what?"

"The usual Debbie. You know, scorched earth. All about you and how much she loved you and how you rejected her and were sleeping with some local cow."

Wyatt groaned. "Perfect."

"Don't worry about Debbie. I can distract her until you're gone. No biggie. Don't sweat it."

"Thanks, Spence. And for the drink."

"And partner, don't let Debbie or Madzilla or anybody else keep you away from that local color. She's a keeper."

☼

SO WYATT WAS GLAD HE'D spent every night save one at Callie's place. She'd only slept in his room once—though she came and went whenever she could get away from working at Sal's Mountain Market—and even then they'd kind of snuck into his dorm room. The bed had been too squeaky, and they'd put the mattress on the floor. After making love, he'd been maudlin.

"I don't think I could live up here in the mountains," he said. "I see those lights in the darkness and each one's a house. I think I'd be afraid. They're so lonely, so far apart."

"Lonely? I don't see them that way at all. I think they're beacons, tiny islands of life in the dark."

"That was poetic."

"It was? Poetic enough for a city slicker poet like you? Hmm? You're blushing." And then she shouted, "Now hear this: the hotshot poet who only wears black jeans and black shirts and even black underwear is blushing."

Wyatt instinctively put his hand over her mouth.

Callie peeled his fingers back. She had fire in her eyes now. "Don't you ever—"

Wyatt started to cover her mouth again, and in the resulting struggle she began tickling him.

"Hey, stop, no tickling."

"And he's ticklish, too," she shrieked. "You're in trouble now. I grew up with three older brothers and there's not a ticklish bone in my body."

"Stop," Wyatt tried to roll away and protect himself, but she was all over him.

"Yeah." She stopped. Pausing. Her fingers at the ready. "You going to write a poem about me?"

"What?"

She tickled his feet.

"Maybe."

She tickled his sides.

"Yes, stop. Okay. I will."

She paused above him with her fingers poised.

"Really?"

"Yes."

She howled and fell on him, her tongue working into his mouth. And Wyatt kissed back and they laughed and rolled around on the floor until daybreak.

☀

WYATT'S BUICK REGAL WAS ALL loaded up. He had a backpack of CDs ready to load for the long drive home. All that remained was the big farewell lunch before the writers left the mountain for another year.

Mountain Girl had fed him earlier, helped him gather his things, and dropped him by the dining hall. They hadn't said goodbyes yet. Wyatt told her he'd stop by Sal's Mountain Market as Callie had to work the morning shift, though they hadn't discussed his imminent departure at all. They both avoided the subject. Wyatt figured once the passion faded, the day-to-day grind on the mountain would be impossible. He couldn't imagine living this far from culture. And what would he do? Could he take Mountain Girl back to

Charlottesville? She would fit in, but would surely wither so far from the mountain. Sal's Mountain Market was a family business. Someday it might be hers.

It was after lunch before the usual round of thanks and memories, speeches and congratulations, and formal good-byes was almost at an end. People were restless, ready to hit the road, when Mountain Girl slipped in the dining room back door.

Spence noticed her first. He elbowed Wyatt, who turned and saw Callie wending her way through the tables toward him, hefting a basket full of peaches, her clogs banging loudly off the linoleum. Debbie noticed her, too, and was in the process of standing, when Spence put an arm around her waist, pulled her into his lap, and rubbed his other hand down the front of her pants. Poor Spence. He would pay dearly for starting that fire, Wyatt thought.

Madzilla had saved her farewell speech for last, using her role as director to subject the participants to another round of self-indulgent aphorisms and psycho-babble. She droned on seamlessly, yet paused when Mountain Girl arrived at Wyatt's table.

"Hey you, I brought you these for the road." She sat down, pulled her blue bandana out of her hair. He'd rarely seen her without one.

"Look, Callie, I—"

"They're really ripe," she said.

"As ripe as—" Debbie started to say until Spence just stuck his tongue down her throat, stood, lifted her in his arms, and carried her quickly out the back. By the time they hit the door, Debbie was responding in kind.

"Yuck," Callie said.

"He's doing it for me. For us," Wyatt said.

"Well, it's not worth it. That's a virus in black leather." She smiled.

"Now who is your friend, I don't believe we've been intro-duced." Madzilla was hoarse from her speechifying so spoke too loud for somebody standing by his elbow. He'd been semi-aware of the applause, indicating the conference was over, but hadn't been paying attention.

"Callie Mae Tyson," she said, standing and shaking hands.

"Do you live on the mountain?"

"Born and bred. My folks own Sal's Mountain Market."

"Do they now?"

"Yes, ma'am."

Here it comes, Wyatt thought, Madzilla's in the wind-up. But before she could say anything else, Wyatt was surrounded by Martine and Martha and Margo and his other students, all of them telling him how much they'd learned, how much they'd written, how wonderful he was, and how hopeful they were that the director would bring him back next summer so they could continue under his tutelage.

"I'll consider it," Madzilla said huffily and exited.

While the rest of the students and teachers left for their cars and rides to the airport in Asheville, Callie and Wyatt sat surrounded by peaches.

"They adore you."

"Well, the director doesn't."

"Big duh there. I mean your students. You must be a good teacher."

"Dunno."

"Oh and modest. Oh my. What a crock," she said beating him with a fist.

"Stop."

"You going to let me read some poems? Now that you're leaving me and all."

"I—"

"Don't worry, I knew you were one of these mountain conference arty types when I met you."

"How did you—"

"That haircut for one thing, and the Buick Regal. God what an awful car."

"You can take NASCAR out of the mountains but you can't take NASCAR out of the mountain girls."

"Damn straight. And you know what else? No? You don't? You won't ever forget me, buster. No how. I own you."

Wyatt rolled his eyes. "Pretty cocky, aren't you?"

"I don't believe so. I've got you wrapped tight." And then she patted her ass. "You want some?" she said shaking side to side in an exaggerated singsong. "You'll be back next year."

"So you knew I was smitten from the start?"

"Here's you," and Callie stuck out her tongue and went all pop-eyed and drooly. "Miss Rhea will be talking about you the rest of her days," Callie cackled.

"And if I don't come back?" Wyatt crossed his arms defiantly and turned away.

Callie got close and whispered in his ear. "Next summer they'll have another guy who wears all black." He turned away, though she hung onto his neck laughing "I'll bet it promises one in the brochure."

"You'll be married with twins by next summer."

She snorted. "Like hell."

"Petty and Dale."

"Ooh, I'll get you." And she started slapping at him. And then just stopped, allowing him to capture her hands. And hold them above her head. And bring them back down to her sides. And just kissed him, and kissed him, and kissed him some more.

"Hey, how did you know to save me that day at the restaurant?"

"Just lucky. You weren't in the dining hall so I gave up finding you and came over to Little Switzerland to kill some time with Jerry and Isabelle. They own Swiss Alps Cafe. And of course when I saw Leather Child holding your hand, I was so jealous I wanted to kick your butt."

"So you came inside to kick my butt."

"Somebody had to." Callie smiled and then looked stricken.

"What?"

"Damn. Now I've gone and told you I was jealous."

It began to rain as she followed him out to the car.

"Drive safe," she said.

"Look Callie—"

"I'm not going to let you talk. Don't say anything. You didn't say anything when we met, so don't start now. In fact, I figured you for a deaf-mute for the first hour or so." She laughed.

"I—"

"No. Don't." She put a hand on his mouth. "You know how I feel. I know how you feel."

Wyatt handed her a copy of his book of poems. They seemed completely inadequate, but they were all he had. Her basket of peaches was on the floor on the passenger side. She'd let him off the hook. How could he leave?

"Thanks for this," she said clutching the book to her chest. "Now get the hell out of here," she motioned to the road.

Wyatt left, "Dark Star" once more blaring out of the speakers, the ripe peaches spilling from the basket and rolling around the car floor with every curve of the winding mountain road.

Confessions of a Literary Editor

During the six-month period from 11/1/85 to 5/1/86, I read eight thousand-plus short stories and novel excerpts as possibilities for inclusion in *Gargoyle* magazine's special Fiction/86 issue planned for later this year. (This is an avalanche of work, compared to the submissions for the Fiction/82 and Fiction/84 volumes.) From this incredible pile of submissions, my assistant editor, Gretchen Johnsen, and three screeners and I took twenty-five stories for what will ultimately be a paperback volume of close to four hundred pages. This is even more astonishing when you consider that *Gargoyle* only pays with one copy of the finished book, no cash.

A word about the screeners. After ten years of reading every submission, I had to call a halt. The numbers are too overwhelming. Our screeners (Cynthia Cotts, Ann Downer, and Susan Weinberg) handled every story by writers I've never dealt with before, new names, etc. I handled all name writers and people with whom I'm familiar. It was a pretty good system, basically freeing me from the influx of new material. But it was difficult to give up even that much power, because a large part of being an editor is playing talent scout. You never know what the mail will bring. I've always tried to read every submission all the way through. If there's a glimmer of hope on page 10, I say so. And I frequently write things like: chop the first nine pages, your story begins there. If a story isn't geared for us or I think it will go better elsewhere, I steer writers to another market; I basically treat writers the way I wish other editors treated me when I send out my poems or stories. Some writers get in the magazine first try (there are several new names in F/86), while others get rejected forty-five to fifty times before we find something we can live with.

On average, *Gargoyle* takes one out of every two hundred and fifty stories we receive and one out of every thousand poems. Through the years, as the magazine matured, as we began to earn a track record and the reviews came in on both F/82 and F/84, the numbers have grown exponentially. During the same period, the short story has become a hot property again for the major conglomerate publishers in New York and the media at large. During the '70s, it was almost impossible to give away short stories, or for any writer to land a book of stories unless he had a novel under his belt or a run of fiction in the *New Yorker*. The advent and growth of the creative writing programs now approaching the status of literary guilds has created an abundance of writers with an urge to see their work in print. The role of certification played by the Associated Writing Program, National Endowment for the Arts, and state arts councils has encouraged more and more people to try their hand at fiction. It's not uncommon now for writers to begin their careers with short story collections. Ray Carver (the most imitated writer in America, from my perspective) is a product of creative writing programs, and he studied with the late John Gardner); a creative writing teacher himself at Syracuse, he's served a long apprenticeship in the small presses. His acceptance as one of the premier short fiction practitioners today is synonymous with the endorsement of creative writing programs. It doesn't matter what you think of him or his new realistic minimalism. He's the major reason students are flocking to Bread Loaf, Iowa, Johns Hopkins, Stanford, Syracuse, Virginia, Brown, Arkansas, Houston, Columbia, et al. Short fiction seems to be the poetry of our day, perfectly geared to short MTV attention spans. The meta-fiction novels of Pynchon, Barth, Gass, Donald Barthelme, and company were bloated to fit the times, the sensibilities of the '60s. Amy Hempel and Lorrie Moore (two of the "Girls from Knopf" and part of the twenty-to-under-thirty crowd) have been described by critics as writers of "sushi-sized" fictions. It's bite-sized entertainment, which goes down with no fuss.

Easily four thousand of the fictions received at *Gargoyle* were close imitations of Carver/Jayne Anne Phillips/Ann Beattie/William Kennedy/Bobbie Ann Mason/Stephen Dixon–styled "Matters of Life and Death." (So named for a book of realistic fiction edited by Tobias Wolff, who teaches at Syracuse with Carver.) Most of the stories are about finding patterns in mundane situations, blueprints for survival, and feature a reductive prose, stripped of emotion and honed to a spare resonance, where details and props are more important than action. Ann Beattie was a precursor of this flat delivery, and she owes everything to Hemingway—as does Carver.

Most of the New Realist stories dwell on one or two characters, usually deal with alcoholism in one way or another, and/or with divorce (has anybody noticed that almost every one of the baby boomer writers is either gay or from a broken home?), and include tragic scenes in trailer parks, condos, or shopping malls. Most deal with family relations or other semi-violent confrontations.

Dialogue is more important than exposition. (Exposition is out in the '80s.) Speakers are almost always designated by "he said" or "she said." Second-person narrators are often featured (both Frederick Barthelme and Jay McInerney have made this legitimate).

Consumer products and brand names have made a big comeback as foundation. TV plays an active role, with actual transcription of what's coming from the screen often relating to or commenting on the action, what action there is.

Other trends? The one I find most prevalent works against that old saw of the '60s: "Write what you know." No longer. Almost every woman is writing stories from the male perspective, and men seem to be writing from the female point of view. This has been a significant development since

1980 or so. And what's more, most of the women have created more convincing male voices than the men, and ditto for the women created by the male writers. Don't ask me how that happened or what it means. It's just what we've been seeing. On top of that, there's a strange new trend among black women to write science fiction–like fantasies. Strange, because I can't think of any black women science fiction writers to speak of. I think it's wonderful! Black men seem to be concentrating on novels rather than stories, while the women explore and expand the shorter form.

Satire seems to be a lost art form, and we didn't see enough well-crafted humor. No sports stories to speak of— for some reason, we don't seem to attract them. Maybe writers save those for assaults on Roger Angell at the *New Yorker*, or other big slicks. Don't know. We'd be interested. So many stories are the same old thing. And I think, generally, that's what we're against...that same old tired story. We get too many submitters who believe that *Saturday Evening Post*–styled fiction is still viable in the '80s. It isn't. We rarely run anything approaching a genre story. And there's nothing more boring than another story about a dying grandmother, cancer victim, or burial ceremony, as though death can be brought to bear for its sheer dramatic leverage. Many of the stories we read wouldn't have been sent to us in the first place if people had ever seen the magazine. We saw the usual post-holocaust scenarios, inscrutable experimental doodlings, bad Hemingway or Bukowski imitations, derivative girl-meets-boy maneuvers, or one-dimensional TV rip-offs. Most were good, with many centering on similar subjects, themes, and very nearly the same experiences. In the end, roughly a hundred stories were serious possibilities. With a few borderline stories, we asked for new endings, fine-tuning, or compression.

By the end of six months, we'd accepted twenty-five stories or novel excerpts that we felt were the best of what's being written today. I'd never heard of seven of the writers before. Nine others have ties to the area. One is an American in Denmark. Those who made the final cut tend toward a poetic synthesis of the New Realism and the surreal. In fact, we've privately called this our "wings and things" issue because so many of the stories have to do with angels, airplanes, winged insects, the shuttle disaster, nuns, priests, and otherworldly visitations. This trend was also seen a lot in the stories we didn't take. (We wonder about the implications.) If, indeed, the short story is the poetry of the '80s, then we're publishing the new metaphysical poets. This new hybrid, part wild experimental art commentary and part realism, is epitomized by writers like Toby Olson and W.P. Kinsella, and seems to be the new direction for those New Realists like Frederick Barthelme, Carver, and Mary Robison, who are moving away from the terrain the rest of the New Realists have carved out. The final product may not be something akin to Ted Mooney's *Easy Travel* to *Other Planets* or Kathryn Kramer's *Handbook for Visitors from Outer Space*, but language is important, sentences ring out like lines of verse, something happens, and—most important of all for me—I get some sense of everyday experience. I don't necessarily want to document anyone's life, but there are aspects of this city that aren't represented in popular novels and have little to do with the government. My D.C. is writers, artists, and musicians, struggling to be heard. Living in cheap apartments (for here), hitting the fern bar happy hours for the free food, hanging out at the 9:30 Club, d.c. space, or the WPA, attending art openings, free concerts, Redskins games, etc. One wishes more people were aware that there are Washingtonians here, be they Chinese, Salvadoran, or whatever, who are not living on Capitol Hill.

Now that it's over, I'm burned out. Time to take my first break in ten years and rest. I'll start reading manuscripts again in December. Until then, I intend to get back to my own writing, read some books (instead of manuscripts for a change), and catch some flicks.

Good Hope Road

The gospel lady who called
for the book buy in Southeast
had taught piano lessons

and owned more sheet music
than I'd ever seen before or since.

Sellers always tell you
"I have a lot of books."
Yet rarely do they own more

than one semi-empty, knickknack
paddywhacked freestanding bookcase.

My helper had as many (if not more)
tats than Harvey Keitel in *The Piano*.
Elaborate Maori ink that wrapped

down one arm, clipped an ear,
and covered his sharp features

like kudzu swallows Carolina red clay.
Zeke hefted boxes out to the van and

I cut the well-meaning and sweet gospel
lady a larger than normal check. And then
I drove from Skyland to the Shrimp Boat.

We ordered mumbo wings and trout sandwiches
and ate while Zeke shared how much he loved

smoking Crack and Angel Dust cocktails.
I studied the pink fingerprints the hot sauce
was sculpting into my forlorn white bread.

Still amazed that the gospel lady had owned
almost nothing beyond her Aerosonic stand-up piano
whose yellowing keys clashed with her wallpaper.

She'd been pretty wary about opening her door
when she saw Zeke and his red and blue tats.

Told me she was letting the sheet music go
because she was getting glaucoma and
besides, she knew all of that music by heart

after teaching in the D.C. public school system
for more than forty turbulent years. I wished

I could have cut her a larger check. And was
sorry I didn't ask her to play something for us,
some music that might have soothed Zeke's

death metal soul, or might have made me feel
less than a carpetbagger on her side of the river.

6
SUGAR MOUNTAIN

(a Triptych)

For David and Vicki Greisman,
who've stood by me through the years.

"Oh to live on Sugar Mountain
With the barkers and the colored balloons
You can't be twenty on Sugar Mountain
Though you're thinking that you're leaving there too
soon
You're leaving there too soon."
    —*Neil Young*

"It's so expensive just to get older."
    —*Nils Lofgren*

HAL
Greetings from the Ether

HAL HAD THE DOG DREAM again last night. There he sits, some sort of shepherd mutt, three-quarters of the way across four lanes at the dip in the road where one hill starts up into another.

The mutt almost made it. He looks like a young gray wolf in the twilight; his huge tongue lolling out, as though he were just trying to cool off—not half mangled. He's alive though—poor guy. And his hind legs are smashed beyond recognition, flattened on the asphalt. But his head is up and his front legs still work—except cars are coming towards him down the suburban incline at forty miles per. The bastards are speeding. Never mind the thirty mph signage. And the dog can't move, just sits there waiting, just waiting, and there's nothing he can do.

On a good night, Hal watches the dog. Moves to lift him out of harm's way. On a bad night, Hal is the dog.

TAYLOR
Bosch & Bruegel = The Original Glimmer Twins

BORED. LOOKING FOR SIGNS. SITTING on the patio riffling art books for ideas. Writing in this journal and trying to finish a paper for art history. Embracing the new dark ages. Absorbing Pre-Millennial tension through my pores. Wondering if the world will really come to an end at midnight December 31st. I think I want to paint the apocalypse.

Hieronymous Bosch (1450?–1516).

His real name was Jeroen van Aeken or Aken or Aachen. Bosch comes from his birthplace Hertogenbosch, a town in northern Brabant near the border with Belgium.

The birds in Bosch's work are malicious. Weird demons with beaks feeding red berries to humans. They are everywhere in *The Garden of Earthly Delights*. The birds in progression through the geometric shapes in *The Creation of Eve* panel. Owl faces appear in many paintings. The crows on the bones in *The Vagabond*.

Pieter Bruegel the Elder (often Brueghel) (1525?–1569)

Born in Breda, also in northern Brabant. Considered by many a Bosch imitator. Perhaps at first but not in the later stages. His engraving of Pride from the *Seven Deadly Sins* features owl faces and birdlike demons, and there are all sorts of crows flying around in *The Triumph of Death*, the paintings which are perhaps the most directly influenced by Bosch's visionary art. But his later work is different. His peasants as timely now as they were then. What faces. You can see the direct lineage from Bruegel's faces in *Peasant Kermis* and *The Peasant Wedding* carried over into the work of Maxfield Parrish.

Still there are ravens in *Christ Carrying the Cross*. One sitting ominously on the death wheel atop the pole. More ravens in the air. Birds circling the hunters returning home in *The Hunters in the Snow*, one of the five surviving panels of the *Months* series. These birds seem to have more in common with Van Gogh's crows in the fields. They're realistic. Perhaps Bruegel just noticed birds more because there were fewer buildings or things to distract him. They are always sitting in the bare treetops, as though looking down, studying the human condition.

What if? Bosch & Bruegel as contemporary pals. Hanging out. Visiting each other's studio. Going to a dance party. Maybe doing the visuals.

If alive today would they go to Kosovo? Chechnya? Paint those scenes?

dad says rent Ken Russell's *The Devils*. More weirdness. King Louis XIII dresses Protestants up as crows and shoots them. But that's just a small taste of what happens. Very off-the-wall. Predictable dad weirdness.

MONA
Wooden Nickel

"I FELL IN LOVE WITH Neil Young the very first time I ever heard his helpless helpless voice. At home in Bethany I was the summery cinnamon girl he sang about you know. I mean I dreamt about guys like him. Not Canadian, or epileptic, or anything like Neil is, but moody broody boys who maybe had a chopper or could help me escape this townie beach life.

"Well, trust me, life at the beach isn't everything. Not after you're in high school anyway. It was bad enough to get married at eighteen, but at least we were in the city. If I'd stayed in Bethany I'd have married one of the charter boat captains or rednecks. Probably have six kids. I wouldn't have landed the degree eventually, wouldn't have become a teacher. Now look at me. Who'd have guessed that the beach bunny would wind up teaching high school English? Not me. Not at eighteen. Not when I was trying to do anything and everything to get the hell out of Dodge, to see the world, to find somebody like Neil Young. Somebody with the answers to all my questions. Of course I know better now. I know that life has more to do with living day by day. I realize the secrets of the universe aren't found in a song. Back then, who knew?

"Hal looked like Neil when we met in College Park. My first husband. He had the same do. We'd hang out at the Varsity Grill or Town Hall and drink scotch. God I could drink back then. Just set 'em up and knock 'em back. I drank most of the boys I knew under the table at the beach when I was fifteen and then when I got to school, I laid waste to them. Hard to believe huh? Me?

"By the time I had my daughter Taylor at eighteen I was old. Not burned out, but definitely been there done that. Hal likes to think that women have power over him and he likes to believe that most women have lived adventurous lives outside of his sphere before they ever hook up with him. That's true I guess. I had lived a pretty wild and chaotic existence before I ever was aware of Hal and his desire to understand everything. I owe Hal my musical education in a lot of ways. Thank you. And he did give me the Buffalo Springfield, which I'd missed. I don't remember all the names of the stuff he played but I recognize songs when I hear them again. I have a good memory for things like that.

"Hal played me the Crosby, Stills, Nash & Young bootleg *Wooden Nickel*. He actually owns a copy. He has almost everything. Tons of old vinyl. Neil talks about this record on another bootleg, *Young Man's Fancy*. I listened to that so much Hal finally made me a tape. It was only after we broke up that I realized Hal was like that, a wooden nickel. Not the real thing at all. He spent all of his days looking the wrong way, backwards, carrying his past around with him like a snail.

"And it's only now that I'm rediscovering my roots, moving back to my folks' place here in town, that I realize Neil Young's songs are all about hope, love, and never giving up. I like that about him. Naïve? Hardly. Nobody's ever called me naïve before. But if you think so, then maybe it's a return to innocence. Something I choose. I pretty much stopped listening to Neil Young after Hal and I split up. Back in 1991. Didn't listen to any music with my second husband. Well, the mariachi bands at the hotel don't count.

"It's funny. I think my subconscious is rediscovering my past and that's why I want to play his songs. Why I want guitar lessons. And at the same time maybe I'm secretly hoping that Neil Young will keep me young in some fashion."

HAL
Truth Squad

HAL'S HAVING ONE OF THOSE really twisted talks with his daughter that he always kidded himself he'd never have.

"So, why did you and Mom split up?" she asks for the umpteenth time. And no fooling, she means it. Taylor's not taking any of his stale one-liners. Dark Judy Davis eyes smoldering the same way her mother's did when she sort of shrugged and left the department Christmas party with the other guy she later married.

"K-Y Jelly and condoms."

"Dad I don't believe you. How can you keep saying shit like that to me. Grow up." She's slung her black leather backpack over her shoulder, shoved the door open before Hal can say another word.

"But it's true," he finally sputters, even though this sounds ridiculous even to him, but Taylor has already turned the corner out of sight.

Later in bed with Taylor's best friend, Sealy, Hal gets asked the same question.

"Taylor told you?"

"She was pretty steamed."

Sealy stretches her arms over the top of the pillow like some James Bond beauty. Hal finds himself staring at her constantly. She's such a scrumptious cat.

"Yeah, well," he mumbles. "The really sorry thing is that I was telling her the truth."

"Seriously?"

"Yeah."

Sealy pulls his black silk sheet up over her chest, mostly to prevent him staring and to curtail his increasing urge to play with her nipples.

"Go on."

How does one end up in these situations? How does one live one's life and end up in bed with your daughter's best friend? And Hal can't resist her. Really doesn't want to. So it spills out. He tells this twenty-something perfect raven-haired beauty all about his self-pitying little life as the patchouli incense clouds the bedroom.

"Oh, I never got into buying condoms."

"Who buys them for you now? No, don't tell me. Taylor?"

"No. I buy them now." Sealy doesn't believe him. No matter. "Back when I was with Mona I was too shy and geeky."

"You're still geeky," Sealy says, exhaling smoke from the joint she's puffing.

"Thanks."

"Poor baby," she looks at Hal and brushes his cheek, the way every woman before her has said "poor baby" and brushed his cheek. "Go on," she says, and kisses him. Her lips ashy and sweet with lip balm. Sealy's secure in her power. Hal will do anything to please her and she knows it.

"I know it sounds incredibly stupid, but I swear to this day that if I hadn't been so young and clueless, had stocked up on condoms all the time so Mona didn't have to, had kept a supply of K-Y Jelly around so sex wasn't such a painful scratchy steel wool ordeal for us, and gotten into the brown door like she'd wanted, then maybe—"

Sealy reared up with glee. "Anal sex. Are you kidding me?"

Hal shook his head no.

"Does Taylor know about that?"

"Not unless her mom told her."

"Omigod. What a trip."

Hal's thoughts exactly.

TAYLOR
A Phalanx of Crows

DREAM: 100 CROWS ON A green grassy expanse, walking with their herky-jerky clockwork motion like tiny T. Rexes. Diligent. Meticulous. Wind-up soldiers.

Cooing mourning doves. Who-Who-Who. Lacy brown and white on the ground beneath the bird feeder. Too big for the delicate balancing act. When one of the pair rises en route to the relative safety of the garage roof, something black streaks across the lawn and slams into it in midair. A crow. And the crow, unbelievably large, takes the dove in its claws and flies away. Crows eat doves? Life is way unfair.

Sometimes crows don't even fly like birds. They take off like black kites blown on windy days, like collections of rags, like ink spots that are almost an affront to sky. Sometimes they hang like broken umbrellas. And sometimes they just seem like a bad joke.

At Buzz last night. Everybody so Plury. (Peace/Love/Unity/Respect) Keep it real. Why? Some of those candy ravers wouldn't know real if it bit them on the ass.

DJ Zodiac. British mum. Part Jamaican. That clipped ta-ta way of speaking. Blue shades. Artful dodger if he wasn't so skinny. Whizz skinny. Sensational vibe though.

Yaba. Poppers. Whizz.

The Chemically Friendly Zoom Mix

Got to watch the fluids more. Too dehydrated.

Listening to: Monkey Boy, Shinobi, Delta 9, MC Storm.

Who is Sealy doing? Cat with cream. Her last guy had a face like old stirrup leather. There she goes bragging about the *Kama Sutra* again.

Why club? To dance? For music? Sell candy? Do candy? Socialize? Pick up?

Ally McBeal clone in design class talking smack about messed-up rave kids.

Road trip to Chicago for party next weekend?

Averaging 5–6 raves a month now. Never ever sleep.

"Sleep is for the Weak."

Carried away by the beat. The beat gets inside my head, my bones, and burrows into my dreams. One with the beat.

Old hippie dad listens to music, loses himself inside the solos, the lyrics. Doesn't dance. He's melody oriented not beat oriented. Mind over body. Big surprise that he and mom named me for James Taylor.

MONA
On the Way Home

"IT'S REALLY FUCKING STRANGE TO be back in town. Yeah, well, you can say what you want but I don't have to embrace everything about the place. There are a lot more yuppies, and there are ritzy boutiques and pretentious dining establishments like Sedona. Anything to get a buck out of the tourists. It's like everyone here has turned into a vampire. Dependent on fresh blood.

"I'm teaching at Wooster Country School. It's a private school. Nothing like Indian River High where I went to school. The kids have bucks. It's kind of depressing. But I needed the job and the bennies. Hell, yeah. What's it like? The kids have certainly changed. The Gen Y kids are pretty different. They're ruder, a little more arrogant. Sort of like Taylor. Well, she's Gen Y after all. And of course I know some of the parents. Just a few. The ones who invested or did okay in real estate or rentals. Nah. Most of my classmates stayed here. A lot of them have five kids now. You wouldn't believe. It's inevitable. I'm bound to run into some old beau or another. Isn't that a great word—beau.

"I don't know. I look at *Chief Little Owl* and I think— C'mon you remember. The wood sculpture. Almost a totem pole. A tribute to the Native Americans. Some beach bunnies appreciate art. A little bit. Honestly it's pretty tacky. Not quite as bad as Tiki art or anything but close. You hated it. I was thirteen when they put it up. It was fun to watch. Little Owl was chief of the Nanticoke Indians in Delaware. What's funny is this isn't even the original statue. Some combo of termites and storms. They put a new one up in 1994. Regardless, when I saw the sculpture as a kid, it was my hometown and that meant something. Now it's just another in a long line of tricks to try to make people stop and spend.

"The beach isn't the same either. Well, there's less of it. The ocean takes away. Erodes. Yeah. And there's not as much as there was, or at least not as much as I remember when I was living down here with Mom. Not Waterloo Street. Close though. Wellington. The guy who beat Napoleon at Waterloo. Well, I thought I'd remind you. Mom's house was/is at the corner of Wellington Parkway and South Pennsylvania Avenue. One of two white houses with mansard roofs in among the coastal pines about a block from the beach. I know you remember staying in the hot attic. How could you ever forget? No a.c. to speak of. A couple window units. The yard is all pine needles and sand.

"Sunshine Octopus is still there. I know that's a blast from the past. The old head shop. They've got a festive mural with dolphins and manta rays painted on the wall.

"No, everything's closed until spring. The Blue Surf Motel, the Bethany Arms. The bookstore is open. And Frog House is open. You can eat pancakes. There's a new addition, Japanesque, that has some beautiful kimonos in their window.

"It's okay. I can walk the beach and of course the place is completely dead in the off-season. I've always loved autumn at the shore. I'm going to have to put a new roof on before winter gets into full swing. There's termite damage. Yep.

"And of course I had to replace the furnace. Yeah, that was pretty hard to deal with. Thanks. I'm sorry, you couldn't make it to the memorial service. I didn't expect you to. That's okay. The rescue squad guys said my folks never felt a thing. They'd already gone to bed and the carbon monoxide just carried them away. So yeah it's weird to be back but the move feels kind of positive, too.

"I don't know, I look out here and watch the kids riding around on their skateboards and bikes and I try to remember what it was like, but it's hard. Even when I was a kid I think I was looking forward to the day I'd be an adult and get to drive and put away the foolish things of childhood. I am too a lot of fun. You just wouldn't know.

"Taylor's birthday? Oh god, I don't know. Sell one of your mom's paintings and get her a ThinkPad. You still have some of her art in storage, don't you? Yeah, that's just a suggestion. I don't have the bucks for a laptop. Well, do what you can."

MONA'S TOP TEN NEIL YOUNG SONGS

Sugar Mountain
The Needle and the Damage Done
Here We are in the Years
I Am a Child
Expecting to Fly
Only Love Can Break Your Heart

Cowgirl in the Sand
Harvest Moon
Wrecking Ball
Heart of Gold

HAL
Space Is the Place

AM I CRAZY, HAL THINKS, or should people who drive SUVs be pulled from their vehicles and beaten with sticks? Which is more elitist—driving your SUV? Biking the yuppie bike path? Reading Proust?

Hal catches his breath after almost being run down on Seventh Street. He's standing on the corner where d.c. space reigned for so many years. Time stops for Hal every once in a while, and he thinks damn, this is where I met Mona. His very own quicksilver girl. And Hal flashes on Steve Miller whose "Quicksilver Girl" has just been called to mind. He loved Steve Miller's first three albums back before Miller joined the hit parade. Man he was incredible with Boz Scaggs on the other guitar. *Children of the Future, Sailor, Brave New World.* They were great. And then Boz left and things went more MOR and the next thing you know thirty years go by and "Fly Like an Eagle" is a saccharine sweet tune promoting the post office. What happened?

Later Hal is sipping coffee with Sealy after playing pool at Whitlows in Clarendon. Whitlows which, in its old downtown location, used to be an after-hours watering hole for so many denizens of d.c. space and the 9:30 Club. Hal is being interrogated. Sealy has been questioning him nonstop for half an hour.

"Taylor told me you don't drive. You don't have a car?"

"Nope. Never got my license."

"That's so weird."

"I've lived at Dupont Circle for years. Don't need one really."

"How long were you and your wife together?"

"From 1980 when we met at a Slickee Boys concert at d.c. space until 1991 when she left me for Ralph, a rich T.A. dilettante in the English Department."

"Ouch. That must have hurt."

"Ancient history."

"What does she smell like?"

"Why?"

"I just want to know."

"Vanilla." And Hal remembers putting snow in ice trays in the fridge for Taylor. Mona adding vanilla flavoring. Taking a swig from the tiny brown bottles. "But after we started sleeping together she'd wear my Canoe men's cologne."

Sealy shakes her head briefly, revealing the tattoos on the back of her neck. Hal flashes on the first time he'd moved Sealy's hair aside and seen the Chinese ideograms. "From the I Ching," she'd said. "What's it mean?" Hal asked, tracing the tattoos with his index finger, then running his fingertips down the assortment of dangling silver earrings punched through the cartilage in both her ears. "Innocence," Sealy said.

"Did you love her?" Sealy asks matter-of-factly, but there's actual tension in her voice.

"Yes."

"Do you still?"

"No, not for some time."

Hal goes home alone and there are new CDs in the mail. The Electric Prunes—*Stockholm 67*. Hal never got to see them live and pretty much only knew them because of the tune in *Easy Rider*. Their first two albums were mostly fey and disappointing. Bubble gummy. But here they are live and they kick ass. Jim Lowe acts and sounds like a Jim Morrison wannabe. The pix look that way, too. But that fuzzy *Nuggets* sound, that garage rock of "I Had Too Much to Dream Last Night" and "Get Me to the World on Time" still work their magic. Other cuts are raw and electric. Nothing like the filler on the first two albums. Nowhere near as trite or controlled. And H. P. Lovecraft—*Live May 11, 1968* at the Fillmore West. A Chicago band. Tony Cavallari's guitar meets Dave Michaels's depraved organ. The double vocals of Michaels (the high notes) and George Edwards (the low notes) augmented sometimes by Jeff Boyan. Two almost-great American bands that nobody besides Hal ever listens to, he's certain.

And then Paul Horn's *Inside*. Paul Horn played flute inside the Taj Mahal one night and got eaten alive by mosquitoes to capture some magic inside the echo chamber–like structure. Hal remembered putting the record on the turntable at Maryland, sitting back to toke some really fine hash or Thai stick, and folding his mind into that majestic ivory space.

He tells himself he doesn't have a sentimental streak, that he keeps all of this old stuff so that maybe one day Taylor will appreciate it. Maybe someday she'll outgrow tape decks and computers, and DJ beat-obsessed overkill. Who knows? Is he lying to himself? Is it just about recapturing the past? Hal couldn't really tell you.

TAYLOR
Rave New World

CLUBBING MORE THAN USUAL AND DJ Zodiac is to blame. 9–10 times this month. Love his bald head. Euro sensibilities. Bought some poppers off him. Some X. Good stuff. When he's not guesting, or hosting, he's zipping by other clubs to check things out.

Up to Baltimore a couple times with Sealy and Zodiac. Danced all night at 1722's Phenomenon Party. Caught Bra Night at DV8 and then drum 'n' bass at the Martian Martini Bar.

Zodiac ran a rave last night in a warehouse in southwest. Pretty wired. The entire space knee-deep in soapsuds. Can't really capture it in words. Lots of Brit sounds. Zodiac draws people from as far away as Boston and Kentucky. He manipulates Massive Attack, Everything But the Girl, Pi, Chemical Brothers, Aphex Twin, Saint Etienne, Bjork, and FSOL. Lots of great stuff in the mix.

Zodiac is a cultural nomad. An alchemist. Almost a shaman. He passes through and collects everything he needs from different forms and isn't afraid to change the mix with ambient noise things, electro, techno, trance, underground house, speed garage, jungle, drum 'n' bass, acid house, straight-up jazz sessions, with heavy doses of Jungle Music, deep deep house, breaks, and old skool hip-hop.

Wears this hip white leather jacket that he bought in London and he's got autographs from all the local talent up and down the sleeves and all over the back in black Sharpie permanent marker.

Crystal Method—"Vegas."

This crazy woman in leopard skin skirt saying, "K would be da bomb about now." Skanky crack ho. Nearly biting through her pacifier. Looked like Lil' Kim on the worst ever bad hair/ bad wig day.

The syncopated strobes are usually overkill. Too hypnotic. Prefer the sensation the visuals provide. Better when they flash still lives. Dreary photos mostly. Fall/winter shots of stark landscapes, railroad yards, urban vistas. Or videos of urban decay. That makes sense. Bleak. Chilly.

To be a part of this community, any community. Everybody X-ing and so fucking cute. Seems like an odd way to find love and happiness. At least to me. $30 to get in and see some skinny guys in size XXXXL clothes dance till they drop. Or else watch leopard-skin woman fucking some guy in the chill-out room only partially obscured by shadows.

Painting: Dark massive. Luray Caverns–like. Crows around the edges. Wall of soapsuds like 5' of snow. Humanoid dancers with crow heads and flappy wings.

Cadmium fingers. Lollipop rings.

MONA
Don't Let It Bring You Down

"YOU HAVE TO UNDERSTAND THAT Hal's locked in the '60s. To the detriment of what's happening now. I mean I like Neil Young a lot but I listen to new music as well. Loved Elvis Costello, Depeche Mode, Gary Numan, the Cure, the Smiths, Human League, Boy George and Culture Club. All those '80s groups. Yes, I went straight from disco queen to new waver. Give me anything with a beat. Still own an Abba *Gold* CD. That was part of my divorce settlement. A joke. But Hal will never go there. He despised disco. Never danced. I couldn't get him interested and I lived to move. Don't get me started. If it's cerebral he likes it. I found that very attractive when I was younger. What? Well, good point. I guess I am getting more and more interested in lyrics now. Guess I'm slowing down. God I hope not. But I think about these Neil Young songs a lot more than I ever thought about the stuff I used to dance to. I mean gimme a break. How deep were the Village People or Donna Summer for that matter?

"Taylor was almost a compromise. Not her name, Taylor Leigh Palmer, but the very fact of her existence. I had to give to get. That's kind of the way I see it nowadays. We both wanted a child and we hooked up at the right time to make that happen.

"I never did get into the drugs like Hal did. When we met he smoked a lot of weed but as time went by he tried a little bit of everything. When I got into coke he got into heroin. We kind of went separate ways after that. Neither of us was anything close to a habitual user or anything. Strictly recreational. But our relationship was definitely on the skids.

"Of course I believe you, I'm sure you never did drugs. Uh-huh. Just like I'm sure most other guitarists have never ever done any drugs. In fact, I'll bet they don't sleep around when they're on the road either. Just bad press. I'm sure. Actually I think it's pretty cute that you can't play guitar with a wedding ring on. I had a vague memory of seeing guitarists remove their rings before a show. Bet it helps beef up the reputation some, hmm? I'm sure it does.

"My ex? Oh I think the fact that his writing's never taken off... I mean he's been working on the great American novel ever since we met back in 1980 and he's never finished it... has a lot to do with his negativity. He's so negative that streetlights go out when he walks past them. Seriously. I've read parts of the novel, it's okay. Not my sort of thing really. I loved *Cold Mountain*, and *Memoirs of a Geisha*. I've read everything by Jane Smiley and Margaret Atwood. Though these days I mostly read whodunits. Not exactly the sort of thing Hal's writing. He's trying to combine realism and magical realism or something. He goes on at length but it sounds like mumbo jumbo and seems to me that he's just going to piss everybody off. Sometimes I wish he'd write mysteries. He's a really funny winning guy when he wants to be, he just needs a reason and I guess lately he hasn't had that many. Which makes me sad when I think about it too long.

"The first time Hal ever saw me in a bikini was a riot. It was like he grew horns on his head or something. I mean I already liked him and all. It's just that whatever mental images he'd had about women, no matter how experienced he was pretending to be, when met with the reality of my curvy teenager's bod, well, we were married inside of three months.

"He peeled my suit off me that day like he was pulling a grapefruit apart. The fabric kind of stuck to my damp skin and came away like sunburned skin does, you know, when you pick at it. A quiet little hiss of the tearing and there I was pretty much buttering my panties.

"Well whoopdee-fucking-do. I don't know what happened. Hal never could stand PDAs. 'Public Displays of Affection.' I can't live without them. And as the writing got nowhere, and he couldn't get tenure, he seemed to give up. Traveled further and further into his imagination and shut out the world. He's the classic guy who hides his head inside a dream. He was always ranting and raving. I never knew how to help him. What to do for him. He just closed me out completely. Nowadays he sits in the dark watching cable. Reruns of *Mystery Science Theater 3000*. Yeah. Who knows?"

HAL
Acme Juicers

HAL WALKS WITH SEALY ALONG the C&O Canal in Georgetown. It's Indian summer and they're enjoying the sunshine. He has his arm around her shoulders. Something he wasn't capable of doing in his younger self-conscious days. Back then Hal would be so stoned that the bricks would ripple shakily under his feet and the restaurant portholes and windows on the canal would create the illusion that he was underwater—a merman, looking in on the mere mortals. Eventually they surface the towpath at Wisconsin Avenue by Grace Church where Hal smoked innumerable joints on the front steps shaded by the tall trees. Sealy spots the Pleasure Chest and makes a beeline for the sex toy shop. While she explores the leather and spandex, Hal looks at erotic postcards and remembers Acme Juicers. The CIA secret underground HQ in the next block underneath Clyde's.

Acme Juicers was never open. The Georgetown rents way too high for a small specialty appliance store to exist in the middle of the shopping sector. An obvious front. So Hal and his pal Tommy went back day after day. They never actually saw anybody there. The physical shop space was cut off just a few feet beyond the door. There was one juicer in the window and it had dead flies and flypaper curled up at its base. Like nobody had been inside the room in years. Pure *Man from U.N.C.L.E.* stuff. So they staked it out. Tommy watched on the Wisconsin Avenue side where a big black barn door faced the street, the mall parking garage is there now, while Hal watched the main door on M Street.

Nothing ever happened and then one day this guy walked up, pure CIA type with the hair, the barrel chest, and the shades, and asked them to move along. Then he waved his hands and the black door swung open and zoom a big black limo sped up the ramp out of there. One second the guy was waving to what? Closed-circuit security cameras of some kind? And the next the guy disappeared down the street. Like nothing had happened. Maybe it was some sort of Underground Railroad system so Nixon could get out of town. He'd hop on a tram at the White House and ride into Georgetown and then disappear into the crowd. Nothing on the block really made any sense— the Fire Engine Museum, Clyde's, and some clothing stores. After their brush with the limo, Hal's paranoia skyrocketed.

When Hal points out the building that housed the old Cellar Door where he was lucky enough to see Neil Young play a solo concert back in 1970, Sealy interrupts his reverie.

"You know, Hal, you keep giving me a tour of the places that used to be here, but you never talk about what's here right now."

"What?" Hal ponders her words. "I guess that's true."

"It's like your D.C. is buried under a layer of India ink. Like you have to scrape at it to show me what you see when you walk around. It's bizarre. Like you're living in the past and the present at the same time."

Hal has stopped walking. He's gazing across Key Bridge now. Watching vee formations of Canada geese fly south. He can't even imagine M Street anymore. The different layers of time making its signs and buildings waver and change like an acid trip. Hours spent at Café de Paris, Au Pied de Cochon, Max's, or La Ruche, all running into one another along with the years. Sageworth House. Emergency. Commander Salamander. The Singer's Studio. The Biograph Theatre. Running in a loop like a Fritz Lang movie in color.

"Oh, I almost forgot," Sealy says, ransacking her bag.

"What now?"

"I bought you something."

Hal can't conceive what kind of surprise Sealy has in store for him.

Sealy turns with a wicked smile and holds up two gold-plated balls. "Ben Wa Balls. Know what they're for?"

Hal shakes his head. They look like instruments of torture.

"Oh goodie. Now we're going to have some fun."

TAYLOR
Crooked Crow Lane

THIS MORNING THERE WAS BLOOD and shit all over the living room, black feathers. A crow got into the house. Came in the heater vent or something. Winged down through the furnace and got out into the laundry room, or perhaps it came down the chimney. However it happened, Max the cat found the crow and had managed to chase the bleeding, half-crazed animal all over the first floor.

The crow was still alive when I followed the noise into the kitchen. Max had the bird backed into the corner near his food dish. How appropriate. And the bird was huge. "Max, have you been playing with your food again?" I managed to say before the bird erupted in a bloody mess of feathers and motion and flew right for my face. Ducked in time and it bounced into the kitchen door with Max in hot pursuit. Incredibly loud. Not cawing but caw-caw-cawing and whirling about the room like a dervish who's done as many drugs as my dad has.

Thinking fast, opened the back door, the kitchen window, and pulled up the screen. Max was a blur. The wings louder than you would think in an enclosed space. A pounding. And the bird's cries, screams, a loud raucous series of low-pitched quorks and knockings. Very unbirdlike.

After much chasing about the house, the bird found the door and skittered, jumped, and smashed its wings together before throwing itself onto the grass. Max pretty much killed what was left of the bird, and I shut the door and proceeded to start cleaning up the blood and gore. This crow obsession might be getting a little bit out of hand.

Dream: Ravens in a smoky moldy landscape. Very Clive Barker. These are predatory birds. Telescopic claws. Shiny like metal parts.

2 sheets Bristol board. Graphite sticks 2B 6B

Le Corbusier = a nickname meaning "crow-like one."

Ted Hughes—*Crow: From the Life and Songs of the Crow* (poems)

"As the many-winter'd crow that leads the clanging rookery home." —Alfred Lord Tennyson

"Light thickens, and the crow/Makes wing to th' rooky wood." —Shakespeare

"If men had wings and bore black feathers, few of them would be clever enough to be crows." —Henry Ward Beecher

MONA
Broken Arrow

"I'M LIVING IN OUTLET MALL Hell. You wouldn't believe it. No, IKEA would actually be a blessing compared to all the crap that's congesting Rehoboth and Lewes. It's mind-boggling. How many more Gap or Nike or Old Navy outlets could we possibly need? I think people come to the beach now to shop. Actually, maybe they always did.

"Oh I've been jogging. Did the beach yesterday but today I jogged around the bike path. They've got a nifty new bike path and it circles around the community. There are all of these new gated communities down here. I knew it would piss you off. We're not the Quiet Resorts anymore, we're the racist beaches. Seems that way to me. Sure, these kids are in my classes. The places have names like The Preserve, Bayberry Estates, Pelican's Punch, Gull's Nest, Ocean Ridge, or the one I think really hits the nail on the head, Cotton Patch Hills. Gimme a break.

"But Sea Colony is this huge megalithic structure covering most of the beachfront between Bethany and Fenwick National Seashore. It's huge. Spreading like communism did on those maps of Europe and Asia in old McCarthy era documentaries. Also reminds me of living in the islands. The tourist trap areas. I'm sure they're all built with drug money. Well, they all were down in Cancun and Isla de Mujeres. Who knows? But Sea Colony has expanded from condos on the beach to a housing development called Sea Colony West. Every square inch down here is being divvied up.

"Where? Rusty Rudder is open. And The Lighthouse. Honestly I've spent more time eating at ChitChat 2 and talking to the locals. Over in Cedar Creek. There's so much to do at the house I haven't really had time to do any drinking. I still have to wade through all the paperwork on Mom and Pop's real estate business and meet with the lawyer handling the estate. I'm not going to sell. I think I may stay here for a while. No, I've given up the Baltimore house. Ralph gave me a cash settlement. We're barely speaking. Don't remind me.

"Mixed. My feelings come and go. And it's strange. I walked up the beach this morning and took a snack. The scent of tangerines outside on a crisp day brings back memories of my pop. Sitting in a duck blind with him when I was a kid. The pow pow pow of distant shotguns, like the sound you hear driving over a metal bridge. Now, you've made me cry. Okay. Thanks.

"Pop's boat? Oh god, probably sell it. I dunno. I haven't been out to the marina yet. Indian River. I spent a summer on it when I was seventeen. Right before I met you. You aren't serious. You? Ha. You wouldn't know which end to scrape. C'mon Hal. You'd put the gas in the bait box and the bait in the engine box. You're nuts. No, I don't even know what kind of shape she's in. Teak needs a lot of work. I'm scared to go look.

"Oh right. When? When was the last time you went fishing? I thought so. With Pop back in 1982. You turned green. You did. We didn't even get out far enough to stop seeing land and you were puking your guts over the side. Tell me about it. I knew it was going to happen. You had sausage for breakfast. Yes, you did. Oh god that was ugly. I didn't know a person could turn that color. You looked like you'd been dead for a—. That was a long time ago. If you want to go fishing, I can book you with some of Pop's friends. They're pros. Well, called your bluff. If you're serious you know I'll always help you out."

TAYLOR'S FAVE ARTISTS

Sally Manhattan
Rimma Gerlovina and Valeriy Gerlovin
Edward Kienholz
Egon Schiele

Joseph Beuys
Max Beckmann
René Magritte
Becca Midwood
Mark Ryden
Dorothy Magik

HAL
Toad Hall

TOAD HALL WAS THIS RAMSHACKLE, messy, Victorian, pseudo-Jefferson Airplane house right smack dab in the middle of Takoma Park. It had an almost Escher-like phantasmagoric vibe because of a multitude of doors. Lots of exits and entrances. So naturally the powers that be tore it down to make way for the Metro. Hal remembered the place as kind of a crumbling eyesore but Nils Lofgren had lived there for a spell. It was right down the street from Maggie's Farm, which was the big head shop on Carroll Avenue.

Riding now on the Metro past the spot and '80s graffiti announcing Cool Disco Dan, Hal remembers days before Mona. Days in Takoma Park with college friends. Days with women whose names blur together. Which one had the green eyes? Which the Marilyn Monroe breathy voice?

The two kids across the aisle look about Taylor's age. Students. Hal thinks the rave kids are similar to his generation in a way. The drug culture part is certainly. The tattoos and piercings are different. As Hal ponders the wallet-sized black scorpion visible because one boy pushed up the sleeves of his gray hooded sweatshirt, he remembers how he lost touch with his friend Tommy once the blue Maori tattoos started creeping onto his cheeks and the evening's cocktail became angel dust mixed with crack. Hal had been forced to abandon Tommy in order to save himself. He still felt guilt. Remembered the last fight they'd had. Tommy looking more like Harvey Keitel in *The Piano* than his old music buddy. Hal refused to go to the funeral and Mona of all people going in his place.

Now here he was fighting with Taylor over something stupid. They'd met in Silver Spring for coffee and he'd argued with her about Tori Amos of all things. Tori Amos a.k.a. Ellen Amos who actually used to go out with somebody Hal knows. Back in the days when her parents acted as chaperones and she played lounge standards at the Lion's Gate Tavern in Georgetown. The world too small a place. Maybe there really are only six degrees of separation from anybody famous. Why, he asked Taylor, does she like Tori Amos so much when Tori is recycling musical ideas Kate Bush was playing with a decade before her? Taylor's never heard of Kate Bush. And Hal wonders if Kate might have made a bigger splash in America if she'd picked two other songs for her first U.S. appearance on *Saturday Night Live* than she did. Why not "Wuthering Heights," "James and the Cold Gun," or even the incest-themed "The Kick Inside" over "The Man with the Child in His Eyes" and "Them Heavy People."

"Tori even ripped off the box from Kate's first and second album covers," Hal said.

"So what, Dad? Everybody knows who Tori Amos is. Nobody's heard of Kate Bush."

And so it goes. The originals sink into oblivion or are torn down to make way for subways. The copycats become famous. So what? Hal had been so self-righteous he'd reminded himself of his own doctrinaire military father. Rigid to the point of paralysis. Why slam Taylor's musical tastes when she was just finding the time to listen to his treasure trove of old music?

When the boys get off at the Brookland–Catholic University Metro stop, they're met by girls who could be Taylor and Sealy. Hal wonders what they see in two doughy-faced immature boys. Refusing to face the thoughts that are trying to bubble to the surface. Refusing to accept that the kids are made for each other. His guilt is getting way out of control today. First Tommy, then Taylor, now himself. He thinks of the clump of hair in the bathtub drain this morning. Then closes his eyes and does some deep breathing. He imagines a grassy enclosure somewhere. And sees horses grazing. Pimlico? Maybe being put out to stud like Secretariat or Native Dancer wouldn't be such a bad thing. A second later he thinks of Ferdinand the Bull, sniffing flowers in a field. *Ferdinand* was the book Taylor always wanted him to read when he put her down for the night. Blink and you miss the years. Blink again to combat the tears Hal feels starting to cascade down his face.

TAYLOR
Counting Crows

HAVE BECOME AWARE OF THE local crow population. Hear their caws every day now. Notice them everywhere.

Wake to crows cawing from the trees. What's with these crows? One sits in a tree croaking more than cawing. Sends shivers up the spine.

The woods near gran's old house in Rockville have a roost, a rookery. Watched them fly into their trees near La Madeleine. Hundreds, thousands of black spots winging past, all communicating with each other. At night when they come back to the rookery, they fly like bombers out of the sunset and fill the sky. Black shapes everywhere. Like something out of Alfred Hitchcock.

Going home to have dinner? To chat? Tell lies?

How odd that there should be rookeries near this mall and also near Tyson's Corner. Crows like malls. What does that mean? What does that say about our culture? Do malls imply dead souls? Crows do gather on battlefields to taste the aftermath. To scavenge on human remains. They are both scavengers and predators.

Gathering at medieval hospitals, execution sites, and cemeteries.

The carrion crows feeding on the dead in *Alexander Nevsky*

Rook. The card game.

Heckle & Jeckle.

Painting: Crows on a landscape of snow. Strutting. Squabbling. Showing off.

Wrote a poem about crows tonight. Not so good. The rhyme is forced but what the hell.

> Ravens in the woods of winter
> soaring high while daylight lingers
> acrobats that claw the air
> pitch black shapes hanging there.
>
> Perched among the graying bones
> of summer's dreary skeleton,
> like kings upon their velvet thrones
> to usher in the midnight sun.

Zodiac doesn't have to make me tapes anymore. Or use his new CD burner. He just sets it all up on his computer and downloads MP3s and ships it to my computer. Sweet.

Counting Crows have a new CD. *This Desert Life.*

DJ Urban, DJ Max Factor, DJ Melt, DJ Burn

BPM = Beats Per Minute. I like 133–180 BPM best. Can dance all night. When it goes past 210 BPM, 230 BPM, it gets too weird, no longer fun. House, Acid House, and Jungle do me well.

Memory: Theo. The way he turned blue after huffing Freon from the fridge. Frozen lungs. How cold the skin was. The body in rigor. The look on my stepdad's face.

MONA
Like a Hurricane

"HURRICANE IRENE BLEW PAST US. Floyd and Gert were worse. But the sea's still rocking and rolling barrels at the boardwalk. Pretty wild to see. Lots of erosion. All of the jetties are visible. Rain got in the house and now I definitely can't procrastinate any longer. Have to call the roofers. It sucks. I mean it. Last thing on earth I want to do is hang out at home and watch the rise and fall of some redneck's butt crack.

"Yeah I'm so pleased. Taylor made me a tape and there was a cover of one of my favorite Neil Young tunes by some group called Saint Etienne. 'Only Love Can Break Your Heart.' It's great. The rest of the tape is all kinds of weird groups she listens to. I don't like it that much. She's into all kinds of trancy dancy stuff. Like somebody turned on a perpetual beat and everybody was forced to dance to it. Reminds me of a scene in one of those movies you made me watch—where death makes them all dance at this masquerade. Vincent Price. You know the one. Yeah, that's it, *The Masque of the Red Death*. Like that. Like nobody has a will of his or her own. Like they're robots or something.

"No. I don't agree. It's nothing like disco. No. Nothing like the stuff I used to listen to. Really? Australian? Okay. *Priscilla, Queen of the Desert*. I'll rent it.

"Oh you'll be proud of me. I went to the Annual Jazz Fest. Hey, we're getting culture down here. In Rehoboth. You laugh but it was four nights and we had a lot of big groups show up. John Pizzarelli, Keb' Mo', Gregg Karukas, and Marion Meadows. I had a blast.

"School? Oh the usual bullshit. Why am I doing this again? I know, I know, I always wanted to teach. Now I understand why you quit being an adjunct. That sucked. No bennies, not to mention no paycheck ever. I'm sorry, hon, but it's true. Well, you know the score even though high school is a little different from college. Same old politics. Same old nitwit academic little Hitlers. Elvis Costello nailed them. Yeah, it's just not what I wanted it to be. Still, I have a couple kids who have potential. That's what keeps me going.

"And this is the best part. I had this kid I couldn't keep in his chair. Just talking nonstop and cracking jokes when he was supposed to be reading or doing an assignment, and I'd snapped at him a few times, but I really wasn't getting anywhere. No, I mean I really really wasn't getting anywhere. So I walked him out in the hall and he went all contrite when he wasn't acting out for his buddies. All beaten down. His folks must punish him a lot. He just imploded. It was so sad. There I was suddenly feeling all of this sympathy for this guy. Well, he's not that big but he's bigger than most of the other tenth graders.

"So I figure I've lost it. Can't teach at all. Go into the office to see my boss and she asks me which kid it is. So I tell her and she tells me that he's got slight Tourette's Syndrome and a steel plate in his head. Can you believe it? And I'm speechless. When were they planning to tell me? And it turns out I have three special ed kids in my class and didn't have a clue. Yeah, well that's pretty fucked up. Suddenly Indian River High School doesn't look so bad after all."

HAL
The Mars Embassy

TAYLOR'S BIRTHDAY WAS HALLOWEEN. ALWAYS. Hal agreed to meet her and was surprised when she showed up with Sealy in tow. They'd both dressed like Jellicle Cats from the musical production of *Cats* and looked like they'd just stepped off stage, while Hal was dressed in his usual civvies. The trio had a dinner of salmon and fries on the lower level of Childe Harold while Hal listened to the two friends laugh about life, school, and classes.

Taylor, unaware of his involvement with her friend, retold the stories of running into Sealy at the Maryland Book Exchange where they both now worked, how great it was that Sealy was a returning junior in the art department, and how Sealy needing another roommate for her group house on Calvert Road saved Taylor at the very last minute from living in the dorms. Now here they sat—Hal, his daughter, and his lover. Hal had a couple shots of Jim Beam and life became warm and fuzzy. He was bewitched by the cat costumes. It was hard not to stare at them. But he felt a little twitchy about seeing Sealy with Taylor. He couldn't figure out what to do. He wanted to get her alone. But kept thinking it was totally fucked up for him to even think such a thing. So Hal almost jumped out of his seat when he felt a leg slide over his leg and across his lap. What? Taylor sat across from him oblivious to what was happening, but Sealy now playfully twitching her tail across her nose and grrr-growling made her intentions and her ability to read his mind clear.

Taylor unwrapped her birthday card and gave a little shriek. Hal had included a check for the ThinkPad and she jumped out of her seat and raced around the table to thank him. The cats tried to persuade Hal to walk into Georgetown with them, to join in the raucous party crowds, but he opted out.

On his way home through the streets filled with costumed partygoers, Hal found himself thinking about Tommy. He'd met Tommy Mason at Maryland. They'd lived in a dorm and had driven consecutive roommates crazy playing esoteric and obscure music. They hooked up because they kept walking past each other's rooms hearing cool new things they weren't familiar with. That was always a key. By junior year it wasn't unusual to drive everybody nuts by leaving the door open to the hall on Parents' Visiting Day and playing weird things like the *Songs of the Humpback Whale* album. That was a hoot. Crank it up and BLEEP and BLOOP and FART and GRSSSSH. Tommy had removed all of their light bulbs and replaced them with red or blue or green so they could fit the music to the mood lighting. A large sign on their door pronounced "Mars Embassy." Campus dealers made them a routine stop. It was one way to survive the mind-numbing routine of school.

Memory: Sealy standing on his porch in the dusk. They'd just gone for pizza at Trio's. Hal's treat.

"You know what I want?" Sealy asks.

"Yep."

"You think you do," she says smugly, folding her arms across her chest. Her Sherpa brown and white coat. Her long skinny arms.

"I get the picture."

Sealy showed a mouth full of enormous white teeth. "Hmm. What if I said I wanted you naked on all fours barking like a dog?"

Hal got down on all fours right there on the wrought-iron porch of the building and howled.

Sealy made a spectacular frown. "You're not naked."

"Not yet."

Sealy clapped her hands and took Hal's face in hers. My very own doggie," she said, and half pulled, half motioned him back onto his feet. She turned away, looking through the street lamp haze as though looking for the moon, then turned back to him. "I'll hurt you."

"Sooner or later."

"You're not scared?"

"Why be scared? Women are always leaving me. I'm pretty used to it."

"I'll let you know before I do," Sealy said and then clomped her Doc Martens up the metal steps, and took Hal by the hand, before pushing open the door to the building and leading him inside.

TAYLOR
Ravensong

BEEN MISTAKING CROWS AND RAVENS. Didn't know there was a difference. Ravens are bigger. The Native Americans have a saying, that if you hear something in the woods and you don't know what it is, then it's a raven. Must have been a raven that got inside the house then. Too large to be a crow. And where crows only seem to caw caw, ravens make all sorts of other weird grunts and clicks and supernatural sounds. They're both pretty group though. And very smart.

Taping the crows. Entertaining actually. They can't distinguish between the taped calls and the real thing. Like the old Memorex ads that crop up on some of dad's home-cooked videos but for real. Taping 2–3 crows eating road kill and then playing it back a few days later when the road kill is gone proves an interesting experiment. Crows appear and answer the tape. They walk around puzzled. Stare at me on the porch. Act nervous. Then they fly away and sit in the top of a nearby tree. Their heads bobbing around. Like they're trying to locate this mysterious crow, the one who's so happy to have found some flat rodent or squirrel, and they just don't get it.

Kind of fun. Some guilt. Some paranoia. Like the crows know what's up. Will catch onto the game.

Corvus = Latin for crow family which includes blue jays and ravens.

Roost can number 40,000 crows. They are family-oriented social creatures. They roost in the fall and winter. Mate in the spring.

Some think they gather for protection against predators, and to share information.

But crows and ravens are competitors. Rarely found in the same locale.

Painting: fuzzy-headed raven perched on a skull in a charnel house. Tone piece, sure. Going after color, mood, and atmosphere. And who says you have to always paint crows black? Why not red? Or blue?

"Reverse the color but not the value."

Didn't realize that Albrecht Dürer (1471–1528) was a contemporary of Bosch. Born of a Hungarian father in Nuremberg, Germany. His *Apocalypse* woodcuts date from 1498.

Oddly, Hans Holbein the Younger (1497?–1543) was a contemporary of Bruegel. Also German. Born in Augsburg. Illustrated Erasmus's *In Praise of Folly* in 1515.

Holbein's 51 drawings for *The Dance of Death* produced from 1523–1526. Died of the plague in London.

Zodiac's rave in southeast was shut down by the cops on Saturday night. Ubiquitous fire code violations. Why do they slap down X-treme experiences? Zodiac was pretty upset. Needed lots of TLC.

MONA
Rust Never Sleeps

"I'VE TAKEN UP GUITAR AND the instructor is too cute. He relocated down here from Wyoming. Hell, he's half my age. But he's pretty fine. Yes sir. He's got a rep though. Yeah, he's been boffing a lot of the married ladies in town. That's the scuttlebutt anyway. You know me, I'd never kiss and tell, but somebody has to or we'd miss out on all the hot gossip.

"What? I hear tell he fucked this one widow in town so hard he drove the legs of her brass bed into the wood floor. Really. Left actual rings in the pine. Deep impressions. So the bed kind of sits there now in its own ready-made coasters. Okay, okay, no more.

"Been going through a lot of the stuff my folks left behind here. Had to get around to it sooner or later. Time to have a giant yard sale before the weather really gets cold. And there's all kinds of stuff. I can give you a set of china if you want. Silverware. A couple of chairs. You want one of the rugs? Braid rugs? Like the one under the kitchen table. Well, they're not to my taste either. And you're right, a lot is kind of old fogey stuff for the most part. There are some hurricane lamps. Maybe you could use them in the group house. A wicker table and chairs. You want a vacuum? They had one on every floor. Well, you're old enough to start vacuuming.

"Of course you're welcome to any of Mom's jewelry. Is there anything else you do want? Okay, you can have the rocker. And Pop's pocketknife. When you come down, you can help me go through some of this stuff. There are wall-to-wall tchotchkes. And you should go through some of the art and the photos. See if there's anything you'd like to keep.

"Right. This is definitely not a case of TMLT. 'Too Much Leisure Time.' Is that what you think?

"Oh there is something coming up I think you might like. You want to come down for the weekend? Please think about it. They have an annual event where they lob pumpkins as far as they can go. I wouldn't make something like this up. In fact, it's the...wait, let me find the newspaper...it's called the Punkin' Chunkin.' Make that the 1999 World Championship Punkin' Chunkin.' Woo. Now it says here that you can use human or machine power. I've gotta go. Maybe I'll learn some techniques for launching some of my students into orbit. Can't hurt at this point.

"Now, you know all those ponytailed men with Cat equipment baseball caps get me so hot. All of them. My what? I think the phone's breaking up. My virginity? The summer I worked on the crab truck. The CRAB TRUCK. That's right. Like a Good Humor man who sells crabs. We rode all over Fenwick Island and we'd set up in parking lots. It was hot, miserable, smelly, and I got sick of crabs. But the driver was Grant Woodloe. He had peroxide-blond hair, a lopsided grin, told stupid jokes, and the tightest little butt. He also had the biggest biceps I'd ever seen. He lifted weights. Had a bench press on the side porch. Was incredible. I'd sit in a chair and eat Popsicles and watch him curl or bench. He'd use weights I couldn't even lift off the floor. Not even one side of the stupid barbell. You had to see this guy to believe it. He was just really something. He could have lifted me over his head if he'd wanted to.

"And despite everything he wasn't a jughead type like the guys who came to town to train at the National Guard training site, he never threw his weight around. I mean, whoa, if he had I can't imagine what I'd have done. But he wasn't a hard-ass. Had a sweet disposition. No idea. Nope I don't know what happened to him, but I'm sure if I stay here I'll find out.

"How? That's a real long story. No, I'm not stonewalling you. It's true, it's a long and complicated story and not one I usually tell sober."

HAL'S TEN FAVE SCI-FI FILMS

Attack of the Crab Monsters
Five Million Years to Earth
The H-Man
The Incredible Shrinking Man
Invasion of the Body Snatchers
It! The Terror from Beyond Space
Metropolis
The Mysterians
The Thing
Village of the Damned

HAL
Rape of the Lock

"HMM?"

"I said, are you gonna see the Squirrel Nut Zippers? Your daughter's gonna be there."

"When is it?" The sun was baking the color out of a pile of books by the bed. Sealy had opened the blinds. So Hal could barely focus.

"Saturday night," Sealy snuggled up to him, swallowed one earlobe in her lips, hugged him, started reaching around for his dick, but Hal had to piss so bad he couldn't think.

"Wait a sec, okay? Just wait a second." Hal struggled to his feet and knocked over the lava lamp, which met with Sealy's laughter.

"Man, you are really out of it this morning."

The hot black ooze cascaded across the floor, and then Hal stepped right in the black lava and singed both feet, jumped up grabbing one foot in both hands, and somehow managed to hop and keep from falling down until he landed his butt hard on the toilet seat.

"I want to go dancing, Hal. I want you to take me dancing. I want to swing and sway to the Zippers."

"Sure," Hal said, holding one severely damaged foot, not having the faintest idea what he was getting into.

Hal decided that if he was going to bite the bullet and go dancing with Sealy and his daughter he needed to clean up his act. He'd been getting a little slovenly. His drab hair needed a trim. He walked to the Hair Cuttery and had a sweet, nearly mute, Chinese woman cut his hair. She didn't actually weigh much more than the scissors. And while sitting in the chair listening to the faraway snip snip snip, he thought of the Alexander Pope poem, *The Rape of the Lock*, a long poem, one that Hal thought he should like, but found too difficult and boring to care about at all. And then he remembered the place in Wheaton that took their name from the poem, going so far as to reproduce this amazing rendering of a woman with long hair, a copy of one of Aubrey Beardsley's illustrations for the poem, on their front window glass. Not that Hal's been out to Wheaton in eons. The space is still there of course, something else now. The barber held up the mirror so he can see how things look on the back of his head. I'm getting way too sentimental in my old age, he thought.

Later, Hal's haircut is the least of his worries. His feet are killing him. He's tried to keep up with Sealy and his daughter but he's a terrible dancer and now he's sitting down. Sealy has been keeping her distance to maintain the illusion for Taylor. But Hal knows eventually they'll give themselves away. It's a real struggle to keep his hands from sliding over her body.

Lucky for him the 9:30 Club is packed with all generations. There are little tots jumping in place to the songs and people his parents' age spinning gracefully across the dance floor. Hal had never heard of the Squirrel Nut Zippers and he knows in the morning he'll go buy everything they've got out on CD. He's seen the Gap ads featuring the Lindy, but he's never ever imagined people coming together like this to dance to swing music.

"C'mon Poppa san," Taylor says, and takes his hand. His feet are bleeding, he's certain. But he tries to move with some semblance of grace. He's never seen Taylor so happy.

"I like your friend," Hal manages between gulps of air. The Zippers are taking a break and Sealy has run off to the bathroom.

"She's a lifesaver," Taylor says.

Afterwards they walk down U Street to get a dessert and some drinks and unwind from the heat. Pam Bricker is playing Sunday night jazz at Utopia. Hal likes the exposed brick. Hal's eyes cut from Sealy to Taylor to Pam Bricker, and something increasingly gnaws at him, something he can't place. His eyes are lingering on his daughter in ways unbecoming a father and he's only had one beer, and then he feels an ocean moving inside him, winds, and a bolt of white light. Taylor is wearing one of Sealy's mock turtlenecks. A heather gray henley that he has stripped over her head drenched in sweat and cum while Sealy bounces back and forth in his lap in her black leather skirt, her high-heeled knee-high boots rocking back and forth on either side of his chair, her matted hair glued to his face. Hal feels a storm is definitely en route.

TAYLOR
Black as a Crow

"CHICKAPOO." WHAT DAD USED TO call me.

Getting used to crows everywhere. Noticing their absence more than their presence now. All quiet at the group house today. A serious dearth of crows.

How do they sleep? Clotted together in bare trees near malls. At night if you stand there the cackling and croaking noises. Startling to come upon them unawares. You don't notice them, you don't notice them, and wham, you realize those blacker than black shapes in the darkness are alive. Something Zodiac should record and add to his audio arsenal.

Dream: Walking through tiny village in a foreign country. Belgium? Twisty cobblestone road. Turning the corner and startling a roost. Hundreds of crows taking off at once. Have to get down on all fours to avoid colliding with them.

Crows live 17–21 years. Oldest recorded crow was 29½ in Ontario.

Second oldest 14 years, 7 months.

Party Pack = 2CBs + X.

Zodiac is packing. Banged me six ways from Sunday. Bruised cervix. Torn underwear. Ruined my best Glamour Sheers mesh top black stockings. Big deal. His skin like butterscotch. His lips not too thick, not too thin.

Caressed his bald head. Every little contour, gradation, beaded with sweat. His voice wispy like a smoker's voice but he doesn't smoke tobacco. Weird.

Total lost weekend. Didn't see daylight save for the water-color pink sky Sunday morning. Zodiac's bedroom curtains black and floor to ceiling. Living my whole life after dark.

Worst part—Zodiac lives upstairs in same building as my dad near Dupont Circle. What's up with that?

Have they ever met? Doubt it. Will they? May be inevitable. Imagine them talking music. dad would hate him? dad would like him?

Can dad hear my voice through his ceiling? Oh no, oh no.

Can't tell him, can't tell either one of them. Not yet. Too soon.

Listening to: Orbital—*Snivilisation*, Portishead, Morcheeba, Tricky, The Prodigy.

Crows can mimic human speech with potential vocabularies as large or larger than parrots'.

Stitches on Zodiac's neck. Tracheotomy? Knife fight?

Walking medicine cabinet. Sells candy. Wall-to-wall CDs. New purple iMac. Owns little else. Fridge empty. Old pizza boxes. Typical guy that way.

Frou-frou gold and white bathroom. Pretty clean for a guy though he calls his place his "Palace."

Women? Oh yeah. You can smell them. Scent marking the place like cats. He'd have to scrape the walls to get rid of the evidence. Use a blowtorch.

Won't explain his name.

Painting: Zodiac as Saint Sebastian with crows circling his head. Patch cords attached to arrows. Attached to computers.

My apocalypse?

MONA
Mr. Soul

"WHATEVER HAPPENED TO THAT NEIL Young songbook of yours? I don't know why I'm asking. You've never thrown anything away. Sorry. I'm not in fighting mode today. I just want you to mail it to me. Which one? There's more than one?

Two volumes. Sure. I'd like the two volumes. Just express them to me. Why? I'm taking guitar lessons. What guitar? For your information, smartass, I went out with my teacher and bought a Martin DXM. That's more like it. I thought you'd be impressed.

"I don't know what brought this on. I'm kind of in a Neil Young phase and wanted to play some of his songs. In the house mostly. Some mornings I go down to the beach and sit there as the sun comes up and play guitar. But I'm pre-it-tie self-conscious about it. Fingerpicking. His name? You've never heard of him. Local guy. Nope, nobody I know from the old beach days. Just some guy with a dream and a small guitar shop.

HAL
The Boss with the Hot Sauce

SEALY IS DOWNING MORE FOOD than Hal has ever seen her eat before. French toast and scrambled eggs. It's raining outside, water droplets pooling on his jeans, and he's forgotten his umbrella. Hal likes Trios. He always feels comfortable in these particular surroundings no matter how surly the wait-resses are. He doesn't know where Sealy stayed last night, or if she took the Metro into the city early just to meet him. He tries not to think about it.

"You know Taylor told me so much about you. You sounded like a fluffy romantic. Did you ever wear a frock coat and scarf?"

"No way."

"So how did you finally meet the wife?"

"Mr. Mateus and Mr. Chianti."

"What happened to Tommy?"

"Couples tend to cling to other couples. We drifted apart. After Taylor was born, the baby kind of put the clamps on other friendships. We stayed in touch for a number of years but the world becomes increasingly made up of friends who have children, too."

"So what's she do now?"

"Mona?"

"Uh-huh."

"Her folks passed away. She's moved to their place at the beach to take care of things. To find herself."

"Wow, the beach. Did you know her folks?"

"Yes."

"So what did you see in her?"

"Well, one day we discovered we were both only children. I think we kind of clung together because of that, because we didn't have brothers or sisters. I felt like I'd finally found a sister. Somebody I could confide in."

"I'm an only child," Sealy said, pausing midchew. "More syrup?"

Hal made a quick sprint through Dupont Circle. The chess players were gone and the park was pretty much abandoned. A couple of street people under plastic bags, though most had fled. As he crossed P Street by Second Story Books he found himself getting nostalgic. For one instant he had a memory of Taylor playing in the fountain. Sun shining and a Willie Nelson blue sky. And then he landed in a puddle and splashed himself rudely. He's late for lunch with Taylor at Café Japone. She's already landed a table by one of the fish tanks.

"She's driving me nuts, Dad."

"Who?"

"Sealy."

"Why's that?"

Hal watches Taylor chew some octopus. She's always been klutzy with chopsticks and prefers to use her fork. He's still drinking miso soup and letting the broth warm him up.

"She's such an immature potty mouth. She's got a lot of talent and she's wasting it all on some guy. She's never home anymore. She's out partying all hours. She never fucking cleans up after herself."

Hal doesn't know what to say. Especially since he knows that Taylor is raving a couple times a week. "Well, do you want to move out? You want me to help you find another place?"

Taylor's lips always quiver a tiny bit when she gets overwrought. She's making herself hysterical. Before Hal can comment, she seems to realize it herself and puts on the brakes. "I just needed to vent a little. I think making another move in my first semester is asking for too many transition problems. It was hard enough moving out of the house in Baltimore."

"Well, I haven't got a lot of space, but you know you're welcome to crash at my pad for the weekend or whenever you need to get away," Hal says. "In fact, take this key. I've got a dupe."

"You sure about this, Dad?"

"Yeah, I'd prefer a phone call before you show up but we can play it by ear. No strings. Just gives you another place to go if she's really driving you nuts." And kills two birds with one stone, Hal thinks, imagining visiting Sealy in College Park if Taylor moves out. Which will make things so much easier. And for some reason he thinks of hipperthan-you'll-ever-be Barry Richards, the self-described "Boss with the Hot Sauce." Hal remembers the open-air parties Richards threw at WHMC, the radio station he worked for out in Gaithersburg. Hal remembers rolling around on a plaid blanket with a dancer he was infatuated with and getting stoned and drinking too much vino in the afternoon sun. Hal had been sunburned places he didn't know you could get sunburned. And he'd almost asked the dancer to marry him. One door closes and another door opens. A different wife, a different life.

After lunch, the rain stops. Hal tries to write a little, bags it. Pops an episode of *The Sopranos* in the VCR but he's too distracted to watch it. There's some hash in his pipe so he lights it and gazes out the basement window. He can see the world go by at street level. Soon he is chuckling, remembering a time at the University of Maryland. Ordering steak and cheese subs with everything at Hungry Hermans. Picking out a spot on the main green with Mona and getting ready to chow down, with the Memorial Chapel on the hillside behind them. But Hal's so fucked up he can't tell the top of the bun from the bottom and he holds it upside down, so the meat and lettuce and tomatoes and everything slide right out the side onto the ground. Mona manages a brief moment of composure, a pseudo-contemplative air, and then laughs so hard that Hal starts laughing too. His mouth gaping wide staring at the food on the grass. And then Mona flips her own sub over so that all of its stuffing falls out. Plop. Then she proceeds to pick up handfuls of meat, or lettuce, or onions, hold them a little above her head and drop them like food bombs into her mouth. Hal joins in and they consume the insides of the subs with sticky fingers and never again touch the bread.

TAYLOR
A Murder of Crows

A FLOCK OF CROWS IS called a murder of crows. Why?

The crows on our street are getting used to me. I feed them peanuts now. And they recognize me. They watch and listen. Wait. Fly down out of the tree when I move to the porch. Kind of satisfying.

Painting: a crow with claws outstretched on the American flag. Pecking at it. Doing that peculiar bob and weave. Glued feathers to the canvas. Find myself thinking wood would be a better medium. An altar piece. A triptych. Something to attempt. Something more in keeping with the art history stacked around the bed.

New issue of *Juxtapoz* came today with more pix from Mark Ryden's "Meat Show" catalogue. He uses bees like I want to use crows.

Crows look up whenever a plane or a helicopter flies over the house.

Today: very distinctive haw haw haw haw haw haw haw

"To have crow to pluck (or pull) with someone." (Brit expression)

Sealy's painting sexy cameos of celebrity nudes. Weird. Elvis doing Cher doggie style on the top of Machu Picchu. Tom Cruise in Native American headdress in a threesome with Marilyn Manson and David Bowie (in his Ziggy Stardust phase) onstage somewhere at the Mardi Gras. And Leo DiCaprio being flayed alive at Malibu Beach by all three Catwomen from the *Batman* TV show—Lee Meriwether, Eartha Kitt, and Julie Newmar.

Memory: Age 12? dad's *Playboy* collection. Breaking into his desk and sneaking a peek. These fabulous women. Thinking it exciting, scary, and strange. Mom making him unload a couple of boxes of them soon after. Did he sell them or donate them to the dump?

Zodiac guesting at Fluid in Philly. Driving us up in his gray Jag. Great story about hanging with Roni Size at Buzz. Says we have to go to New York. Check out Baktun on 14th Street and Wetlands. Philly and Baltimore are real cities. More fun than DC. People are less inhibited, less goal oriented. None of the hill wonks to contend with.

Crows have been up on the roof. Went outside and noticed they're digging in the rain gutters. Why? Watched them for a time. Sketch pad. Got a ladder out of the garage and climbed up to look. The gutters haven't been cleaned this fall. Poked around in the leaves. Yuck. Found a dead vole. They're putting food up there. Storing it? Caching it away?

Memory: Actually believing that sports teams (football, basketball, soccer, hockey, you name it) lived together in a group house/dorm/stadium/coliseum like in old gladiator movies I watched with my dad. And being surprised later when discovering it wasn't so.

MONA
Powderfinger

"WELL, I HAD TO GET out from under your daddy's influence sooner or later. I was eighteen when I had you. I've told you that before. I carried you all summer and it was hot. Come August I wanted you out of my body. It's true. But you hung on until Halloween. The last trimester was hell.

"Of course we wanted to have you. You weren't an accident. I swear you drive me crazy sometimes.

"It's just that those were hot days in an apartment that didn't have air conditioning. It was awful. One tiny window unit. And we were in the basement with all of the sinks hooked together. Nobody had a garbage disposal so if somebody upstairs stuffed food down their sink... Oh please. The sinks would overflow straight down the line from top to bottom. It was nasty. I mean it. You could tell what the people on the third floor had for dinner. Looks like chickpeas and broccoli again. What's that over there—smegma? We'd come home to a foot of disgusting standing water and their dinner flotsam on the top like an oil slick. Your dad would put you in the crib and I'd gather the buckets and mops and we'd roll up our jeans and start brushing everything out the back into the alley. The landlord never did squat about it. The place was pitiful. Still is, I'm sure. Well, just pray you're not there next time it floods.

"You were so cute. You had no idea that we both had a lot of mileage and had been around the block a couple times. You'd make these scenarios about how in love we were.

He was twenty-five and I was seventeen and I knew a lot more about sex then he did at the time. But you'd make up stories about how we'd met in the sandbox or something. Like we were the same age and we'd always been sweethearts. Hardly. But you always had a vivid imagination.

"What? Why do you ask? We used to use these weird birth control Fizzies. They were unbelievable. They sounded like Fizzies sound. You know how they sound? Crackling away but inside me. Really. And they got hot. Effervescent. Tingly. It was like doing it with Pop Rocks in your twat. I mean it. Just awful, but your dad would look so lovelorn and into it how could I complain?

"Okay. But you asked. I don't want to imagine my folks having sex either.

"No that's pretty much true. He had a real problem buying condoms. God knows why. I used to buy them by the ton so I wouldn't embarrass him and so he wouldn't get me pregnant again. After you. I said after you.

"You were a difficult labor. I never told you that? Whew, it felt like days. Nope, your father wasn't allowed in the delivery room. That's a pretty new thing, honey. They kept him out and he must have paced deep ruts in their carpet. I resented not having any say in the process. But that's old hat. Oh, they strapped me to the bed and wouldn't let me move around or anything. Plus it was a teaching hospital. G.W. So there was a constant parade of young students poking their heads in the room to take a look. Drove me nuts. And for future reference—take the epidural. You say that now. Just trust me on this one.

"Your daddy has always loved you. We both did. Do.

"You want to come down to the shore? Any time, sugar. You don't even have to call. Just try to be here before dark if you can. I know it's getting dark earlier and earlier. But you're welcome. Of course you are. You can bring Sealy, too. I'd love to meet her. You've told me so much about her.

"What are her paintings like? You know, compare them to somebody I might have heard of. Seriously. I'm not laughing at you. I'm not. You know I'm just old and in the middle of nowhere out here."

NAVELS ZODIAC DREAMS OF DRINKING SHOTS FROM

Christina Aguilera
Tyra Banks
Sarah Michelle Gellar
Salma Hayek
Jennifer Love Hewitt
Ashley Judd
Jennifer Lopez
Rose McGowan
Shania Twain
Vanessa Williams

HAL
Fuck This Shit Let's Go to the Vous

"SO?" HAL SAYS AND SHRUGS.

Sealy is sitting on the edge of the bed, popping purple wine grapes into her bright red lips. She's wearing one of

Hal's two white dress shirts. She hasn't buttoned the front. Her legs are crossed and she's kicking one of them while she talks, like she's using the leg to power the conversation. Her large thin bare feet and red painted toenails bobbing into and out of his view.

"So last night your little minx of a daughter—"

"Do I really want to hear this?" Hal can see that Sealy is being patient with him as she nods her head a few times. "What now?"

"She got blasted, had a fight with Zodiac, and then she basically Tawny Kitaened herself across the front of his Jaguar."

Hal doesn't like this image. It reminds him of too many straight-to-video movies he's seen. And it's not the way he likes to imagine his daughter. He wants her to be strong. He's never felt comfortable with needy women. Should he phone her for a heart to heart? Should he tell Mona? "Why tell me?"

"It's just not right."

Sealy lobs a grape at him; Hal tries to catch it but doesn't open his mouth fast enough and it bounces away across the carpet. When he turns back, Sealy has tossed another, softly this time, and he latches his teeth onto the skin and likes the satisfying pop of the flesh in his mouth. The grape is tasty. Fresh. He swallows the seeds.

"Taylor was going on and on about you and DJ."

"We have nothing in common, flyboy and me."

"Taylor thinks you do."

"Really? Like what?"

"Well," Sealy says, her ferocious eyes glittering. "You both sleep with children."

Hal's entire being stops, like he's run into a jersey wall or the proverbial brick wall of middle age, and he can see hints of colors around the edges of what seems to him at this point in time like the end of the universe. Intense, killer colors. He's hurt, incredibly so. His stock college line comes to him— "Fuck this shit let's go to the Vous." The Rendezvous, a student dive on Route One where he could play Foosball and drink his troubles away. And yet he wants nothing more than to fuck this smiling, almost sneering, young woman until his heart explodes from the exertion and he blasts off into some sort of space, some unknown space beyond the everyday world he feels so defeated by on an everyday basis. Somewhere in the heart within the heart of everything.

"Sorry," Sealy finally downcast her eyes. "I'm sorry, Hal. That was uncalled for."

"I don't need to be reminded how old you are. I know I'm just a fling."

And then Sealy curls herself up from the floor, from the soles of her feet, reaches for Hal and pulls him down onto the futon, and then recurls into his lap, "Baby, I'm sorry, really, I do care about you, I do love you. C'mon, smile for me."

Hal begins thinking about Sealy's other lover, Maxwell, a slam poet on the scene. Maxwell makes him feel edgy, because he's a little bit dangerous. Hal knows he'll never be dangerous, never make Sealy feel edgy. He's safe, and despite all of his old-timey hippie glory-day leanings, he's really kind of a microwave dish, a pushbutton dinner best enjoyed when she's feeling pretty cocky about life, love, and herself.

Still, he knows that Sealy knows she's hurt him by stating the obvious. She knows he's self-conscious about being with her, and she also knows part of him resents spending what money he has on her whims. But he does it because he wants to and their lovemaking, while not the kind of stop-and-go freeway ride she probably has with Maxwell, is still great for both of them. Hal is a generous lover; he does care about pleasing her. And as if on cue, Sealy lifts her arms and sheds the white shirt like a large seagull flapping its wings, and her long black hair covers Hal's face, and she tongues his cheeks, his lips, and begins forcefully to undo his belt. And Hal is in heaven. He loves that Sealy takes what she wants from him and he knows better than to regret anything about this gift, this gift of an amazing younger woman, even though he knows that sooner or later she'll pour a glass of wine on his head, like one of the characters in that Cher movie he can never remember the name of, because he's not the perfect father, because somehow someway he's disappointed her, and she'll be gone. He buries his face in her black hair, marvels once again at her blue eyes, that rare combo, like Kerouac, and knows he will never ever ask her about her father. Never ever think about anything but the way her nipples sear into his chest like hot coals, the way her breath comes in hungry gasps, the way she fits on top of him like a limpet.

TAYLOR
Ravenna in Vulture

CROWS ON BARE TREES LIKE tumors in delicate filigree of lung.

Ravenstone = Old English for place of execution.

They keep pet ravens in the Tower of London. Generation upon generation.

The crow's only enemies—owls and humans.

At school. Looking out the window and seeing a crow standing on a dead squirrel. More than that. One clawed foot planted in the middle of the squashed squirrel's white stomach. The claws spread. And the crow had enough of a grip that he/she (it's almost impossible to tell without an autopsy) could drag the whole sorry mess with one foot. It would caw caw and then dip its beak down to tear into the fur and guts. The red and gray mass. Quite the feast. Another crow joined the first. Would dip and bob its head and caw caw caw. Sometimes four caws. Sometimes five. And it would hunch its shoulders.

This went on the entire class. Couldn't take my eyes off the crow, the dead squirrel, life in the face of death. Barely touched my brush to canvas.

Gallows Tree Crow.

Why do people hate crows so much? They're one of the smartest birds yet people have always hunted them. Reminiscent of medieval cat inquisition.

Big surprise. It's illegal to own a pet crow. Yet orphaned crows can be raised as pets if subsequently freed.

Delightful. One of the crows banging on the kitchen window. Trying to entice me outside to feed it peanuts?

Listening to: Stereolab, Vanessa Daou, Autour de Lucie, the Egg, Ozric Tentacles, Pizzicato Five.

Playing with paint: acra violet, venetian red, dioxazine purple, titanium white, cadmium yellow.

"I don't believe in subsidies, but I don't see why art should think we owe it a living. It has to start defending itself and saying what it thinks it does for us, particularly since the arts that do tend to get subsidized are generally those that people are not that keen on." —Brian Eno

Going with Sealy to see *Blair Witch Project*.

Fight with Zodiac. He's off to Los Angeles for the week. He's always talking about raves in other cities. Always talking about Europe. He was at the Eclipse '99 Rave in England in August. Got drunk and made an ass out of myself. Sealy holding my hair out of the way while I worshipped the porcelain goddess.

Bound industrial dance party, the dungeon club Sealy dragged me to last month, is having Catholic school girl night. Where's my plaid dress?

MONA
Down by the River

"I THINK THE FIRST TWO Neil Young songs I ever heard were 'My My Hey Hey (Out of the Blue)' which was oddly blended into 'Down by the River.' Some garage band was playing it at a frat party on the row and I was blasted on vodka and weed. A hilarious evening as I recall. Some Sig Matchi frat club guy was trying to get in my pants and me dancing every dance. Not stopping until my bladder was so full that I was going to splash right there in the basement of this mildewy brick building filled with skanky sluts in clothes that were several sizes too tight considering the amount of healing fluids they were all trying to force into their anorexic bodies. Can you say pukearama. You could always smell stale beer and old puke in those places. It was unbelievable.

"But the band struck up this slow 'Hey Hey My My' chorus and that turned into a louder mostly plodding chch-chchch chchchchchch chchchchch chchc chunky sound and I was hooked. I mean it became a battle of the wills—was I going to pee myself or race up a flight of stairs to the girls room and elbow my way through all the big hair until I could sit down, or was I going to grind to this song until Mr. I Lust Therefore I Am creamed in his jeans. No contest. Neil won that first time. Mr. I Lust came. I split to pee and snuck out the back. A big success all around. But I didn't know the name of the song. The next day I only had to ask one of my snob job friends who worked at the Student Union and first she looked down her nose at me like I was a stupid bitch who listened to old out-of-it music, and then she told me who Neil Young was. I looked in the CD rack and discovered at least ten CDs. I bought the one with 'Down by the River' on it and so begins a tale.

"I guess I met Hal a couple weeks after this began and I couldn't come right out and tell him what I was thinking—that he looked like Neil Young. Hal must have been trying to model himself on the guy. I mean he parted his hair in the middle like Neil and he wore flannel shirts and had the whole grungy look before it took off in Seattle. I mean he looked like Neil, the godfather of grunge. And he told me about Crosby, Stills & Nash, Buffalo Springfield, everything. He had the early stuff and that's what I ended up liking the best. Partly because that's what Hal had and what I basically just absconded with from his collection. And partly because the middle-period albums like *Live Rust*, *Hawks & Doves*, *Re-ac-tor*, *Trans*, and *Everybody's Rockin'* suck so badly. I'm sure Neil knows it, too.

"You have to understand, hon, it's not like we had a lot of money and could go out and buy every new CD. That's why after we had you, we kind of lost touch with what was going on. Your daddy was teaching at the university and I would pop you into a stroller and roll you around campus. I always liked the Book Exchange because I could sit on the floor and read while you dozed in the stroller. No, I didn't go with him every day. I dropped out of school once you were a bun in the oven.

"Your daddy saved me from Cumberland Hall. That was a zoo. We almost rented a place in Berwyn Heights. One of the streets with an Indian name. That's a long time ago. Dupont Circle? He'd crashed in a group house made up of people arrested in the Pentagon march. He'd been living there ever since and finishing his MA. Life was good even if the first time he had me over the one bathtub had actual green moss growing on it. You don't know. It was like bathing in a mountain stream under a roof. Very weird. I almost ran screaming out the door. But he'd been living there a long time, and the owner decided to renovate and turn the house into individual apartments. That was perfect for us at the time so we stayed on. Well, the place fit him like a glove even if it was too cramped for three of us."

HAL
Iguana Coffee House

KEGEL EXERCISES. THAT'S THE ONLY thing that can explain how Sealy manages to hold onto his cock and work it the way she does. Hal continues to be stunned and amazed at how she flutters her vagina. She gets his cock inside her and her body clamps down on it and tugs at it. She works him like he used to work his fingers to get them out of those Chinese finger cuffs when he was a child. No matter how much he pushed or pulled he couldn't get himself free. And Sealy's contortions and contractions pull him and stretch him and please him in ways he'd never dreamt before. But what does she know about Kegel exercises? Sealy's never had a kid. Not that he's aware of? Not with that body. And when he thinks of Mona actually practicing the same exercises, on the bed, her belly growing almost visibly from one change of clothes to the next, he marvels that she never used the same muscles on him. Why not? Maybe she didn't have the same control? Again why not? He can't think about Mona without a pang of remorse.

Hal walks the apartment and makes a pot of green tea, and ponders this worrisome fact all morning, the sky as gray as the proverbial battleship. He wanders out to the front steps and watches the gay couples walk hand in hand down P Street toward the tiny stone bridge over Beach Drive and P Street Beach. Most of the leaves have fallen now. Autumn such a good time to be in D.C. But now that winter look, the bare trees showing all the buildings and roads that stay hidden beneath the canopy of leaves most of the year.

Flash: His mother has a show at the Art's Club on I Street. Hal must have been ten. So it's about 1966. Hal is more interested in the fact that it's a Friday night and he's missing *The Wild Wild West* and *The Man from U.N.C.L.E.* But his mom wants him at the gallery for some reason, and he walks around the glitzy interior and peeks at the men and women in suits and ties who applaud his mother's work and seemingly laugh at her every word.

Afterwards they pile into the car and drive forever and instead of going home end up in a church basement where Hal hears poetry for the first time. He's disappointed there aren't any real iguanas. The name of the coffeehouse has impressed him. What he encounters, nothing like the rainforest atmosphere he'd longed to find. And he remembers that there weren't any potters at the Potter's House. Still, he likes this much more than the gallery. He doesn't understand all the words but he realizes later that this is where his desire to become a writer was born.

Hal inspects Sealy, looking for evidence that she's been painting. He pulls her ribbed sweater down, revealing one shoulder. Annoyed, she begins to fidget out of his arms.

"What are you doing? I can't watch the movie."

"Hmm. Taylor's covered in paint. It's under her nails, on her jeans. I can't find one speck of paint on you."

Sealy, laughs, kisses him. "I work hard to be a clean beast for you."

Hal sniffs for paint or turpentine fumes. "Maybe you don't really paint."

Sealy smacks his hands. "Of course I do."

"You ever going to show me some of your work some time?"

"I'm way too shy."

"Right."

Sealy gets out of his lap and walks to the fridge. Pulls out a Corona. Pops the top. "You going to let me read some of what you've been writing?" She clicks her nails on the bottle. Waiting. When she gets no response, she takes a long drink, comes up for air, and says, "Uh-huh. That's what I thought."

TAYLOR
Attending Ravens

DISCOVERED MEANING OF MURDER OF Crows. "...Based on the persistent but fallacious folk tale that crows form tribunals to judge and punish the bad behavior of a member of the flock. If the verdict goes against the defendant, that bird is killed (murdered) by the flock. The basis in fact is probably that occasionally crows will kill a dying crow who doesn't belong in their territory or much more commonly feed on carcasses of dead crows."

Worried about how much Sealy smokes. The queen of nicotine and caffeine. Makes me look like an amateur.

Sushi Taro with Zodiac and Sealy. Wore slate blue silk shirt, short kicky black skirt, and new Skechers. Zodiac had the new Abercrombie & Fitch catalogue. Banned in Boston. Hotter than last year. We pointed with chopsticks and laughed and generally made a fuss. Almost got thrown out.

dad, quoting Oscar Wilde, said that the 19th century dislike of Realism was the rage of Caliban seeing his own face in the glass. The 19th century dislike of Romanticism was the rage of Caliban not seeing his face in the glass. Wilde was being a smartass, but he was probably right.

Noah sent out a raven before the dove. It didn't return to the ark.

Muslims call ravens *Abu Zajir* or father of omens.

In Peter Beagle's first novel *A Fine and Private Place*, a wise-guy talking raven waits on the protagonist.

Neil Gaiman's Sandman/Morpheus comic character always attended by ravens.

Crow's nests are shabby, sloppily built things (like Sealy's room) and don't hold up well in wind and rain. Sometimes crows do return and reuse nests, but very often they will nest in the same tree, or adjacent trees for many years, usually constructing a new nest.

Painting: crow as icon in something textured, maybe pebbly or teethy. Crows in a tall, narrow box. A coffin? But shape it like a pointed gothic cathedral window. Backdrop of stained glass?

Shrinko keeps asking me about Mexico. How can I not think about five years of my life? Sometimes it was like living in a hotel. Boring. Theo. Poor Theo. We had adventures in order to stay alive.

Zodiac told me about some kids in Pittsburgh back in '92 or '93 who decided to have a rave in one of the tunnels. They would have been busted but they had the genius idea of calling the police and getting a permit to film a movie. The big Rave Tunnel Scene. They got one and instead of being busted for having a rave actually had police protection during the party. We represent, ya know.

MONA
The Last Trip to Tulsa

"ME? I'M HAVING FUN. SPENT some time hanging out with this woman who owns Cinnamon Owl Antiques and Collectibles. She came over and looked at some of Mom's things. There wasn't much of value but she cherry-picked through what she wanted and she took some other stuff on consignment. The wicker stuff. No big treasures. And then I ran into my old friend Bootsie. I don't know if you ever met him. Not a beau, just a sweet guy. He owns a barbecue place in Ocean View. Who? Spencer? You remember him? Lord, he was an old friend of my pop's. They'd known each other during World War II. If he's still alive he's probably running a place called Pawn and Prawn. That would be about his speed. He wasn't a crusty old salt type. More like a stray dog. I'm surprised you remember him.

"Oh, I got a little nostalgic today. Well, I'm allowed. Found myself thinking about Hard Art, MOTA., d.c. space, and the BBQ Iguana. Some of the places you dragged me into.

"And I almost forgot to tell you. I went to the second annual Rehoboth Beach Independent Film Festival. Yes, that is a mouthful. It was great. Over a hundred films. They've got a film society at Rehoboth now. Well, lots of gay and lesbian films. Of course. I saw some I think you'd like. *The Red Violin*. And they showed Rory Kennedy's documentary about the dirt poor in Kentucky—*American Hollow*. *The Secret Life of Girls* is perfect for you. And the feature was the original silent *Ben Hur* with an eleven-piece live orchestra. Oh, it was incredible. I had a blast.

"Oh come on. If you hadn't met me, you'd have knocked up that blonde from Angel Flight. Oh yeah. You didn't think I knew about her. Get a clue, Hal. She left her fucking white epaulets or whatever the fuck they were under the bed. Well, it was a surprise. You couldn't have had anything in common with her politically speaking. I'll bet. God, she must have been slumming. One look at that dump you lived in and she signed up for life in the Air Force. And right, you've listened to my advice. When? I just want to hear the words from your mouth. But when didn't you? Like I dunno, hon, did you ever read the books I gave you? Did you ever see any of the films I told you about? The answer's no. You don't care about my advice or anybody's advice. You've always done whatever you wanted to do no matter who you hurt. End of story.

"What? Well, I'll tell you. When we spent that week in the mountains. You remember. In the Shenandoah Valley, right. And you yelled at me most of the way home because I'd screwed up and left the food in the fridge. I'd packed it all up and just forgot to bring the bag out to the car. Not that you'd helped one bit. And Taylor was tired and screaming. Your voice upset her. Right. Not to mention I had to drive because you never bothered to learn how. Do you know what a pain in the ass that was? And you were pissy and just awful the entire trip back home. And when we filled up in Front Royal, you went to the bathroom. And I thought about leaving your ass right there. Just driving away. What? I'd have packed up things at the apartment and drove back here to my folks'. And that would have been that. Yes, you did. You yelled at me all the way home. It wasn't right. We were a team, Hal. I know nothing was going your way, but that's no excuse. There wasn't any reason to take it out on me. Or your daughter. I never forgave you for that."

SEALY'S FAVE KAMA SUTRA POSITIONS

The Pair of Tongs
The Rising Position
The Splitting of a Bamboo
The Crab's Position
Fixing of a Nail
The Turning Position
The Widely Opened Position
The Mare's Position
The Yawning Position
The Position of the Wife of Indra

HAL
Marco Polo

HAL IS MEETING SEALY IN Bethesda for Greek food. She's trying to get him to fly somewhere warm for the holidays. The idea is pretty appealing. He hates D.C. winters. The restaurant is off Wisconsin Avenue and in walking from the Metro he recognizes the building that used to be Marco Polo. Hal never really comes out to Bethesda anymore but this was one place where he went to buy see-through shirts. Even men wore them in the '70s. Some with Hobbit prints on them. They sold the usual head shop paraphernalia and he was sure the owner must have been dealing drugs out of the space, because it had been at the same location next to the Army surplus store with an impossibly high rent for years and years. Places like the Sixth Sense in College Park had died by the mid-'70s but Marco Polo had stood the test of time way into the '80s. Hal is more than ever aware that living in one town turns everything into a time portal of some kind.

Sealy's already grabbed a table and Hal kisses her cheek. She's wearing a sleeveless black dress and sheath and how something so simple can look so good on her tan skin boggles his mind. They order grilled smelts, stuffed grape leaves, spanikopita, and share a giant Greek salad. Sealy wants ouzo and they drink a little bit and graze a little bit and Hal almost spits an olive pit across the table when he feels Sealy's toes in his crotch.

She's smiling. And she applies pressure. Rubbing the pad of her foot up and down, probing with her prehensile toes while looking as nonchalant as possible. The crusty old mustached waiter pours more water and she presses even harder. Hal's getting aroused and Sealy knows it. She's having a blast.

"So, Hal," Sealy says, there's a sparkle in her eye but she's totally disconnected and not letting on what's up with her footplay.

"Hmm?" Hal couldn't formulate a sentence if his life depended on it.

"I'm worried about Taylor." The pressure is a constant. Green light. Red light.

"What about?" Hal imagines his daughter at a club making out with nameless beautiful strangers. He feels a twinge of jealousy. But his hard-on is growing.

"She's really down. She's painting these horrible crows."

"Crows?"

"Yes, black birds. Everything she does is related to these horrible black birds."

Hal thinks this is funny. He laughs. Sealy pushes her heel down harder. He stops laughing. She looks hurt. Like he's making fun of her.

"She's stopped seeing the DJ."

"Hmm?" Really? Hal's surprised that he's not overjoyed.

Sealy sips some ouzo. She's poking at her salad a little, the foot keeping the stroking motion.

"Last night at the club she was sitting at a table with some guy she'd just met."

"And?" Hal is getting tired of this conversation and Sealy knows it. She sighs. Pulls her foot away. And just as Hal starts to relax, slides her other foot into place. He looks startled.

"Actually, she was pretty toasted and she crawled across the tabletop—"

"What?"

"Literally. Crawled right across the top of the table and sat in this guy's lap and pretty much fucked him right in his chair."

Hal imagines it and the image, on top of what Sealy has been doing to him all this time, is too much. He feels himself coming. Knows Sealy can feel it happening through the sole of her foot, see him go a little pale, his lips quiver, put down his fork. Hold onto the table. Hal is embarrassed and wonders if Sealy shouldn't be disgusted. She did this to him. She made him come in a restaurant full of people. And her copulatory gaze says she's thrilled.

Now Hal's upset. Why on earth was she telling him this stuff about Taylor? What's that all about? He's shaky.

Sealy removes her foot. Hal finds himself tearing up. He oddly misses Sealy's foot, the pressure. He feels incredibly attached to every single part of her, every single cell of her body, every molecule, every atom. Yet she's across the table from him a million miles away. He feels so alone. So alone. And he realizes for the first time that all they have in common is sex. This is like dawn's early light creeping across Hal's reptile brain, and he knows just as suddenly that they're almost fini. That both of them are bored. And that all Sealy can think of to do anymore is to shock him. To please him she thinks she has to shock him. And that will never ever last, Hal thinks. And he remembers that he'd tried this same tired routine on Mona so many years ago.

That night Hal has the dog dream again. He can't move his legs. Turns his head to hear the approaching engines. Hear the whirring tires.

TAYLOR
Raven's Knowledge

THE IRISH SAY THAT "RAVEN'S Knowledge" is to know and see all.

Memory: Age ten? First hearing the phrase "screenwriting" thinking it actually had something to do with screens. First a sculpture with multi screens, then the idea that you wrote on screens, perhaps with crayons. The idea of writing on all of the screens in a house say, or in a skyscraper, so that all of the windows together, the screens, spelled out messages, words, sentences. Quite upset later to discover it meant writing scripts for movies.

Crows in flight dropping clams and walnuts on the highway pavement to break open the shells.

Sealy dragged me to the East Wing today. Almost nothing in there inspires me. Too clever by far, not art half the time. Art history? "It's history" more like it. Who's going to remember this stuff in five years? In five minutes?

Finnish ice fishermen have discovered crows pulling their baited fishing lines with their bills, and walking away from the hole, then putting down the line and walking back on it to stop it sliding, and pulling it again until catching the fish on the end of the line.

Woman in England whose pet crow walked her spaniel around in the garden by its leash.

Tell dad about trailervision.com site. They make trailers of outrageous fake movies. Send things up à la *Mad* TV.

Ravens play toss with themselves in the air, dropping and catching small twigs. They also lie on their backs and juggle objects.

Crows play a brand of rugby, wherein one crow picks up a pebble or a bit of shell and flies from tree to tree, taking a friendly bashing from its buddies until it drops the token.

Crows also avidly rub their bodies with squashed ants. They wallow amid busy ant colonies and intentionally squat on disturbed anthills, allowing (inviting) hundreds of ants to swarm over their body. Something about the formic acid? Nobody knows why.

Been reading eCRUSH horror stories. Zodiac is more than a crush to me. But Sealy (who never ever washes the fucking dishes in the sink) says that's all it was. So disappointing. Sex for her is like perpetual bubblewrap. You just keep pop-pop-popping those sexual bubbles one guy at a time.

Crows mate for life.

So do penguins. Wolves. Swans. Hawks. Whales.

What's wrong with people?

MONA
Long May You Run

"MY CAR DIED. I IMMEDIATELY flashed on Neil Young's song for his old hearse Mort. Love that, too. It was funny though.

"You keep talking about crows and this was weird. At first it was one crow, I'm pretty sure. I don't see that many around here, honey. I just don't. And this one crow would be sitting on my car. I'd see him when I looked out the window, or took a walk. And he'd thrash his wings and fly away. First he was on the roof. Then later he moved to the hood of the car. And then I saw him kind of pecking at something. It turned out to be the windshield wipers. The first time I caught him messing with them, chewing on the rubber, I ran outside and shooed him away. The next day there were two crows on there. Each one had a wiper in their mouths. Beaks. Whatever. And they were tearing at the rubber. So I flew out the door again. Stupid birds. Maybe they are smart, but you wouldn't know it from their behavior. What? You guessed! There were three crows. The very next day. Is that predictable? Families, huh? I guess that makes sense.

"You know what happened? Crow vandalism. They tore the wiper blades off my car. Really. They tore them off and flew away with them. Why do you say that? They hate me?

Because I tried to chase them away from my car? Nonsense. That's the sort of thing your grandmother used to say to me. My mother. No, it really happened. They can hate me all they want. The car's dead, too. Time to find something newer. Another Yota. Absolutely. They last forever. Though what I'm going to do now about protecting my wiper blades I have no idea."

HAL
Maggie's Farm

HAL'S FLASHING ON A LEAFY forest path to a seemingly familiar lake. Where? Hal can't place it. A cabin on the opposite shore beneath some pines by the water's edge. Was he in a canoe? He feels the sensation of rowing. Somebody has plowed a small garden behind the place. There are a couple of apple trees. Smoke from the red brick chimney.

Hal does smell smoke, realizes Sealy is awake, and slowly becomes conscious. Sealy is puffing on a bidi cigarette. Hal remembers the pungent aroma of the Indian cigs from his college days. Twenty years ago. He didn't know they still made the things. Something like triple the nicotine. He used to buy them at Maggie's Farm. Tommy thought you could get high on them, but mostly they just got nauseated. Though the bidis did give you something to smoke between bong hits.

"Hey," Sealy says. She puts her warm hand on the small of his back. Caresses him. Hal has been sleeping on his stomach with both arms under a feather pillow that he's been hugging to his face. Sealy exhales a cloud of smoke and kisses his ear. "How you doing? You were jerking around in your sleep."

"I'm fine," Hal says, and reaches an arm out and runs it down her endless legs.

"So who created that piece?"

"Hmm." Hal turns his head to the left and can feel his neck muscles pull. Shit. It hurts and he's going to obsess about having a Jacuzzi at the YMCA for the rest of the day. "Which?"

Sealy's pointing to the red and yellow abstract assemblage hung in the living room above the stereo equipment just visible through the cracked bedroom door, the one that has vinyl LPs melted into various shapes all across its wide expanse. They look like mountains and craters, fissures, geological shapes on the surface of planet jazz. Hal has been living with his mom's artwork so long that it's just become another piece of furniture.

"My mother."

"What? Get out."

"My mother did that piece."

"Really. Your mom's an artist. Why didn't you tell me?"

"Was."

"Not anymore?" Sealy is stubbing out the cig, and she turns to face him, the sheet dropping to reveal her breasts, Hal's hand still planted on her thigh.

Hal is thinking he wants more of this fine body, what his college buddies called "screwdola," so he says, "Long story, let's talk about it later," and rises up on his right arm to lift the sheet and lean into her waist which smells like ripe Bosc pears. Hal momentarily luxuriates in Sealy's scent and begins kissing her navel, slowly working his way down her exquisite skin.

And oddly the Dylan tune from which the head shop took its name pops into his brain and he wonders why he should suddenly equate making love to this young woman and working on a farm in the same breath.

TAYLOR
Rain, Tree, Crow

SHRINKO SAYS DAD IS THE crow.

MONA
Journey Through the Past

"WELL, I LEFT YOUR FATHER for Ralph because Ralph looked like my ticket out of here. The East Coast I mean. You have to understand I was younger than your father and the eight years seemed immense back then. No, it wasn't something I thought about when we got married. Why? I was like you, exploring every possibility. And like most women I thought I could change him. He was a fixer-upper if I've ever seen one. But one thing I have learned is that people are the way they are. You can't change them. I hadn't learned that yet when I ran off with Ralph.

"Let's see. You know I was your age when I had you. Eighteen. And I'd only known Hal a year when you were born. My eyes were open, but obviously not open wide enough. I thought he knew everything of course. Bzzzt. Wrong.

"Your dad and I stuck it out until you were ten. A major miracle for us. And that's why you miss him so much. Sometimes I think if I'd split before that you wouldn't. That may very well be cruel but it's true. I think so. I'm glad you love your daddy but I think you have to realize that you might not be as close to him if I'd left sooner. And you might be more attached to Ralph. It's kind of a terrifying thought to me, too. Old Ralphie was a loser, wasn't he. It's so hard to get everything. You can get love, or sex, or money. But you'll be lucky to get two out of three with anybody.

"And your dad still hasn't figured out that he's always dating women in their twenties. He's been through scads of women since my day, honey. The problem is that women always change around thirty. Some get serious, some get wild. But they change. And poor Hal hasn't figured that out yet. He always hooks up with them and then is surprised when they change. Maybe someday, if he experiences the same thing over and over again enough times, he'll finally get the picture. Don't hold your breath.

"Why hasn't he remarried? I dunno, honey. No idea. Of course he talks about me all the time when you're there. Of course he does. And I care about him but I'm way too independent now to ever consider getting back together. Really. My god hon, he works at Borders. I mean he's just a register jockey. You can defend him all you want to, you always have actually.

"Oh I meant to tell you, I did run into somebody who told me what happened to Grant. The guy I told you about last month. The weightlifter. Yeah, drinking and driving don't mix. He flipped his Jeep in a drainage ditch. Drowned. Sad. He was so handsome."

TAYLOR'S TEN FAVE HALLOWEEN COSTUMES

Peter Pan
Pirate
Madonna
Agnetha Faltskog
Emma Peel
Jackie O
Gypsy
Charlie Chaplin
Scarlett O'Hara
Grizabella

HAL
Food for Thought

HAL IS STRAIGHTENING UP THE New Arrivals paperback section when Sealy comes through the doors. She's been in the sun or the tanning booth, and even though he missed her the past week because of her schoolwork he's glad she looks so healthy.

"You're what?"

Sealy's eyes are starry and laughing. "I'm spending Thanksgiving with Taylor and your ex."

"Oh, don't kid around about stuff like that. Are you serious?" Hal can see Sealy nodding her head, arms out at her sides, her jaw slightly open.

"What's the big deal, Hal?"

"I, I just don't like it."

"Maybe you should come with us then. Be my chaperone."

Hal likes this less and less.

"Look lover, I'm not going to tell your ex that I'm sleeping with you almost every night. Every night, that is, when I can get away from your daughter."

"She doesn't—"

"Nope."

Hal is relaxing. Beginning to take deep breaths again. Remembering his meditation lessons. Exhaling through the top of his head and all of his pores.

"No that's fine, just miss having you around."

"Hal, you know I can't stay over more than a couple nights a week. I actually do study some when your rave fanatic daughter allows me to. Plus the semester is winding down and I have some paintings I have to complete."

"What do you tell her?"

"Whaddya mean?"

"What do you tell Taylor. As an excuse."

"That I'm going to go fuck your dad now Taylor, gotta run—"

"I should spank you."

"Ohh," Sealy purses her lips and arches an eyebrow, "you know I'd like that."

"That's why I don't."

"Oh spank me daddy daddy, please."

"Come off it."

Sealy winks her drawstring pants down part way in the bestsellers aisle and shakes her booty at him. "This mighty fine little butt is begging you to spank it, spank me, please, spank me."

So Hal takes a half-hearted swat at Sealy but she moves quickly out of the way, sticks her tongue out at him, and races across the shop, with Hal in slow pursuit. She's laughing up a storm like he's never heard her laugh before and he wonders how she can move so fast in her platform wedges.

Hal flashes on Food for Thought. A folk singer is passing the hat after a so-so set of Joni Mitchell covers. Taylor sits opposite in Deadhead tie-dye and sandals eating a crunchy granola sandwich. Her short sandy brown hair now long and braided. The waitress arrives to take their order. Sealy. But how she'll look in ten years. Fifteen? And just as Hal's jaw drops open, he realizes the folk singer thrusting out her hat is Mona.

TAYLOR
Crow with a Broken Wing

LISTENING TO: TLC—"NO SCRUBS," CHEMICAL Brothers— *Surrender*, New Radicals, *The Miseducation of Lauryn Hill*, Beastie Boys.

Norse mythology—Odin's two ravens, Munin and Hugin.

Munin = the memory

Hugin = thought or the intelligence

They flew out and brought back news, which they would whisper in Odin's ear.

Sculpture: Crow Woman. Something gran might have done. Owing more to Greeks before her turn to abstraction. Bronze. Not exactly Corcoran School stuff. Subservient eyes. Woman as Laocoön.

Both crow parents take turns sitting on the eggs. All family members help in the care of the brood. Older children from earlier broods even help gather nesting material for their parents.

Crows can make and use tools. In Australia, a naturalist observed a crow make a hooked tool by plucking and stripping a barbed twig. He also observed the use, but not manufacture, of what he described as a "stepped cut tool" with serrated edges. He took photos of leaves from which crows had started to cut such stepped tools.

Ravens are also known as *yel, txamsem, hemaskus,* and *tsesketco* by Pacific Northwest Native American tribes.

Lattes at Zi Pani after work. Long talk with Ally about Martha Clarke's dance troupe. She saw *The Garden of Earthly Delights* at the KenCen. Now I'm jealous.

Great News: Mariposa's Center for Artistic Expression, a coffeehouse open mike place in Berwyn Heights, wants to lease student artwork. Not a lot of bucks but an excellent ego stroke. One that I needed. Running a couple of my crow paintings in January. Fantastic.

Hanging at Xando with Sealy. Her studio is knee-deep in books, notebooks, canvas, oils, watercolors, brushes, pens, pencils, and papers. Barely room for her easel and drawing table. Remember Albrecht Dürer's engraving of "The Scholar"? "The Student"? A young man (maybe Dürer self-portrait?) writing or reading at his desk, surrounded by stacks of books? Makes me think of Faustus and all his stuff.

"All art is at once surface and symbol. Those who go beneath the surface do so at their peril. Those who read the symbol do so at their peril." —Oscar Wilde, *The Picture of Dorian Gray*

Actual crow with broken wing walking down the side of the road. Shuffling favoring one side. The wing out of place. Like an umbrella that won't fold up. Doomed.

Feeling that I've plateaued with shrinko. I understand that I'm responsible for my actions. Duh. Nothing more to be gained right now.

Visit Mom at the beach? Paint? dad? Sealy?

Chocolate. Some shrooms. Paint. Crank up Madonna.

MONA
Sleeps With Angels

"ACTUALLY ONE OF THE REASONS I moved back down here is that I'm having a hard time accepting that some of the women I was at school with in Baltimore are just having their first kids. I mean they're in their late thirties, some are even in their forties and they're just starting out. I couldn't do it again, no way. I haven't met a man who makes me want to do that. No way no how. It just got to me a little. All that talk of doulas and breastfeeding.

"We've got a girl who had to leave the fall semester at school already. She's seventeen and she's preggers. No, she won't abort the kid. Not down here. Way too conservative. You forget what you want to forget, hon. These trailer park honeys; they get married and start pumping out the babies right away. By the time they're my age, they're grandmothers. Not that you couldn't make me one soon. That's what I like to hear.

"They've got a billboard down here that reads: 'Being a teen parent is like babysitting every day for free.'

"How's the painting going? Good. And that's great news that somebody wants to lease some of your work. Well, it's not a sale exactly, but every little bit helps. You know, I think I'm going to keep this house for a while, so if you want to come down for the summer and do some painting you're more than welcome. I'll try to stay out of your way. I seem to have a pretty active social life all of a sudden. Up to you.

"The Dance of Death? I think immediately of one of the Bergman films your daddy showed me. *The Seventh Seal.* Death dancing away with everybody across a hilltop at the end. It's funny, that was one of the very last things we did together. Uh-huh. And I think that's one of the reasons I think that the Dance of Death is the dance couples do when they unwind their relationship. When everything just comes apart. Well, if dancing brings a couple closer together. If you can get the man to dance. Then the Dance of Death is like a counterclockwise dance that couples do when they separate. Somehow it erases everything that ever mattered, that ever happened between them or held them together. I guess that is pretty heavy. Sorry.

"Which reminds me of this place on Route 1 just past the Beltway, that sold garden statues. It was there for years and years. I couldn't drive past there with a straight face. There was a head shop nearby called Electric Head or something. Your father worked there back before we met. Oh, he's full of secrets and surprises. You don't know. I'm sure he's never mentioned the topless dancer he used to see who danced at the Starlite Inn. No, he wouldn't. That woman had some serious mileage on her. Ahem. That's another story. Anyway, he worked for this odd couple who owned the statuary business. I'm not sure you can imagine what I'm talking about. There must have been fifty garden deer alone. And there were all sorts of other animals and things. Thousands of statues and birdbaths. An army of tacky horrible white stuff all poised to march onto somebody's lawn and take over. It could give you nightmares. Who knows? Minimum wage. Your daddy's job was to load the pieces into the car whenever they did manage to sell something. One of the worst jobs in memory. Most of the time he had to listen to the couple bicker and be their captive audience. They used to rent out rooms to students, but it was a pretty spartan existence he said. And he had to hose down the statues. Took him hours. That's when he decided to go back to grad school and just before he met me.

"Yeah, his father died around the same time. I never met the man. Heard stories. He sounds a lot like my pop. They'd both been in World War II. My pop in the Pacific. His dad in Europe. Actually, the more I think about the statues, the more it gives me the creeps. It was like a giant graveyard in a lot of ways."

HAL
Booeymonger

HARD TO BELIEVE THIS PLACE still exists. Like so many parts of D.C., Hal enters the door expecting to flashback into some drug-addled dream of the past. To stand watching himself order food, like looking in the mirror at the McDonald's that used to be on Prospect Street in Georgetown, spotting some long-haired fuckwad in the mirror staring back, and in the moment of discovery, when he's about to say, "What the fuck are you looking at?" realizing that it's a mirror. That it's him.

So Hal's in Chevy Chase because Sealy wanted to cruise Mazza Gallerie, and she kind of wanted to go to the Cheesecake Factory, but they have too many times before for

Hal to stomach, he doesn't really like supporting the mob that much and the mob owns the Cheesecake Factory he knows for sure, just like the Nazis own W. R. Grace, and besides they feed you alcohol so you'll order sugar, and he's had all the sweets he needs for a year at least. So Hal stands there in this old haunt of eons ago and wonders what to order. He hates all the names. The Duke, the Patty Hearst, the Scheherazade, the Tina Turner. They're as corny as the biz in meditation class where he has to om ah hum. Drives him crazy. He gets the deep breathing but not the clichés. So maybe just a fruit salad with yogurt and a cup of tea. He finds it hard to concentrate in the bright light and remembers that the lights in here have always bothered him. He'd like this place a lot better if it had softer lighting and realizes that's why he stopped going. He clenches his jaw and plods ahead. Hal wants to charge everything but they don't take plastic. He counts his bills. Nope. Sealy smiles and plucks some bills from her purse. Hal hates moments like this one.

At the table, Sealy, sucking on a Diet Coke and playing with her roast beef and brie sandwich, the so-called Gatsby Arrow, begins another of the interrogations he's become almost used to. He knows she's read some book on how to deal with men and that she thinks the thing to do is just let him talk about himself, though the truth is he really hates talking about himself. It seems ridiculous that he does it only to please her. That's totally cockeyed but that's the way this seems to him, now in a pretty good mood, though squinting a little in the bright light in Chevy Chase.

"So how come you never finished telling me that story about your mother?"

"Hmm?"

"Your mother, Hal. I know you have a father. He died in a car wreck when he hit a deer, but you never talk about your mother, ever."

Hal ponders the question. He can picture Dorothy's gray pageboy haircut immediately. In his heart of hearts he knows he loves her. Always has. Always will. But how to begin. A crack about *Blade Runner* comes to mind but he reconsiders. Ahh fuck it. He can feel the tape loop in his head begin as he punches the mental button.

"You want to know about my mom. Well, Sealy, I'll tell you. She was an artist, is an artist I guess in a way, not that she paints anything anymore."

"Does she live in the area?"

"Live? I'm not sure you can really call it living. No." Hal pictures the rest home where they take quality care of his mother; her mind burned out on plastics, a victim of her art. Hanging onto her life in a sterile cocoon.

"I'm not sure I get—?"

"My mom was a trailblazer, an artist before her time. She worked with a lot of solvents and plastics and metals and nobody knew anything about that stuff back in the '50s and '60s."

"That's so cool. Your mom was an artist. No wonder you're a writer."

Hal comes to a screeching halt. What do writing and art have in common? He thinks for a second, his mind doing a jackknife remembering the times in his life where he's been at events with artists most of whom seemed to think in colors or shapes and who were for the most part fairly inarticulate. Like words made them uncomfortable. Certainly it had been that way for his mother. While he was growing up, it would have been easier to get his mother to paint a picture of how she felt rather than get a verbal response. That's if he could get any response at all. You never knew with his mom.

"Yeah. You see, the chemicals did a job on her. She's not right in the head. She just melted things and sprayed things in a grubby little garage studio. The fumes ate away at her brain like termites did the garage. Nobody had any idea how toxic that stuff actually was."

"Ohmigod, I'm so sorry."

"She wandered around the streets for a number of years. It was strange, one day she was in her studio and the next she disappeared."

"How old were you?"

Hal flashes on a photo of himself at ten. Standing on the porch of his aunt's place in Chevy Chase. His jeans had holes in them even then. "Ten. Ten years old."

"What happened?"

"You finished?" Sealy hasn't taken more than three bites of her sandwich. Hal wants to split. He could be wrong, but he thinks people at the next table are eavesdropping. He's got to get out of here.

"Sure, I guess." She puts her hand on top of his. "Sorry."

"S'okay. Why don't we wrap that up and take it home. Let's split this pop stand."

Sealy nods her head, lifts her hand, wraps the sandwich in a couple of napkins, and shoves it into her expensive Italian purse. Hal has never understood this about Sealy. She's capable of putting anything in her black purse. He imagines the horseradish and mustard glooping out onto her money and hairbrush and thingamabobs, and shivers.

At the door on the way out, a group of students march in and one of them knows Sealy. She says hi, introduces him, and Hal can see the looks, the double takes.

"This your pop?" the one wearing the charcoal cargo pants and reversed Yankees cap holding the door asks.

"Nope," Hal says, and walks outside into the night. Hal's aware that Sealy is behind him, waving to her friend, but he's feeling kind of sorry for himself and weird. He hates being judged, especially when he didn't think he was doing anything particularly wrong. He spies a couple crossing Jenifer Street. The woman has the bright platinum hair of somebody who gets her hair done every two weeks. She's wearing a camel-colored jacket of some kind. The light brown and the platinum playing off of each other like a shiny bauble. She could be any age. She reeks of money. The man is wearing a black leather jacket. It looks ridiculous on him. The guy's gone gray and thin on top. He's at least fifty-five, maybe older. And then Hal realizes it's the exact same black leather bomber jacket that he's wearing himself. The man catches his eye for a second as he walks past. And Hal notices the man noticing Sealy as she embraces him from behind and air kisses his cheek.

TAYLOR
The Patience of Crows

WASHINGTON MONUMENT LOOKS BETTER WITH the aluminum scaffolding than it does normally. The objet d'art in progress. Reminiscent of the Eiffel Tower.

Mom and the beach. How the sand seems to live beneath her skin. If you cut her grains would drain out.

Sealy and her impossible breakfasts. Where does she put a serving of pancakes and sausage? Her stork-like legs. If she lost any weight she'd look like a midget walking around on stilts. A beautiful midget. With stilts.

Crows are smarter than seagulls. Flying rats. Mom's copy of *Jonathan Livingston Seagull*. Nostalgia. The way gulls beg.

Great story about crows counting hunters in a blind. Crows scatter. Two hunters leave. Crows wait because they know there are three hunters. When third hunter leaves, they return to their normal routine.

And another. Watching the crows on Route 1. Walking by the side of the road waiting for traffic to subside before attacking the road kill. Flying away again to wait until a car had gone past. Again and again for hours while I sketched them.

Painting: Ravens gorging on seagull innards. Some Boschian replay of the end of the world. Very Francis Bacon.

Mom on gran. We went through some of the accumulated junk. Boxes of photos. Mostly of gran and grandpa. Funny pix of Mom as a sun bunny. No memory of most of this stuff. Mom gave me gran's pearls. Double strand. Like a flapper. And I get to keep her collection of shot glasses from all over the world.

Mom preachy on carbon monoxide detectors. Poor gran.

Mom looks happy being back home. Teaching. Lots of horror stories about the kids. Duh. She can be so clueless. She's old now. Kids can't relate. Not shore kids.

Great eats at Ocean View Deli.

Sealy asked a lot of questions. Got on my nerves. Riding bicycles to calm down. The place is totally dead this time of year.

Went to the movies. *Being John Malkovich*. Hilarious. Reminds me of my temp jobs. Sealy has too much in common with Catherine Keener for my taste though. A drawback. What a great idea though. The kind of thing dad might think up if he ever stopped his endless self-pity party and got off his ass.

Listening to Alanis and Tori all the way down and back. Sealy annoying with bathroom stops. Her bladder must be the size of a walnut. Her brain, too? Just a pain all weekend. Stopped at Harris's Crab House on Kent Island. Excellent as always. I owe dad for that one. Sealy ordered a hamburger. Incredibly lame.

MONA
Deep Forbidden Lake

"HELLO HAL. MY WEEKEND VISITORS are en route. D.C. bound. I'm just sitting here watching the seagulls cruise a surprisingly clear sky. And I wanted to call because I wondered does she remind you of me? C'mon, Hal. You know damn well whom I mean. Taylor's friend. What's her name again? It'll come to me. Little Miss Posturepedic 1999. For God's sake, Hal, her parents named her after a mattress! What are you thinking?

"Well, you know I always like it when you tell me the truth. I assume Taylor doesn't know. Of course, I know you're not a rocket scientist, hon, but you are smart enough to realize she will find out sooner or later. Aren't you? Now don't get huffy with me. I'm not going to tell her. Regardless what you think of me I'd never do that to you, I actually respect you most of the time and besides you've dug your own grave. You can get yourself out without any aiding and abetting from yours truly. Just don't hurt our daughter with this one. Promise me."

MONA'S DREAM LOVERS

Harrison Ford
Mel Gibson
Tommy Lee Jones
Ruben Blades
Denzel Washington
Gary Oldman
Vanessa Redgrave
Ralph Fiennes
Sting
Young Elvis

HAL
Fort Reno

THANKSGIVING ALONE. HAL CAN'T BELIEVE it. He hates the holidays and ever since Mona left him he avoids celebrating them. He doesn't know what to do with himself and ends up seeing *American Beauty* even though he swore he wouldn't. Couldn't bear the idea because the young Brit director has stolen all of his ideas. So much for the novel I've spent twenty years writing, Hal thinks, seeing way too much of himself in Kevin Spacey.

Afterwards, Hal doesn't want to go home right away, so he wanders around. Walks and walks in the twilight and finds himself at Fort Reno. He used to go to free concerts here. He's always liked the park. When Hal was ten, he actually believed it was a real castle. He loved seeing the tower from afar. Wants this to be poignant or meaningful somehow, but in his present mood it just feeds his current assertion that his life hasn't mattered at all.

Hal remembers the first time he knew that Mona would marry him. They'd been making love in the dark for a week, she wouldn't let him in the bathroom when she was alone in there, they never showered together, and then one day something changed and suddenly it was okay. Like Mona had flipped a switch and made a decision about him, about their future, and she woke up that morning and displayed herself for him, doing ballet exercises around the bedroom. Hal remembered laughing himself silly. It was so incongruous. Sans tights it looked almost ridiculous and still somehow provocative and serious because of the tight concentration on her face. And she had pretty good form for somebody who hadn't had a lesson in years.

Mona ended by going en pointe and Hal applauded. She made a proper curtsey and then jumped on top of him on the bed with a big whoop and began showering him with kisses. He felt like he'd died and gone to heaven. Mona had been a godsend, like Sealy was at present. Hal knew he was lucky. He wasn't god's gift to women or anything but he tried to listen, and he'd discovered that was enough in most relationships.

As he walked toward Tenley Circle, Hal thought of the Balloon Man. When Tommy lived at McLean Gardens, they used to get high in his apartment and then walk over to Roy Rogers when they got the munchies. They used to buy shit from the Balloon Man. He had a step van parked outside Johnson's Flower Shop right there on the corner and the best-kept secret in town was that you asked for a silver balloon when you wanted to score some smack.

The Balloon Man's shtick was always on WHFS. "Make the children happy, make the ladies happy." They'd buy pot, or pills, or whatever they needed for the drug du jour and settle into Tommy's pad. Tommy played drums and had been exposed to more jazz than the rest of his friends. His father taught music. So he'd play all this wild stuff like Sun Ra, Harry Partch, and Soft Machine. It was a musical friendship that Hal sorely missed. Man, this holiday was getting him down. Plus he worried about what Sealy was going to say to Mona. He kept conjecturing worst-case scenario after worst-case scenario. Finally, hungry, cold, and almost in despair, he stopped at Armand's and ordered a spinach and garlic pizza.

One of Hal's favorite writers died two weeks ago. Paul Bowles. He'd lived in Tangier for eons. And as Hal folds slice after slice of pizza into his body, he feels himself being weighed down by insurmountable losses. And for some reason he thinks of Arthur Lee and the L.A. group Love. *Forever Changes* is one of his favorite all-time records. The title sums up everything Hal knows at this moment in time. There is no such thing as being rigid or static in the world. The river of time bypasses anything that stays the same, that refuses to change.

TAYLOR
Glazed Crow

THANKSGIVING WITH MOM AND SEALY at the beach. Total disaster. Sealy the grand inquisitor. Talking too much about my dad. What? Told her way too many family stories. Loose lips sink ships. Gotta watch the intake. Can't be faced all the time.

Turkey and stuffing like old times. Chestnuts. Oysters. Glazed yams in orange halves. Pecan pie. Ate too much. Drank too much vino. Slept past noon.

Neil Young? Mom has gone retro. She's wearing flannel shirts and cowboy boots. She thinks she's Emmylou Harris or something. She's playing guitar. Next she'll become a FOLK SINGER. Gag.

Sealy sketching mom. Too freaky. Walking the beach. The boardwalk. Mom's doing her best. House needs serious work. She seems pretty happy. Neither one of us miss Baltimore. We're both glad to be on our own. Might be nice to summer at the shore though. Do some bonding.

Poe's "The Raven" published in 1845. He meant for his poem to be a psychological study in self-torment, since the narrator knows in advance that the bird's answer will be negative and keeps on asking questions anyway.

Pallas Athena was the Greek goddess of wisdom. The raven on the bust of Pallas signifies the ascendancy of despair over reason.

The Baltimore football team is called the Ravens.

Crow-boy = the predecessor to the scarecrow. A boy hired to chase crows away.

I like the Symbolist painters, esp. Redon, but a lot of them are so anal I want to get away from that and be more free, loose, like Van Gogh, but not such thick, abrupt strokes like his.

Schizophrenics love complementary colors together, like pale yellow and lavender. They must live for Easter.

Indo-Tibetans developed a fortune-telling technique from crow calls and positions.

Crow on right: good journey
Crow on thorn bush: enemy

And on and on. As complicated as Chinese fortune telling or Tarot cards with different possibilities for every variation of compass point.

Listening to: Sarah McLachlan, Ani DiFranco, Liz Phair, Belle and Sebastian.

Sealy's never around anymore. Clubbing with Maxwell or where? She can't be studying. She's not bringing anybody home. She's not painting. And the basket of condoms she keeps under her bed is untouched since I took some. I know she's getting laid. But who? The mystery continues.

MONA
Nowadays Clancy Can't Even Sing

"REMEMBER THE EMERSON PREP SCHOOL? You don't? You were so funny. All the losers and bad boys smoking on the steps even then. You can walk by it now Hal says and it looks the exact same as it did twenty-five years ago. Anyway, you were so funny. All those bad boys and girls would wave to you and you'd wave back. You were like a mascot to them.

"Baltimore? It was strange for you. I thought we'd do better and your daddy could still see you okay. It wasn't so far away. So much for plans. We only stayed there the first year before Ralph landed the big hotel job. That's how we wound up in Mexico. Your daddy didn't mind. We were very civil and he was okay with your being in the sun since he was going through a hard stretch himself. His mom was really deteriorating at the time.

"I spent a lot of time taking you to Baltimore museums that first year. You loved the aquarium. We went there almost once a week for a while. Don't you remember?

"And you had a thing for the statue of Poe. It's on campus near the Lyric theater, where they hold the ArtScape festival every year. Well, it used to embarrass me because you pointed at the statue's privates. What's wrong with that word? Okay, his dick. You pointed at his dick. God you're funny. Anyway, it used to embarrass me all the time. I couldn't imagine that you really knew what you were doing. Why is it funny? Because the sculptor had an overactive imagination. No real man has ever had a member that big. Dick. No man has ever carried something that large between his legs. That's what makes it such a scream. God, that statue is built like an elephant.

"Your stepfather meant well. He provided for you and me. He was a bit of a loser. In a different way from your daddy. They were nothing alike. That's why I went with him in the first place. He was everything your daddy was not. Why did I marry him? I don't know. It was just easier, I guess. Made things smoother. A smoother transition.

"And life was good in Mexico. Sand, sea, and plenty of sunshine. All a sun bunny like me needs to keep her engines running. After a couple years of skimping with your daddy, it was nice to have all the fruit and veggies and fresh seafood we could eat. Ralph was a provider. We stayed with the rest of the hotel staff in the compound and a sort of amnesia set in over the next five years. I was drinking margaritas all day and didn't stray far from home, so it wasn't until the fifth year that I noticed the poverty all around the so-called paradise. Very sad. And of course there was Theo. Do you have any memory of what happened? You still seeing the shrink? I just write the checks honey, it's not like they call me and tell me what you talked about. It's not like that at all.

"I guessed you were huffing inhalants, too. No, I didn't know. And you managed to stop afterwards? I'll bet that was difficult. Whatever possessed him— Okay, enough. I won't go there. It's not like you two didn't have enough other adventures. Rosita kept an eye on you. But somehow you two managed to almost drown yourselves one time. You've never been afraid of anything, child. That's what scares me the most. You climbed up one of your daddy's bookcases when you were barely two and yanked the entire thing over on your head. We heard your screams and the sound of falling books and came running. That's why you had stitches on your head. Yes, you do have a very tough skull. Hard for me to believe you made it this far. Knock on wood.

"In 1996 I decided to leave Ralph, go back to school and finish my degree, and move back to Baltimore. We'd been in Mexico for four years, and it was like the land of the Lotus-Eaters. Time to get real. Do something else with my life. I was thirty-three. Making arrangements with myself. Well, you got to go to high school and I got to go to college. It all worked out for the best."

HAL
Sunshine House

HAL FLASHES ON THE SUNSHINE House in Bethesda. He never actually had the cojones to go into the surfer hangout when he was of age, so he's popping out of his skin a little that he should have invaded the turf in his dreamscape. Kids are skateboarding on the sidewalk. It's summer. And Hal feels like he's found some sort of holy relic. He's fingering a cross of some kind. Celtic? Maltese? It keeps changing shape in his fingers like the almonds the teacher made his meditation class explore. The shape shifting continues. Mona in her old ponytail days steps out the door in black leotards, Barbie-pink pullover, and black Nikes. Her usual everyday garb. They haven't been introduced yet. And Mona is looking backwards, holding the door for somebody. When she turns to face him, the light compresses into a sort of haloish tunnel.

Now, kissing Sealy, her lip gloss reminding him of the flavored Yardley lip slicker worn by gals in the '60s, he thinks of birds feeding in the nest. His hunger for her sweet lips, her tongue, that taste, filling him, and yet the more he feeds, the hungrier he seems to be. He needs so much. He's almost afraid that he wants to eat her up, literally, consume this young flesh and spirit, and his passion overflows, like air being forced out of his body on the outcry, and Sealy's blue eyes seem to breathe him in. She's excited by his surge, by how much he wants and needs her. Not afraid at all, which he momentarily thinks she ought to be. Is almost disappointed that she isn't. He amazes himself now, their passion almost a living thing, and he wonders if it's real or delusional, if he's really perceiving what he thinks she is and if it means anything at all. And he wonders for the first time as they head for the bedroom with clothes flying and hips and sweat and skin, if he loves her even a little bit or if he really just hungers to possess her youth and energy like some Hugh Hefner wannabe who can never be truly happy because static in the face of such electric beauty. Or if he should ultimately be afraid of Sealy, who could just be using him? But why should he be afraid? And of what?

"She's cute Hal, in her embroidered denim shirts, her overalls, and cowboy boots. And you know what—she still loves you."

Hal inhales his orange juice up his nose. Coughs. Blows into a napkin he reaches across the table to grab. "Boy, are you cracked," he says.

Sealy is grinning. "No, Mona's a real woman. I liked her, I liked her a lot."

Hal doesn't know what to say. He realizes he's never been comfortable with the idea of his lovers meeting up. And wonders if it's ever happened before. Maybe not.

"You wanna know what she said about you?" Sealy leans over conspiratorially and almost licks his ear.

"Do I?"

Sealy nods her head quickly. "Say yes."

"Yes."

"She said you had a really big cock—"

Hal starts to push Sealy away, but she grabs him tight.

"And she said you were the best lover she'd ever had."

Hal laughs.

"You don't believe me?" Sealy says.

"Why should I?"

"Because it's true," Sealy says.

"Why am I with you again?" Hal says, going for a joke.

"You need me, Hal," Sealy says, cupping her coffee in both hands. "Sex with me is the only thing that keeps you grounded in the here and now. Without me you'd float away."

TAYLOR
For the Love of Crows

CLICHÉ-VERRE—A DRAWING ON GLASS. Camille Corot an early practitioner of *cliché-verre*. Asher Brown Durand, the American painter. His etching, "The Pool."

Hajek-Halke—Experimental photographer (1898–1983). He used *cliché-verre* technique. Some of the shapes look like things you would see in deep space or under a microscope lens. Snorkeling off Isla de Mujeres.

Dream: Dorm as a freshman's idea of the descent into hell. All-glass dorm rooms. Riding a conveyor belt down endless hallways. Everybody doing it in clumps. Girls. Boys. Everybody selling flavors. Broken parts in my hand and no way to reassemble them. Not knowing what they are or what they're for. Carrying them anyway. Broken glass everywhere. Windows cracked with jagged edges. Winding round floor after floor. Like Bruegel's *Tower of Babel*.

House of Musical Traditions. Buying bodhrán. When in doubt bang on a drum. Vague memories of being on this street as a child. Looks different and not much changed. Takoma Park so precisely alternative. Stopping in Savory to see Ally's photo show. Mostly landscapes from Ireland. Eating veggie at Korean restaurant. Metroing back to College Park.

Memorial Chapel on the hill at Maryland. Where my parents got married. Never been in there. Fear of running into myself. Erasing myself. Stepping on the cracks. The threads that hang life just so on gallery walls.

Story of "eating crow" has origins in the American Revolution. A redcoat caught a patriot and had him take a bite out of a crow. (They supposedly taste vile.) Not to be outdone, once the patriot got the upper hand, he forced the redcoat to consume the rest of the crow.

Painting: Someone biting a crow? Alive? Or a dried-out one? How weird is that? Too weird for whom? Who the hell cares? Maybe it's too boring, though. Or too Ozzy.

Zodiac. Our new revolving door relationship leaves a lot to be desired. It's taken me more than a month to figure out that what I hate the most is how he's trapped in the DJ booth and can't dance with me. Driving me nuts.

Lou Bega—A *Little Bit of Mambo*.

Santana—*Supernatural*.

Clubbing: The Spot, Nation, Element, Zei, State of the Union.

Maybe time to make myself scarce and throw myself into my classes before the semester ends. Can always go swing dancing instead. Different but lotta fun.

The Jennifer Lopez poster in Zodiac's bathroom that he won't take down and put away.

MONA
Flying on the Ground Is Wrong

"I WANT TO BE THE first to tell you so you don't get all upset about it later. I think you need to hear this from me first. Well, you know after my folks' death, I did a lot of soul searching. No, not about you or us, but about my life decisions and me. And I decided I needed to write more. You're not the only writer in the family. I teach English for god's sake, and I played editor for you for years. Not that you ever gave me any credit or said thank you. Too late now. No, that's sweet and I do appreciate it.

"I've started writing features for *Coast Press*. I'm well aware it's just a local rag. A cash cow for adverts. I know, I know. But I'm having a lot of fun doing it. I get to meet all the people who own the local shops and it's integrating me into everyday life here.

"The features have recently evolved into essays about my shore roots. I've also put them together as a manuscript during the past six weeks. A nonfiction book. And I showed it to one of the other teachers at the high school and he has connections in publishing. What I'm trying to say is he showed it to somebody in New York and they like it a lot and it looks like I'm going to have a book out.

"You're pissed. I knew you'd be pissed. No? Look, I don't want to hurt you and I don't want to be your enemy or anything. I know how you have this target mentality sometimes but I wanted you to know that this has nothing whatsoever to do with you and me or our relationship. Taylor? She crops up now and again in terms of Mom and life at the shore. A chick book. Yes, now that you put it that way, yes, it is a chick book. How much? Well, shit, deal with it, Hal. They paid me twenty thousand up front on the advance. I'm sorry, hon. I know you've been banging at that particular door a long long time, but this all just kind of happened spontaneously—I realize that doesn't make it any better. I'm really sorry. But I wanted to be the messenger. I wanted you to know so that you didn't hear it from Taylor first or see it in the paper in a review or something. No hard feelings. Well, thank you. I'm glad you're happy for me. You know that does mean a lot after all we've been through. I know Mom and Dad didn't like you that much, and we didn't make it easy for them to, but that's all in the past. And hey, some of this money will go to Taylor. Take some of the pressure off you. I'm not implying anything—

"Hal, honey, we've been over that. Over and over again. I'm gonna go. I didn't want to upset you. I just thought you should know. Bye."

HAL'S TOP TEN PLAYMATES

Henriette Allais
Tanya Beyer
Sandy Cagle
Terri Lynn Dross

Marianne Gravatte
Echo Johnson
Rita Lee
Barbara Moore
Susie Owens
Lisa Marie Scott

HAL
Old Ebbitt Grill

HAL IS WATCHING *KING KONG*. It's late and he can't sleep. Sealy's at McKeldin Library. Why, he has no idea. So he eats pasta bows with Classico spicy red pepper sauce in a big plastic bowl. Damn. He always wears a white shirt when he eats pasta. Why? No learning curve whatsoever. He sets the bowl down, wets a paper towel in the sink, and tries vainly to soak the spot enough to get it out, gives up, and sit back down just in time to see the brontosaurus flip over the raft and send the doomed crew into the inky black prehistoric water. He's pretty delighted. He remembers vague outlines of the movie's plot, but the little details are long forgotten. The dinosaur looks fake here, several sizes too small compared to the men fleeing now through the jungle, but he marvels at the animation anyway, so well done for so early on. He realizes he hasn't seen the movie in more than thirty years. Yet parts of it remain in his memory banks. He anticipates the log sequence before it happens. The movie must have worn some grooves into his kid mind long ago.

Oddly, he finds himself thinking of Taylor when she was in her onesies. The yellow ones with the funny furry bears. And then she's older, and Hal is maneuvering the stroller in a slight drizzle. The spring showers that always seem to go on too long in D.C. He's pushed her over to the library in Georgetown. The one she loves with the kiddie room. And he's walking back now, pushing her as she sings little ditties and points at dogs, down the cobblestone streets past Dumbarton Oaks and Montrose Park and down the hill to P Street where they'll stop at the drugstore and he'll buy her M&Ms. Even though she won't eat the red ones for some inexplicable reason, and he surprises himself by chuckling. Taylor always had issues about something or other even from the very start.

Hal and Mona had finally agreed on a name for the baby after eating chili at the Old Ebbitt Grill. Hal had always liked the dark interior of the old place. The new place sucked by comparison. Where the old location had been a stack of increasingly smaller rooms connected by a winding stair-case over a varnished dark wood bar, complete with a bear and hunting trophies, the new space was light and airy and featured interminable yuppie scum. Hal loved their chili with its combo of vinegar and brown sugar, back before Clyde's version of sweet Cincinnati chili became the staple. They always used lots of onions, and Hal would have eaten there every night if he could have afforded it.

So what's in a name? The chili is different. The restau-rant forever altered. And then he starts thinking about Mona. How he'd been stoned with his friend Tommy listening to Quicksilver Messenger Service. *Happy Trails*. And how right after hearing the metallic call and response of "Mona," they'd made their daily exodus to check out new music. Somebody yelled "Mona" from behind the counter. Hal had almost jumped out of his skin, but turned just in time to see a pony-tailed sandy-haired blonde stop in the doorway and wave to the clerk before leaving the shop. Hal took it as a sign. This was a woman he had to get to know.

Why Taylor? James Taylor's "Fire and Rain" had meant a lot to him. His father died. Tommy died. And Hal found himself going increasingly mellow. Pulling out old Leo Kottke albums. James Taylor. Revisiting songs that had staying power. He was glad that he and Mona were having a daughter. Glad that he could break the chain of endless males in his unwieldy family tree. So he fought for Taylor. Mona had wanted something more normal like Debbie or Alice, but gave in and added Leigh (her mother's maiden name) to the mix.

TAYLOR
As the Crow Flies

RAN INTO DAD'S MOM. CHECKING out the new show at Gallery K with Sealy, hopping from gallery space to gallery space.

Poor Dorothy standing in front of Teaism. Like a bird that fell from the nest. Sealy's eyes bugging out. Why talk to her? Some homeless woman. I took Dorothy's hand, spoke very softly. She may have had some awareness. Dunno. Bought her a cup of hot tea. Some muffins. She said thanks. When she walked off down the windy street we headed back to the Metro. Sealy wanted to eat but that was enough for one day, time to go home.

Sealy was blah blah blah blah until told who it was. Then Sealy went silent. People huddled on subway platforms. Coats zipped tight. Getting colder. And then Sealy mumbles something about taking a walk and wanders off. Girlfriend is acting mighty strange. After all it's not like it was her grand-mother.

Painting: Dorothy with her arms outstretched balancing a family of multicolored crows on her arms. Why not at Hain's Point with *The Awakening* for a backdrop? Too corny?

Adam Duritz and Counting Crows borrowed a traditional folk saying about crows from the graphic novel *The Crow*.

"One crow for sorrow,
Two crows for joy,
Three crows for a girl,
Four crows for a boy,
Five crows for silver,
Six crows for gold,
Seven crows for a secret never to be told."

Suggest St. John's Wort to dad.

Children's book: *Johnny Crow's Garden* drawn by Leslie Brooke circa 1903

Get a stash of objects, textures. Sticks, twigs, stones, feathers, shells, sea glass, glass frags, brick rubble, flattened aluminum cans, broken metal things, etc. Shark's teeth. Fossils. What works, what doesn't work? Like that poet who came to school in Baltimore and pulled out a bag of toys. Made us pick one object and write a poem about it. Imagine writing a poem about all of the objects instead.

MONA
The Emperor of Wyoming

"I DON'T KNOW WHAT TO tell you. He always listened to such depressing music. Took me years to figure it out. Two in particular—Nick Drake and Syd Barrett. Lovely voices but just lost causes. Down and down and down. Like they had a hotline to hell. You would like Nick Drake. Really? A commercial? For what? A Volkswagen? 'Pink Moon'? Can't say I remember the song. But now, all these years later, I realize I've had to scrape off a lot of influences to get back to basics, to get back to the core me. I think this happens to women all the time, honey. It just does. I don't know why. Maybe we didn't have as strong a sense of ourselves as your generation does. Punk rock. Well, you forget that I had you and that I'm really a cusper. I have one foot in your dad's generation and one foot in Gen X.

"I suppose everybody is a mix of influences, as you put it. God knows I am. I'm a beach bunny who reads. I mean, c'mon. What? I read mysteries these days by women writers. I think my days of reading men are over.

"Where was I? Oh, that's why this rediscovery of Neil Young is so meaningful. I'm well aware he's a man. I don't recall saying anything about not listening to male singers. I just don't particularly want to read books by male writers. What's the difference? Of course they write the song lyrics. What's the difference? What is the difference? Okay, point taken. Well, I'm generalizing. You know me. Vast generalizations are us.

"My point is that Neil's music is upbeat, hopeful and about love. At least eighty percent of it is, I think. And that's what made me start thinking about what your daddy plays all the time. I believe strongly in a musical education. I was all for you listening to his collection of CDs and records. I'm glad that you've found a way to bond with him after all these years.

"One of Neil's songs, 'Change Your Mind,' is all about being true to yourself and the magic healing touch of the person you love. It also gets into how love can hurt you and destroy you. And then makes a full circle back to square one. I'm sorry, hon. I'm sorry to hear you're having such a rocky time with your love. I think a lot of times it's how we view each other. Sometimes you just need a little distance. Like a new set of eyes. I guess it does sound pretty trite. But there's some valuable truth there. That's what makes a cliché a cliché, I guess. See if you can work it out. If it feels right in your gut, then ride the wave.

"Regrets? I think life's too short to have regrets. I loved your daddy with all my heart. I loved Ralph for saving me from your daddy. Now I love myself a lot more. Trust myself.

And I don't think I'll give everything away in the future. I'll hold more back. At least that's how I feel right now about my guitar teacher. He's such a cowboy. He's turned me onto some pretty cool music. Lyle Lovett, Steve Earle, Tom Waits, Gillian Welch, Lucinda Williams, Kelly Willis, and some folk stuff like Carrie Newcomer and Dar Williams. Of course, I'm probably driving him nuts making him teach me how to play all of these old Neil Young songs. Oh lord no; he can play rings around me. I'm just a beginner. He's really something special. I can send you a tape if you want. He hasn't made a CD yet.

"I think he's running away from his muse. Some kind of baggage back in Wyoming. Why here? I think it was as far as he could drive his pickup truck before he hit the ocean. And he wind surfs. You'd like him. Of course he's about your age, so hands off."

HAL
Surrender Dorothy

"IS THAT SO?" HAL SAYS. He's got the phone clenched to one ear, all the while grating cheese, making some tostadas. He's lined up tiny bowls with onions, lettuce, tomatoes, and guacamole. "I know, honey, it's awful. I'll call them. What? Okay, I'll call them tonight and I'll drive back over there tomorrow. They can't seem to keep track of her. She walks right out of the place all the time. I know, I know. Of course I care. She's my mother." Hal turns off the burner under the refried beans, and prepares to put some more tortillas in the toaster oven.

"Look, Taylor. I hope you do half as much for me when I'm out of it and playing with myself in front of the Lincoln Memorial. Okay. I'll try. I'll take a walk after dinner and see if I can spot her. She usually haunts the Circle. She likes the chess tables. I will. I promise."

No sooner does Hal put down the phone than the microwave dings. He's just starting to spread the tortilla with beans, then onions, when his door opens. It's Sealy.

"Hey babe, I'll have dinner here in a jiffy."

Sealy isn't running, isn't taking off her coat, she just sort of stumbles straight for him, he can see the tears, and then she lets loose a torrent.

He drops the tortilla bean side down on the linoleum as she slams into rather than folds around him, and he tries to console her. She's left the apartment door wide open. He can hear the wind blowing around the stairwell.

"What's wrong? Are you okay? What happened?" Hal kisses her forehead, helps her off with her long wool coat, sets her on the couch, and swiftly shuts and bolts the door. "What's happened, baby?"

"I saw your mom."

"What? Where?"

"With Taylor. Today."

Hal can't believe this. His entire world is becoming the size of a small needlepoint on a tapestry of tears.

"I'm sorry, Sealy."

"Oh my god," Sealy moans. "Why didn't you tell me."

"What?"

"Your mom. Your mom is Dorothy Magik. She wasn't just some woman who paints. This…" and Sealy began motioning to the paintings and sculptures that actually do clutter the apartment now that Hal thinks about it. At least what he hasn't sold to pay for Taylor's college education or stuffed into storage. "She was Dorothy Magik. We read about her in school. She was so good, she was so beautiful, and she's gone, she's just…nobody's home."

Sealy is shaking out of control. Hal wraps her in his Pendleton blanket. Does his best impression of rubbing down a shock victim.

"I know Sealy, shhh, it's okay."

"But it's not," she gasps in a tiny little voice. "It's not okay. That could happen to me—"

"No, no, no, you're fine, you're okay."

"Or Taylor—"

"No, not Taylor."

"Oh god, Hal, if I start to lose my mind like that, just shoot me, please, will you just shoot me."

"Shh shh—"

"I want you to promise."

And then Sealy is simply gone, heaving and crying and Hal doesn't know how long he strokes her and strokes her and waits for her to calm down.

Hal knows now that Sealy has never suffered—as much as she tries to be the voice of experience, and as much as she's experienced, in the realm of death and dying and disappointment, she's a relative novice. Hal realizes that he has suffered too much, and remembers the first time he saw the graffiti over the Beltway bridge by the Mormon Temple that read "Surrender Dorothy." And he finds himself right now wishing that somebody would do just that. Surrender his mother from her pain, surrender his broken heart, surrender Sealy from the pain she's yet to experience, and save and protect his daughter and his ex-wife from any more of the pain that Hal feels expand and contract like ice, becoming incredibly thin at the spot where he is trying to stand and catch his breath. The idea that a vision of his mother could reduce this dream lover to a soggy, shaky shadow of herself is incomprehensible and more than he can bear.

Only after Sealy is finally asleep does Hal realize that dinner is truly ruined.

TAYLOR
Raven Calls

ZODIAC PULLING HIS SWEATER OFF, cig dangling from the corner of his mouth like some French detective. How he thinks of himself for sure. The quintessential noir guy. Difficult not to hate the size of his ego at times. Sleeps by the door. Difficult not to wish him torments and troubles.

"The crow thinks its own bird fairest." Brit expression.

Watched *The Crow* with dad. Gruesome. Brandon Lee actually died during the filming. The urban decay. The landscape of death.

Painting: Zodiac with a crossbow. Large canvas. Huge. Crusades-like. Very Zoé Oldenbourg. Naked. Surrounded by floating black crows. Not going for Saint Sebastian here. More likely the guy who shot Saint Sebastian

Other words for crow: *kangi, karasu, koronae, voronae,* and *rocas.*

Phoebus Apollo is sometimes associated with the crow in Greek myths. Also Hermes. In the myths crows were white until angry Apollo changed them black for being wicked messengers.

Crows and ravens are separate entities in Native American folklore. And often mess with each other with raven usually getting the upper hand on crow.

Evil omens? Crows and ravens are often seen as popular symbols of death and evil. Just because they're black? If crows gather or caw in the vicinity of a house in folklore it is expected that someone will soon die. The idea being that all birds carry souls to the land of the dead, or perhaps heaven, but crows seem best suited for the job because they look like pallbearers already due to their plumage.

Listening to: Moloko, Wink, Enigma, Digable Planets, Spearhead, Skylab 2000, Plastikman.

Funky Buddha Lounge in Chicago.

Maxiclogs by Phobos Deimos.

DJ Junior Vasquez

Books: Charles Mingus—*Beneath the Underdog*

Luigi Russolo—*The Art of Noises*

MONA
The Old Laughing Lady

"OH SHIT, HON, I'M SORRY. That sucks pretty big time. How long did it take you to find her? I suppose Washington's finest were a big help. Yeah, I figured. I'd assume she looked like hell living on the street like that. And it was cold last night. Well, that's good. Now what are you going to do? Well, what I don't understand is why they can't keep that woman on the premises. Go figure. It's not like she breaks out in a big prison escape or something.

"Miss mattress? What about her? Well, Hal, I don't think about your twisted love life very often. What do I think? I think she'll wake up one day and walk out on you. Someday soon. And then she'll probably spill everything to Taylor. I have no idea. Just a guess. Not a certainty. Why? I'd guess she wants to play muse. Wants you to write about her. Wants to fulfill your fantasies. Oh Hal, you always tell a woman every-thing there is to know about you in the first couple weeks of the relationship. You did with me. I knew all your buttons by the end of the first month. There's a difference between having no secrets and giving your lover ammunition.

"No, I never mentioned that Taylor was seeing a shrink. See, how did you find out? Right, Sealy can't keep her mouth shut. Why Taylor confided in her I have no idea. So what do you want to know? A couple of things happened down there in Mexico. Taylor and Theo were the same age. He was one of the manager's kids. He was trouble from day one. They almost drowned together one time. The sea. And they ran away from home one night and we found them near the sleaziest whorehouses you could ever imagine. Well, maybe you could. What? Wandering around. Playing with street kids and their dogs right beside the open sewers. She was only thirteen. No, I don't think they had sex. Maybe. It's a possibility. Theo was a little advanced for his age. He was one of those bratty kids who'd spent his entire life in hotel environments. He wasn't my kid, who knows why. Look who's talking. Look who's talking about being a bad influence. Hal, you were shooting up when I left you. Right. Pot and kettle.

"So, however it happened, Theo and Taylor were into my stash and getting stoned. I have no idea how often. I was so happy in the sun down there, I didn't do anything but drink margaritas and sit in the sun all day. I didn't smoke at all. It was my idea of paradise for the first couple years. But to make a long story short, yes, the two of them were doing drugs together. And somehow they graduated to inhalants. God knows. Why does anybody do inhalants? I think they did glue. And maybe spray paint. But one day Theo got it into his head to snort the fridge. Would I make this up? The Freon killed him dead. Ralph walked in literally just after it happened. Well, thank god Theo didn't browbeat Taylor into going first. He froze his lungs. Well, it's not something I've ever thought about. I mean, how do you child-proof a fridge? Or teen-proof?

"There was a reason I started telling you this story. I wanted you to be gentle with Taylor. Not that you aren't. And I wanted you to understand some of what she's already been through. Why? Because I think that it was while she was down there that she determined to become an artist. I think she just finally focused on your mom and it was like a mental snapping of the fingers. What had once been silly little sketches in that last year after Theo died turned into full-fledged works of art. Some sort of compensation. Maybe she linked Theo's death with Dorothy's deterioration. I dunno. She did love your mom. But she also hardened up. When we moved back to Baltimore, it was like pulling teeth to get her to go with me to visit and I finally just gave up. I don't know. I think they finger painted together once or something. Whatever they do in there. The place gave me the total creeps. Taylor was a serious teenager by then with hormones pumping and as much as she admired your mom, I think she'd made some sort of disassociation between this deranged woman with white hair and the cool artwork she'd seen now and again through the years.

"I just wanted you to know. Agreed, no more secrets. And Hal, remember me at eighteen? Try to realize that Taylor's the exact same age. Okay. Just consider that before you criticize me. Yes, I think we've been pretty lucky in the long run. She's a good kid. I think she'll make a fine artist, too, before it's all said and done."

ZODIAC'S PLAYLIST FOR NOVEMBER 1999

The Dragon—Dragon's Theme
Dunno—Blind Alley
DJ SS—Step Off Remix
DJ Die—Drop Bear
DJ Hazard—Year 2000
Roni Size—Snapshot
Dred Bass—New Destiny Remix
Swoosh—Only You Remix
Photek—Bleep
Molten Beats—Gridlock

HAL
Ellen's Irish Pub

HAL'S COMING HOME FROM THE night shift at Borders. There had been a reading tonight. A D.C. thriller writer. The crowd had been huge. Hal couldn't believe so many people would turn out to meet and greet the writer of such worthless shit. But then that's what's wrong with the Washington Independent Writers. They take Kitty Kelly seriously. It eats away at Hal, stuck in a dead-end job at Borders where he stocks and rings the register like kids Taylor's age. He used to want to rise up the ladder and get a good job, but this has never been in the cards. His current boss is half his age, and Hal knows his days are numbered. He hates retail. Hates waiting on people who buy books because they watch *Oprah*. He's never watched *Oprah* and he never will and he'll go to this grave refusing to accept that a talk show host has any influence or say on anything in America.

At the circle he spots a young man with a baby jogger and remembers popping into Ellen's Irish Pub with Taylor in tow to down a quick Guinness. Ellen would be in true form. She was a wisenheimer, but whenever she saw Taylor she'd go all Irish sentimental. Taylor loved Ellen's expressive face. And the lines etched into her skin delighted Taylor, who reached out to trace them with her pudgy little fingers. More relics of D.C.'s past.

Sealy is sitting on the steps outside his digs, smiling and talking with a slim black man. Hal tunes into the conversation.

"Hal, I don't know if you've met Zodiac before," Sealy pushes him to be nice and he shakes hands with the guy before his brain really registers that this is Taylor's current lover. He's as tall as Sealy. Thin. And instead of the dreads Hal had halfway expected, Zodiac shaves his head. He looks like the Uncola guy, "You know you do...ha ha ha" Geoffrey something. Hal can't find the name. Was in one of the Bond flicks.

"Hey man, nice to meet you," Hal says.

"Wha's up?" Zodiac says back, before standing up. "Check you later on, Special K," he says to Sealy, waves to them both, and then walks up the stairs and into the dark.

"Sorry to be late. The reading went on forever. We couldn't get them to go home afterwards." Hal bends to kiss her. Points at the door and asks "What's he like?"

"Zodiac's a 3M kind of guy—*The Man Show*, *Maxim*, and masturbation."

Hal subscribes to *Maxim* but thinks better of saying anything. "So, you serious about seeing the artwork I have in storage. My mom's stuff?"

"Absolutely."

Hal pulls the lock off the door of the atmospherically controlled storage facility and swings the metal door wide enough to reach the light. There are rows of canvases wrapped in brown paper and padding. Some are more accessible, and Hal slides them out for Sealy to view.

"You know she wasn't really very well known outside of the area."

"She definitely is now."

"Not widely. Some of the instructors at Maryland knew her and her work and have campaigned to get more attention paid to her. They keep her candle burning. Mostly too little too late in a way."

"Still, it's certification that your mother was an important artist. That matters."

"Does it?"

"I think so."

Later in his apartment, Hal made stir-fry with broccoli, asparagus, red peppers, and tiger shrimp, while Sealy oohed and ahhed from the living room.

"Oh god, Hal, these are fantastic. I never knew she did representational work."

"Well, she worked her way through all sorts of styles. Like you will."

"I can't sculpt at all, and etchings? I dunno. Look at what she did here," Sealy says, flapping an etching his way. "It's the Minotaur. The detail. Like alabaster. She was incredibly patient. And gifted."

"Take it, it's yours."

"Really?" Sealy says, speechless for the first time Hal can remember.

Later Hal can hear Snoop Doggy Dogg blasting down from the ravemeister's apartment. Suprisingly, he thinks of Snoopy, and Charles Schultz, ill now at the end of the millennium, and then of Snoopy's doghouse. It's the perfect image for everything unseen. There are strips where Snoopy realizes he's left the light on over the pool table. Or he gets a globe for a present. Even one where Charlie Brown and Pigpen or Linus haul an oriental carpet up the winding stairs so it can be cleaned. And Hal wonders how long his daughter has been sleeping with the matchstick-thin DJ upstairs. Wonders if the noisy woman he's often heard through the ceiling might have been his daughter. Wonders why Taylor has never mentioned this before. Or Sealy? And finally Hal begins to worry about his past, and what other possible surprises might lurk at the bottom of his own stairs.

TAYLOR
A Crow Never Forgets

LISTENING TO: MOBY, THE ORB, DJ Spooky, PJ Harvey, Nick Cave, Garbage, Deee-Lite.

(Lady Miss Kier is from the area dad says.)

Zodiac met dad. So embarrassing that dad still shakes hands "like a soul brother" from the '60s and says, "man."

Snarfing French toast with dad on Sunday mornings and watching really bad black and white sci-fi films.

dad showing me *2001: A Space Odyssey* and forever after using the Hal computer voice when he wanted to get rambunctious and try to tickle me.

Letting me watch *Pulp Fiction* at 14. *Star Wars*. Thank god he didn't name me Leia. Total disappointment of new *Star Wars* movie. Like a two-hour trailer for the sequel and then they kill the best new character.

Listening to music at dad's apartment. Old stuff. Weird stuff. Can. Amon Düül II. Magma. Captain Beefheart. If it's obscure dad likes it. The more obscure the more he likes it. His Patti Smith and Laurie Anderson collections are excellent.

Possible Christmas presents? *Magnolia* soundtrack with Aimee Mann. New Counting Crows despite his dis that they were just recycled Van Morrison. New Beck CD.

Seeing *American Beauty* and thinking this is my mom and dad if they'd stayed together.

Seeing dad at Borders is like seeing a rock star waiting tables. Kicking back at his apartment while he's at work, sneaking a peek at some of the great novel. "Gloom Patrol." Hoping against hope that it's not autobiographical. Highs & lows. Good & bad. Ultimately frustrating and disappointing. Not a masterpiece after all. Wanted it to be for his sake. Breaks my heart.

MONA
See the Sky About to Rain

"I HAD A DREAM WHERE you joined us in Mexico. Ralph was gone. We went scuba diving. All three of us. You, Taylor, and me. Just gorgeous. Rainbows of coral and darting fish. And in the dream we found a sunken galleon. And there were all of these statues littered around the wreck. And in the midst of these sculptures, we found your mother. Her hair was white like a statue, but the rest of her was pink and alive though her feet were encased in a block of marble. And the three of us rigged some netting, and a ship above began to hoist the statue. We were all excited, and the sun shining down through the almost clear water was sensual and alive. I remember feeling that anything was possible. And when the statue was breaking the surface, the line snapped and, as we watched, the statue in the net sank back beneath us into the sand beside the wreck. And the sea went dark all around us and we couldn't find each other.

"I've had a lot of crazy dreams lately. What with my folks and all. You want any of their books or anything? I don't know that there's much here you'd want, but if you think of anything I'll ship it off to you.

"Taylor? Seeing some DJ or something. That's about all she tells me. I know it has been on-again off-again. Why? Small world. Ha. I think the universe is trying to give you a message, hon. Well, c'mon, the fact that your daughter's sleeping with a guy literally over your head. That's too much. Sure. I won't laugh anymore. I just think it's poetic justice.

"Me? Why yes, I am seeing somebody. None of your business. I guess that was transparent. Yes, he does play guitar. He's not from around here. Nope. Wyoming. I have no idea. I don't make long-term plans anymore.

"Nostalgia, Hal. Au Pied de Cochon. I remember that it was open all night. I remember salads and pomme frites. I remember snooty waiters. I remember waiting for you to show up. I remember changing Taylor's diaper in their bath-room. A lot of fun, you bet. So what brought this on? I do think of you, Hal. I think of all the times I prayed that you'd get your act together and stop taking it out on me. I prayed that Taylor would bring you to your senses. I prayed you'd be happy writing. You never are. It's like blood from a stone or something. I've watched you. You beat yourself daily. Whatever. Yes, to answer your question, I do actually think about you, about us, the way we were when we got married in College Park. And I also wonder what went wrong. But I don't waste a lot of time on these thoughts.

"No Hal, condoms and K-Y Jelly. That's rich. No, it was more than that. And the sex was good, when we actually had sex. Ohhh. Got ya. You just got so depressed, hon, it was difficult to sit there and watch. I did try to help, and nothing I ever did worked. You made fun or criticized everything I suggested. I happen to think it's a big deal that we can still talk at all. Like this. Ever. Not everybody does. Not every-body even gets a chance. Oh Hal, you were always my best friend. You always will be. Now, enough of this. Oh, you're crying. Don't cry. Sorry, hon. Don't give up. Something good will happen for you. Believe me. You've paid your dues and it's gotta happen. Trust me. Okay. Now I gotta run. Be good."

HAL
Gaston Hall

"YOU NEVER HEARD THAT STORY?" Sealy asks, her eyes incredulous. She's downing another of her daily five or six coffees. Arabian Mocha Java this time, Siren's Note Blend before that, preceded by Caffé Verona. Hal marvels at how often a walk with her becomes an episode of Starbucking down the avenue. And he can't begin to comprehend how she can tuck into all that caffeine.

"What?"

"The night Taylor and I bonded."

"No, should I have?"

"She must have told your ex all about it."

"My ex and I don't share all information."

"Well, we were at a frat party on the row."

Hal can see the row. Remember eating ice cream at the Dairy, seeing the Pretenders at Ritchie Coliseum, the Book Exchange, the lemonade at Albrecht's with the old-fashioned counter like something out of *American Graffiti*.

"Some asshole slipped her roofies."

"What happened?"

"Typical bullshit. She kind of stumbled into me and asked for help, said she felt terrible. I'd seen her come into the Book Exchange and ask for a job application. I sort of vaguely knew her. The guys surrounded us and said she could lie down on the couch and you know the drill. Predictable. I managed to get her into the bathroom. Saying she's gonna puke. They moved back and gave us space then. Pathetic. And once inside, thought about going out the window. No way. They had bars over it. So, reasons to have a cell phone. I called the firehouse and told them there was a fire at the frat. Then I called for an ambulance and explained the situation."

"And so you made your escape."

"In style."

Hal kissed Sealy tenderly. She gave him a piece of her lip. "What?"

"Thank you. Thanks for saving my little girl."

Sealy looks actually embarrassed for the first time Hal can recall. She turns a little pink, her jaw clenches. And she lets out a deep breath. "You're welcome," she says in a choked little whisper.

Flash: Hal's at Georgetown University's Gaston Hall seeing local bands Grits and Itchy Brother. He's never been there before. Squeezed onto the stairs in the back. Somebody has opened the windows, and a cool summer breeze toys with the heavy brocade curtains. The paintings remind Hal of the Library of Congress, but this could be the set of a play within a movie or a dream. Perhaps his dream of what the inside of the tower at Fort Reno should look like. Hal's eyes scan the room and occasionally light on an incredible blonde in a red leather jacket. She's a black-eyed susan with dark brown eyes. She's alone. Why? Hal can't fathom. Screwing up all of the courage he can muster, he squeezes close to her.

"Hi, I—"

"Fuck off kid," she says.

Hal doesn't fight. He moves away. Though he can clearly see that she's no older than he is. The word "kid" sticking in his craw.

TAYLOR
Stone the Crows

CROWS ARE MY BROTHERS AND sisters from now on.

Zodiac has flown the coop. Found a 20-year-old. An older woman (ha) who works at Bohemia in Georgetown. A joke. No clubs for now. Bastard. Asshole.

Got sloppy sentimental drunk. Cried for Theo. Cried for Dorothy. Cried for my dad. My sorry life. Said no to any and all offers. Took a cab back to College Park. Wrecked my ThinkPad by crying too many tears into the keyboard. How ridiculous.

Long admired Sealy's I Ching ideogram tattoos (Wu Wang, Hexagram #25) on the back of her neck. Most people don't realize they're hidden beneath her long hair. She went with me to Great Southern Tattoo to get a crow tattoo of my own design on my left shoulder. I needed her support. The pain not as bad as I expected. The biker tattoo artist saying that guys usually cry more than women do. But my tears were mostly about Zodiac and how lonely I feel these days.

Dad used to go to a coffeehouse called Crow's Toe near 10th and K Street he said. How weird.

"Embrace your environment and let it reflect into your artwork."

How can it be that we come together as couples and give everything we have and afterwards we cease being friends? Or stop caring about them, their thoughts, their needs, wants, feelings?

My Valentine spreads passion like pâté.

Trying to explain to dad that my friends don't know past music and books not because we're not interested, but because we're too poor to buy beyond the stuff popular right now. That and the radio doesn't play anything outside of Top 40 hits.

Cobalt shades
Little black dress
Red leggings
Black ballet flats

The lobster at the Sushi Chalet in Baltimore. Trying to get away. Moving inexorably across the sushi bar. Mom and me rooting for him.

Artists and toxins. A report? Got too fucked up and worked in my studio and passed out on the floor. Huge welt on my forehead. Don't want to wind up like Dorothy. Oh god, I see how it happens. You just forget time. Don't eat. Don't sleep. Just wade into the work. And the work is always there. Always hungry for your attention. The unconscious like the sea. You need a lifeguard to make your way back.

Doing a painting with Dorothy at the home. She recognized me. Painting fingers. Disembodied fingers. Flying fingers. Finger trees. Bird fingers. Couldn't go back. Way too sad.

MONA
Down to the Wire

"OHHH, I THINK I'VE MET one this time. I really like this guy. No, I'm not as bad as your daddy is. Well, he's had scads of experience; this is my first time round the block with a younger man.

"A friend from Coastal Kayaks told him about this natural phenomenon. I can't wait to do it. Have to wait until late spring. But at Cape Henlopen during the first full moon in May, it seems that most of the horseshoe crabs from the East Coast gather offshore and spawn. You really know how to ruin a mood. Yes, I guess they do look a little like the face-huggers in *Alien*. So what. I think it's romantic. Out in a canoe on a moonlit night with all of these prehistoric creatures mating all around you. Well, it doesn't give me the creeps. Makes me feel like a small part of something larger.

SEALY'S TEN FAVE BOOKS

Patricia Albers—*Shadows, Fire, Snow: The Life of Tina Modotti*
Rufus Griscom and Genevieve Fiel—*Nerve: Literate Smut*
Anna Kavan—*Ice*
Laure—*The Collected Writings*
Kathy Lette—*Foetal Attraction*
Alma Mahler—*My Life, My Loves*
Geoff Nicholson—*Footsucker*

HAL
Camphor Dreams

SEALY IS WALKING AROUND THE house sans clothing again. Hal has never forgotten their first meeting. On a warm October day, he'd gone to the group house to meet Taylor for lunch. All of three months ago. The front door was open, but Hal had knocked and kind of leaned over to look through the screen. Max, his Burmese cat borrowed by Taylor at the beginning of the school year, shot off the couch and raced to the door. Sealy had been on the gray couch hidden from view. First one arm rose above the couch top and then another. As Hal watched, Sealy linked her hands and stretched her arms over her head before rising completely naked and turning his way to walk toward the door. He had never imagined a scene quite like this one in his entire life. The Fat Mattress tune "Mr. Moonshine" slipped into his brain. He did indeed wish for a way to make this mysterious beauty his own. And so Hal met his current lover. She was obviously a total nudist. Hal was so hot and hard and randy and ready to go that he almost pounced through the screen and jumped her.

"Hey there," Sealy said, and flashed him a set of unbelievably large white teeth.

Hal couldn't get over Sealy not being shy or embarrassed or worried about him, let alone some kid riding by the house on his bike and catching a peek. Not to mention his daughter. Sealy was completely comfortable and unfazed. It was amazing. Nothing like Mona had been. Mona may have wanted the unconventional, but she was still a child raised in a very conservative household and she could only really party with the lights off.

"I'm Hal, Taylor's dad," he managed, thinking college had sure changed.

Sealy made no effort to cover herself. One arm was propped on the doorjamb. "C'mon in, Hal," Sealy said. "Your daughter's running a little late, but I'm sure she'll be here soon."

Then Sealy surprised him by pushing the door open but not moving out of the way an inch, forcing him to compress himself in order to shuffle past without brushing into her.

And he was afraid to touch her, as though the very real electric current between them could destroy them both. He was afraid of what could happen, and wanted it and needed it and loved every minute of the possibility. By the time Taylor got back from class to meet him, Sealy had gone upstairs to her room, leaving Hal on the couch with Max rubbing against his ankles, a case of blue balls that would take a week to cure, and his daughter none the wiser.

"SWEETIE, I'M GONNA TAKE A hot bath," Sealy says. She's wrapped both arms around his neck. He's trying yet again to get somewhere on his manuscript and her interruptions and distractions make it almost impossible. He blames himself. He blames her. I'm such a weakling, he thinks. She disengages, and he turns to watch her sashay across the burgundy carpeting, her tight butt, her slinky legs that go on for miles, and he's sucked right out of the room in her wake. She's fast. She's already in the bath-oily water. She'd drawn it first. He hadn't noticed. She's lighting candles and she's got them in a *portacandele*, ten or so, and she's lighting them from the water. Long kitchen matches. He flashes on the candlelit love scene in *Barry Lyndon*. A terribly overrated Kubrick movie. And he's hot. He can't stand that she's submerged and he's standing around with his clothes still on. And thinking about her naked in College Park has added spice.

Sealy's eyes sparkle when he sits on the toilet.

"Hmm? What's up, lover boy?" She's giggling.

"Nothing," Hal says. "Just came to keep you company."

"Okay." Sealy has started squeezing shaving gel out of a green bottle and she begins smoothing the lather up and down her legs. The movement is a seductive one. Her abdominals are taut and her breasts are turning pinker than he's ever seen in the additional light from the candles and the temp of the water.

Hal reaches for the razor. Sealy puts a hand out, expecting him to give it to her but he hesitates. He's never attempted anything quite like this before.

She cocks her head. Curious. Wondering what's going on.

Hal gets down on his knees on the black bathroom rug and leans over the side of the steaming tub. He takes one of Sealy's glistening legs in his hands and begins to shave her. He puts the razor gently against her skin.

"No," Sealy whispers. "You go up." She reaches over and turns the razor around.

Her legs are warm now, she smells of roses, and Hal pulls the razor slowly up her leg.

"Hmm. You do this right and you'll get a reward," Sealy says. She's teasing.

Hal begins to imagine his reward. He wants a reward. He imagines her tongue on him, her lips swallowing the head of his cock, and now he's getting really excited. His breath is coming in tiny gasps. He knows Sealy can see that he's getting turned on.

So far he has managed not to cut her.

"Watch around the ankles and shin bone."

"You cut yourself there?"

"Usually." She's relaxing, leaning back against the white porcelain tub. "And the knee."

"You shave your knees?"

"Yep."

"Do you always cut yourself?'

"Oh, about half the time."

Hal is shocked. He stops. Cleans the razor off. Begins another swipe. He'd never imagined what a pain in the ass it must be for a woman to shave all the time. None of his girlfriends had shaved when he was at Maryland. Before he met Mona. And his wife had never shaved in front of him.

The first trickle of blood appears. He feels the goose bump he's hit but he's applied too much pressure, and the red stream folds back upon itself like red ribbon candy, gradually going pinker and pinker in the steamy water. Sealy's a trooper, though. She doesn't make a sound. Smashes her lips tight together, and he continues. She's a southpaw and her left arm is out of the tub. Her hand on his arm. And she begins to lower her aim, to go for his pants.

"I don't know if I'd do that if I were you," Hal says. Worried that he might lose all concentration and really tear her skin up.

"I'd feel less inhibited if you took your clothes off, too," Sealy says. She's wrapped her fingers around his belt. She's good at this. She can remove the black leather braid with one hand in seconds and she does. Hal places the razor on the edge of the tub, steps out of his jeans, and then pulls his Wizards T-shirt over his head.

"You've never been inhibited in your entire life."

Sealy flicks a little water at his erection and laughs. Once he's finally naked, Sealy rises from the steamy bath, and begins to lather her pubic hair.

"What are you..." Hal says, amazed, but Sealy stops him with one hand on his shoulder and gently pushes him back down into a kneeling position.

"Now," Sealy says, "watch closely." She takes the razor from the edge of the tub and makes a downward sweep through the lather. "See."

Hal can't speak; he's eye level with the shaving gel. Sealy grins. She reaches out and takes his hand, leaving him on his knees on the bathroom rug leaning ever so slightly over the white porcelain of the tub, and holds his hand down on the razor with her own. She pulls down and Hal pulls with her. This is like nothing he has ever experienced.

"Okay?" Sealy asks. The look on her face smug and sophisticated.

Hal gets it now. Okay. I can do this, he thinks. And he rinses the razor in the steamy bath, wraps his left arm around her leg to pull her closer, and makes another pass with the razor. But this time he presses his face into her creamy aromatic thigh, gets shaving gel in his hair and on his face, pauses to clear some away from her labia, leans forward, and teases her with his tongue. This is exactly what Sealy was after. Now her hands are fused to the top of his curly head and she's rearing up on her toes to press into him. But Hal will make a game of it. He pulls back, amazed at how a few strokes with a razor can make Sealy's familiar body look so entirely unfamiliar, and uses the razor again, kisses her leg, her thigh, the newly shaven area, buries his face in the lather, and uses his tongue again, and so he proceeds until Sealy surrounds him and in a couple of motions they're lurching toward the bedroom, pulling back the sheets, the electric blanket on and already warming up the bed, which they both fall into eagerly, wet or not, and minutes turn to hours and time ceases to matter.

TAYLOR
Eating Crow

"HEY POPPA SAN. I GOT out of school early. Want to go see the new show at the Phillips?"

Taylor wanders down the hall, past the bookcases. Dad's not in front of his computer or kicked back in the stuffed chair like she'd hoped. Nope. Max (the cat) had done a job on the stuffing and her old man had never bothered to replace it.

He likes it that way. The yellow foam peeks out through the burgundy and black weave of the fabric. He would like that, she chuckles.

Hal's not in the kitchen. He must have been up all night writing again. "Wake up, sleepyhead." She nudges the bedroom door open. And her eyes blink—once, twice. What? Shit, he's got a woman in here.

Taylor freezes in the doorway for seconds? Hours? Concentrates. Holds her breath. Balances all the weight on her right foot, leaning too far into the room to back up. The woman is on top. Naked. Facing the doorway. Both hands pushing powerfully against her father's chest. Mad black hair hides her eyes, sweeps back and forth, covering his face. His head down by the foot of the bed. The sound of skin slapping skin more audible now. The liquid sound like teasing an egg with a fork. And the woman rocks in slow motion, and then her torso rises as she comes with a noisy "yes, yes," a grunt from her father, another, both of them shaking as her long black crow hair whips up and back with an audible crack, revealing her glistening face, as her blue eyes spring open

Sealy?

And Taylor crying, shell-shocked, runs down the hallway and out the door which she leaves open and into the stairwell and pounds up the metal fire stairs, past Zodiac Douchebag's black barred door, and then back down the front steps and off into the street where she runs, she just runs.

MONA
Tonight's the Night

"I WOULDN'T BE TOO HARD on your father, hon. What did you expect, after all? He's weak. He'd fuck anything that was nice to him. Inanimate objects. You name it. He's a hedonist. He was bound to sleep with Sealy sooner or later. Well, you threw her in his face. What did you expect?

"Did I know? Yes. I figured it out when you guys visited at Thanksgiving. Forgive her, Taylor. God knows your dad can be irresistible when he chooses to be. Just let it go.

"You know you've never asked me why I left your father. I think in the end that I just let him go. Like that Sting song. I set you free, too. No, really. I wanted you to be okay. I wanted him to be okay. And for both of you to grow up. For him to finish his damn novel. For you to stop sleepwalking and get a life.

"You'll laugh, but you have to understand that I've discovered the secret of the universe. I know it's the kind of thing we used to think when we'd done a lot of drugs in the '70s. We'd discover something meaningful and profound and try to write it down in rapid speed scribble, or else try to retain the thought until morning, sometimes repeating the same phrase over and over until it deconstructed into nonsense. Not so silly, after all, I'm the gal who once tried to take photos of the colors and shapes I saw on my jeans while I was tripping. Imagine my disappointment when the photos came back from the lab. Yes, that's what happened.

But I've actually learned the secret now. I've figured it out. What? It's easy. Like Neil says, "Don't let it bring you down." Don't let anything bug you. Simple isn't it. Because if you let something bug you it will. And it'll keep bugging you. And the more power you feed it, the more it will bug you until this little thing, this pestering thing, is blown all out of proportion. It's like road rage, and the foibles of your lover, and everything. So that's it. And where your father's concerned, I learned long ago not to let it get to me. You have to just let go. Let it ride. Let his weirdness play itself out. And that's what I believe. Works for me. And besides it's NMP. 'Not my problem.' Definitely not my problem anymore.

"Yes, blow off the spring semester and go to Europe. I would if I were you. Go to the Prado. Go to the Louvre. Go to Vienna. See the museums, sleep with a Frenchman who eats bouillabaisse and smokes Gauloises, and weep in the Tuileries. Springtime in Europe is the best possible thing that could happen to you, my sweet. Book your flight and I'll charge it for you.

"And you can email me now. Yes, I got email. I've entered the twentieth century just in time for the twenty-first. I'm cinnamongirl@aol.com so take your laptop and email me after you land."

HAL
The Dog Dream Redux

THE MUTT SITS IN THE middle of the road contemplating the traffic.

Hal pushes the pedal to the metal.

Free at last.

ACKNOWLEDGMENTS FOR
SUGAR MOUNTAIN

THANKS TO RON BAKER FOR caring enough, and kudos to Sharlie West Bouic, Barbara Grosh, Margaret Grosh, Derrick Hsu, and Karen Kovacs for being my eyes and ears on early reads. I owe Karren Alenier, Jenny Badman, Nicole Blackman, Jodi Bloom, Lucinda Ebersole, Heidi Glenn, Dorothy Hickson, Bill Holland, Casey Kane, Sara Levy, Joyce Nalejwak, Elaine Orr, Gregg Shapiro, and Rose Solari for assorted data and for answering my frantic emails. And I owe a considerable debt to Karen Kovacs (again) for understanding exactly what I was up to here and sharing additional background culled from her own life. A special tip of the hat to the American Society of Crows and Ravens whose Crow FAQ Taylor quotes from, Hyper Rust Never Sleeps, Ravedata: the Definitive Source for Rave Information, and Urban75 UK Underground. Plus lots of love to Henry Allen and Jane Bradley for the great blurbs on the original.

Appendix: Timeline

1951   Richard Myers Peabody born March 14, a Pisces, at Georgetown University Hospital in Washington, D.C.

1969   Ohio University, Athens, Ohio

1973   BA, University of Maryland, College Park

1975   MA, The American University, Washington, D.C.

1976   *Gargoyle Magazine* Founding Editor and Publisher

        Founds Paycock Press

1977   Board of Directors, The Writer's Center, Glen Echo, Maryland

        Financial Coordinator, The COSMEP (Committee of Small Magazine Editors and Publishers) Book Van Project (Chapel Hill, North Carolina)

1978   Magazine grant, Coordinating Council of Literary Magazines

        Co-host, *Garfield Street* (aka *Writer's Workshop on the Air*), WPFW 89.3 FM, Pacifica Station, D.C., 1978–79

1979   Staff Writer, *The Futurist Magazine*, Bethesda, Maryland

        I'm in Love with the Morton Salt Girl, Paycock Press

1980   *Monaural*, Kawabata Press

1981   Magazine grant, Coordinating Council of Literary Magazines

1982   Editor, *D.C. Magazines: A Literary Retrospective*, Paycock Press

1983   Editor, *Mavericks: Nine Independent Publishers*, Paycock Press

        Member, Poetry Committee of the Greater Washington Metropolitan Area, 1983–89

1985 *Diet of Earthworms,* Northern Pressure Press

   Echt & Ersatz, Paycock Press

   Nominee *Esquire* Register, *Esquire Magazine*

   Begins teaching at St. John's College, Annapolis, Maryland

   Poetry and fiction grants panelist, D.C. Commission on the Arts and Humanities, 1985–89

1987 Begins teaching at The Writer's Center, Bethesda, Maryland

   Special Larry Neal Writers' Award from WDC Mayor Marion Barry

   Board of Directors, Washington Project for the Arts, 1987–89

1988 Editor's Award, Coordinating Council of Literary Magazines

   Fiction Judge, Larry Neal Writer's Conference, Washington, D.C., 1988–89

1990 DCAC Arts Award

   Sad Fashions, Gut Punch Press

   Suspends publication of *Gargoyle Magazine*

   Fellow, Virginia Center for the Creative Arts

   Fiction Grants Panelist, Wisconsin Arts Board

1991 Co-produces Kathy Acker, 15 Minutes Club, Washington, D.C. (Twisted Pisces Productions)

1992 Fellow, Blue Mountain Center

   Co-produces, "Why? A Reading & Response to the Verdict & Turmoil in Los Angeles," Chapters Literary Bookstore, Washington, D.C. (Twisted Pisces Productions)

1993 Co-editor, *Mondo Barbie,* St. Martin's Press

   Begins teaching at the University of Maryland

   Begins teaching at the University of Virginia

   Begins teaching at Georgetown University, Washington, D.C.

1994 Co-editor, *Mondo Elvis,* St. Martin's Press

1995   Co-editor, *Mondo Marilyn*, St. Martin's Press

Co-editor, *Coming to Terms: A Literary Response to Abortion*, The New Press

Begins teaching at the Johns Hopkins University Advanced Studies Program, D.C. Campus

Paraffin Days, Cumberland Press

Buoyancy and Other Myths, Gut Punch Press

Editor, *Loose Change*, a posthumous book of unpublished poetry and prose by the late British poet Tina Fulker, Bogg Publications

Artist-in-Residence, Woodstock Artist's Guild's Byrdcliffe Arts Colony, Woodstock, New York

Co-Owner Atticus Books & Music, U Street, Washington, D.C., 1995–99

1996   Co-editor, *Mondo James Dean*, St. Martin's Press

Resumes publication of *Gargoyle Magazine*

Fiction Grants Panelist, Massachusetts Cultural Council

1997   Editor, *A Different Beat: Writing by Women of the Beat Generation*, Serpent's Tail/High Risk

Fellow, Blue Mountain Center

Individual Artist's Grant—Fiction, Montgomery County, Maryland

Fiction Grants Panelist, Rhode Island State Arts Council on the Arts

Maryland Individual Artist's Grant—Fiction

Award Presenter, Firecracker Book Awards, Chicago, Illinois

1998   Final Judge, Writer's Voice (New York) Capricorn Novel Award

1999   Marries Margaret Grosh

Open Joints on Bridge, Argonne Hotel Press

Mood Vertigo, Argonne Hotel Press

2000   *Sugar Mountain,* Argonne Hotel Press

2001   Fiction Grants Panelist, Maryland State Arts Council

Publishes *Ed Cox's Collected Poems* (Paycock Press)

2002   *Rainflowers,* an ahadada online chapbook

Fellow, Virginia Center for the Creative Arts

2003   Project Grant for Individuals, Arlington County, Virginia

2004   *Last of the Red Hot Magnetos*, Paycock Press

Editor, *In Praise of What Persists*, a posthumous collection of stories by Joyce Renwick, Paycock Press

Editor, *Grace & Gravity: Fiction by Washington Area Women*, Paycock Press

Editor, *31 Arlington Poets*, Spoken Word CD, Paycock Press

Fellow, Blue Mountain Center

2005   Co-editor, *Conversations with Gore Vidal,* Part of the Literary Conversations Series, University of Mississippi Press

The Johns Hopkins University Faculty Award for Outstanding Professional Achievement, Master of Arts in Writing Program

Final Judge, Inaugural Gival Press Novel Award

2006   Fellow, Virginia Center for the Creative Arts

Co-editor, *Sex & Chocolate: Tasty Morsels for Mind and Body,* Paycock Press

Editor, *Enhanced Gravity: More Fiction by Washington Area Women*, Paycock Press

Editor, *Alice Redux: New Stories of Alice, Lewis, and Wonderland*, Paycock Press

2007   Editor, *Kiss the Sky: Poems and Stories Starring Jimi Hendrix*, Paycock Press

Editor, *Electric Grace: Still More Fiction by Washington Area Women*, Paycock Press

Fiction Judge, F. Scott Fitzgerald Short Story Contest, 2007–11, 2014

2008   Editor, *Stress City: A Big Book of Fiction by 51 DC Guys,* Paycock Press

Fellow, Blue Mountain Center

2009   Editor, *Gravity Dancers: Even More Fiction by Washington Area Women*, Paycock Press

2010   The Johns Hopkins University Excellence in Teaching Award, 2010–2011

2011   Fellow, Blue Mountain Center

2012   Editor, *Amazing Graces: Yet Another Collection of Fiction by Washington Area Women*, Paycock Press

        Speed Enforced by Aircraft, Broadkill River Press

        Blue Suburban Skies, Mint Hill Books

2013   Beyond the Margins "Above and Beyond Award"

        Nylon Soul, downloadable spoken word CD (Eat)

2014   Editor, *Defying Gravity: Fiction by DC Area Women*, Paycock Press

Acknowledgments

I am gobsmacked by what Rose and James have produced here. Where, but for you, go I? Note to self—it's nice to be the talent and go along for the ride. Thanks to Lucinda for making the hard choices, to Andrew for being the trail boss, to Nita for copyediting and design, to Steve W. for print savvy, and to Randy for the astonishing cover. The entire team of folks who participated in the making of this object are rock stars in my book. And I can't possibly thank Mike Dirda enough. I just hope I can live up to the hype. Mucho love to my wife Margaret and my daughters Twyla and Laurel for understanding why I was so spaced out and stressed out while this came together. And this project has been quite the rollercoaster. Whew. Want to go again?

I hope my students can forgive me riffing on some of their unpublished work in "Letters from the Editor"; the photo that lends its title to "Stop the War or Giant Amoebas Will Eat You" really did make the rounds of the Internet during the Bush (the son) push for war, and the "Yellow Rose" entries in that story are cleverly adapted news items from the *Washington Post* and other online news sources; "The Ten Most Misleading B Horror Movie Titles" is a found poem grabbed from the Astounding B Monster (www.bmonster.com) site. Italic lines in "Civil War Pietà" are by Walt Whitman. The following works are reprinted as follows:

"Trysting," *Speed Enforced by Aircraft* (Broadkill River Press, 2012); "Everything According to Plan," *Whiskey Paper* Dec. 2012; "Honeysuckle at Night," *Speed Enforced by Aircraft*; "The Other Man Is Always French," *Buoyancy and Other Myths* (Gut Punch Press, 1995); "Walking on Gilded Splinters," *Carve* 7:2 2006; "Bag of Bones," *Manila Envelope* Summer 2012; "Astro City," *North American Review* May–August 2003; "As Bees in

Honey Drown," *Buoyancy and Other Myths*; "Reasons to Live," *Mood Vertigo* (Argonne Hotel Press, 1999); "I'm in Love with the Morton Salt Girl," *I'm in Love with the Morton Salt Girl* (Paycock Press, 1979); "E Is for Elephant," *Blue Cathedral: Short Fiction for the New Millennium* (Red Hen Press, 2000); "She Discovers Jazz," *Buoyancy and Other Myths*; "Fiji Water," *Eskimo Pie* March 2012; "Bad Day at IKEA," *The Literarian* 6 (2012); "Introducing Snakes to Ireland," *Echt & Ersatz* (Paycock Press, 1985); "For Zelda (Forty Years Gone)," *Sad Fashions* (Gut Punch Press, 1990); "Audrey in the Rain," *Sad Fashions*; "Another Stupid Haircut," *Sad Fashions*; "Louise Brooks," *Sad Fashions*; "Waiting for the Popeye Effect," *Mood Vertigo*; "Essence of Mitchum," *Open Joints on Bridge* (Argonne Hotel Press 1999); "King of the Zombies," *Word Riot* October 2012; "Spaghetti Western Sestina," *McSweeney's Internet Tendencies*, November 2006; "The Stillness of Apples, or Jean Genet Meets the Spinx," *Bone Parade* #2; "On the Road to Georgia O'Keeffe," *Mood Vertigo*; "Chimichanga," *Echt & Ersatz*; "Valley of the Gods, 1994," *Main Street Rag* Fall 2006; "The Ten Most Misleading B Horror Movie Titles: A Found Poem," *Rain Flowers* (ahadada, 2002); "Hillbilly Music," *Speed Enforced by Aircraft*; "Civil War Pietà," *Speed Enforced by Aircraft*; "Peppermint Schnapps," *Wilderness House Literary Review* Vol. 6, No. 4, 2012; "Are There Any FBI Agents in Heaven?," *Margin* Dec. 2005; "A More Level Playing Field in Fallujah," *nthposition* July 2006; "Stop the War or Giant Amoebas Will Eat You," *Blue Suburban Skies* (Mint Hill Books, 2012); "Torture Splinter #1," *Speed Enforced by Aircraft*; "Photo Realism," *Speed Enforced by Aircraft*; "Military Fantasia," *Poetic Voices without Borders* (Gival Press, 2005); "Empathy Lesson," *3QR: The Three Quarter Review* May 2013; "Flea Wars," *Open Joints on Bridge*; "Princess Daddy," *Lit* 9 (2004); "What I Learned from Being a Stay-at-Home Dad," *Last of the Red Hot Magnetos* (Paycock Press, 2004); "Folding Laundry in My Dreams," *Chattahoochee Review* Winter/Spring 2006; "It's Always Raining on the Pennsylvania Turnpike," *Connotations Press* Sept. 2012; "Empire Building," *Speed Enforced by Aircraft*;

"Reston Zoo, 2004," *Speed Enforced by Aircraft*; "Walking to Dublin," *Dogs Singing: A Tribute Anthology* (Salmon Press, 2010); "From 'Twyla Tales,'" *Keeping Time: 150 Years of Journal Writing* (Passenger Books, 2009); "Last Call in Mohican Hills," *Red Ochre LiT* Summer 2012; "Nuages," *Speed Enforced by Aircraft*; "My Cheating Heart," *Speed Enforced by Aircraft*; "Dresden for Cats," *Blue Suburban Skies*; "The Forgiveness Device," *Buoyancy and Other Myths*; "Letters From the Editor," *Neotope* #2, Fall 2001; "Gunpowder Divertimento," *Blue Suburban Skies*; "When She Walked in the Room," *Speed Enforced by Aircraft*; "Ginsberg Comes to Garfield Street," *Ludd's Mill* 16/17 1981; "Letter to George Myers Jr.," *First Person Intense: A Prose Anthology* (Bandanna Books, 1978); "Mind Grenades from a Broken Body," *Poet Lore* Fall 1999; "Country Porch Lights," *Blue Suburban Skies*; "Confessions of a Literary Editor," *Washington City Paper* July 4–10, 1986; "Good Hope Road," *District Lines* Summer 2013; *Sugar Mountain* (Argonne Hotel Press, 2000).